RED HERRINGS

A Cautionary Journey for Citizen Opposition Groups

JOHN FILCHER

ISBN: 978-1-60414-709-4

Published by

Fideli Publishing, Inc.
119 W. Morgan St.
Martinsville, IN 46151
www.FideliPublishing.com

*"Truth is often stranger than fiction
because fiction has to make sense."*

— Mark Twain,
Summerlin v. Stewart, 341 F.3d 1082 (9th Cir. 2003)

Table of Contents

Preface ix

Chapter 1   Zero Day — The Red Flyer 1

Chapter 2:   Day 1 — The Band Starts to Come Together 5

Chapter 3:   Day 5 — Genesis 9

Chapter 4:   Day 17 — The Open House 17

Chapter 5:   Day 22 — Biomass Opposition Committee (BOC) 28

Chapter 6:   Day 83 — Incinerator Free Brown County 38

Chapter 7:   Day 93 — Problems on Hurlbut Street 44

Chapter 8:   Day 133 — Oneida Nation,
                        General Tribal Council Presentation..... 55

Chapter 9:   Day 134 — Department of Energy Hearing................ 63

Chapter10:   Day 164 — Distinctions Without Differences 67

Chapter 11:   Day 175 — DNR Says, Come Again? 69

Chapter 12:   Day 266 — Economics 76

Chapter 13:   Day 337 — Ask and Ye Shall Receive 80

Chapter 14:   Day 367 — Proper Decorum for a Public Forum 83

Chapter 15:   Day 367 — "Scary" Threats of Litigation 86

Chapter 16:   Day 412 — Upping the Pressure 91

Chapter 17:   Day 445 — Information as a Weapon 93

Chapter 18:   Day 455 — Strategy and Tactics;
                        They Start a Changing........................ 97

Chapter 19: Day 477 — Rally Time! 103

Chapter 20: Day 490 — Media Loves a Good Controversy 112

Chapter 21: Day 536 — Tweaking 123

Chapter 22: Day 597 — Reeducation 129

Chapter 23: Day 687 — Rescission Hearing 138

Chapter 24: Day 687 — Beers for the Brouhaha 143

Chapter 25: Day 694 — The People Have Spoken 147

Chapter 26: Day 717 — Like a Good Neighbor,
                     OSGC is There 150

Chapter 27: Day 772 — All Lawyered Up 158

Chapter 28: Day 772 — Fallout Zone 165

Chapter 29: Day 776 — Hot Potato 168

Chapter 30: Day 798 — Clawback 176

Chapter 31: Day 820 — Moving on over to Morrison? 179

Chapter 32: Day 830 — All You Need is Love 184

Chapter 33: Day 833 — Appealing 186

Chapter 34: Day 846 — Keeping the Pressure On 190

Chapter 35: Day 888 — Halleluiah Chorus 195

Chapter 36: Day 954 — The Gathering Storm 202

Chapter 37: Day 1110 — Judgment Day:
                     Doctrine of Just Desserts 207

Chapter 38: Day 1172 — Undead 213

Chapter 39: Day 1193 — The Bills Come Due? 216

Chapter 40: Day 1220 — New Life 218

Chapter 41: Day 1421 — Very Appealing 221

Chapter 42: Day 1498 — Follow the dollar 225

Chapter 43: Day 1501 — Sloppy Mistakes Continue to Haunt 231

Chapter 44: Day 1642 — Decision Day 233

Chapter 45: Day 2081 — Watching and Waiting 236

Chapter 46: Day 2272 — Second Bite at the Apple 240

Chapter 47: Day 3117 — For Whom the Bell Tolls 243

Chapter 48:   End of the Beginning 246

              About the Authoe 249

Preface

This is a factual accounting about a remarkable sequence of events. You might even call it a factual accounting of a wildly dubious tale. Once upon a time those words would have made me and the others involved uncomfortable to utter aloud. But if we had not overcome our natural reticence about speaking so impolitely, our homes would today be likely be an uninhabitable, contaminated mess.

Befitting Mark Twain's wry observation, because the fictions in this scandal failed to make sense, an even stranger truth finally prevailed. It took a lot of help from *We the People* who cared enough to keep speaking truth to power. The scandal was patently unbelievable and often nonsensical, yet ironically those fictions somehow still seem more believable than some people's willingness to believe in implausible fabrications. In the end, the willingness to suspend disbelief itself seemed more bizarre than the fabrications that we were told; believing feel-good green energy fairy tales made less sense to us than recognizing deliberate misrepresentations and deception.

How does one make sense of this bizarre, chaotic situation, and why did it happen? What were the motives? This book invites you to make your own judgments as it provides the context for why everything plays out as it does, including the final emergence of the truth. You, the reader, are cautioned that nothing in this book constitutes legal advice, nor is any of it to be construed to be legal advice. For that, consult your own attorney.

It is my hope that this sordid story will give you a sense of the frustrations and fears experienced when our small group of ordinary townsfolk suddenly found ourselves in a dreadful situation, and an understanding of our decision to fight for our neighbors, our homes and our families. This is an inside look at how ordinary people like us, who might never have come together were it not for the struggle to stop an environmental abomination, stood up and told the truth. As you experience this journey from our point of view it will give you a realistic sense of our uncertainties and our anger, and how we overcame the lack of information bedeviling our efforts. It is our fondest wish that you will experience how learning to overcome our inexperience and fear influenced our journey as we grew into the roles that were needed to effectively fight back.

In a way, corporations resemble individuals. Some are good, some not so good, and some completely lose sight of both their founding ideals and their sense of right and wrong. Oneida Seven Generations Corporation (OSGC) belonged in the latter category, for it strangely saw nothing wrong with a proposal that would contaminate neighborhoods in exchange for money. The OSGC proposal was the catalyst which prompted citizen action.

During our long campaign by inexperienced, ordinary citizens, the public image and behavior of this corporation came to remind me of a mashup of stereotypical tropes about bad science, villainy and evil personified. OSGC, an Oneida tribal government owned economic development corporation located on the Oneida Indian Nation reservation,* was a wayward outfit lurching forward with self-inflicted wounds which were gradually exposed when it went all-out on a hot new profit scheme designed to make everyone else bear the burdens. It appeared that this corporation attempted to achieve its goal by using 'creative' solutions; combining industrial efficiency with trash incineration near a residential area. Once embarked on its checkered odyssey, OSGC would brook no dissent as the company positioned itself as some sort of good-idea-fairy peddling 'new' solutions; solutions that would solve the separate problems of power generation and trash disposal. OSGC was now in the business of peddling fantasies and falsehoods about recycling trash into ash for cash.

What was new about trash incineration, you ask? Merely adding a second stage to the incineration process whereby the trash's poisonous fumes would eventually pass through a generator before the highly contaminated exhaust would then be vented into the surrounding area. The fantasy underlying this new 'solution' never addressed the reality that, by semantically relabeling these minor process tweaks, this solution would protect neighborhoods about as well as rearranging Titanic's deck chairs would have kept the ship from sinking.

I also learned, and saw with my own eyes, as a practical matter few were ready to believe that heating up the garbage a second time would remove the contaminants — when the first time did not do it. And the few who did believe were only deluding themselves.

Before I had ever heard about the proposed project, OSGC stumbled out of the starting gates in a mad race to finish construction before the truth could catch up. However, once we learned about the project, our little group ensured that OSGC would keep stumbling.

During our long struggle, I realized that these events were also a cautionary tale about using sophistry, corruption, techno-babble, and fraud to grab taxpayer money that should never have been directed into a fake green energy project. In the end, this story models what a few active citizens can accomplish when they applied their sense of responsibility and accountability. This sense of responsibility wasn't difficult to embrace for residents who would otherwise have found an unwelcome solid waste incinerator in their midst. Our thriving communities certainly did not need a dirty trash incinerator foisted upon them in the nearby corporate business park of the Village of Ashwaubenon, which is a highly desirable suburb of just under 20,000 in the southwestern metropolitan area of Green Bay, Wisconsin.

If you prefer comfortable stories about happily singing kumbaya and drinking hot chocolate by a campfire, this is not the story for you. But if you are interested in a blunt, factual tale replete with the ugliness of inelegant language, accusations, attempted intimidation, conflicting points of view, bungling bureaucrats, and in-your-face confrontations emphasized by litigation, then buckle up cupcake. This ride is yours.

The adventure begins with a little red flyer.

*The Oneida Nation of Wisconsin is a federally recognized tribe of Oneida people, with a 65,400-acre reservation located in parts of two counties on the west side of the Green Bay metropolitan area. The reservation comprises portions of eastern Outagamie and western Brown counties, and some of the reservation is included within the boundary of the city of Green Bay. The Village of Hobart, in Brown County, is completely located within the boundaries of the Oneida Nation reservation.

CHAPTER 1

ZERO DAY

The Red Flyer

"Be the Change you wish to see in the world."

— Mahatma Gandhi

It was three days after Thanksgiving, and I was relaxing on the couch in the family room watching football. The weather that evening was the typical result of northeastern Wisconsin days in late November. Chilly but not unseasonably cold, combining to create a day with just a glimpse of sunshine before twilight settled in. My trees were bare by now and all the leaves had been raked up. Grass in the sizable neighborhood yards was now dormant but not yet covered by snow, and overnight temperatures were falling below freezing.

It had been a relaxing weekend day at home for my family. We had enjoyed foraging through the holiday leftovers in the kitchen, and the house was humming with the normal sort of ruckus a busy pair of high-school-age daughters and a lanky eleven-year-old son are so adept at creating.

It was on that Sunday evening that trouble came knocking at my front door. Trouble in this instance took the form of a nearby neighbor, Greg Kujawa, as he waited patiently in the chilly soft twilight for someone to answer the door. An avid cyclist and father of two teenage boys, Greg is an inside sales manager for a local corrugated machinery and paper cutting manufacturer. Greg and I both enjoyed cycling a lot, but I'm just not quite as avid a cyclist as Greg because I have yet to figure out a successful way to combine biking with beer drinking. The Kujawa's lived in a beautiful two-story home just around the corner from mine, and our children all knew each other at Ashwaubenon high school.

In Greg's hand was a red flyer, delivered to his home by person or persons unknown. Greg had found the red flyer in his mailbox and was about to toss it into the trash when its message caught his eye. The flyer warned of a new industrial waste plant styling itself as some sort of bio-mass facility, and the proposed site was the Ashwaubenon business park, only a short distance away and adjacent to our neighborhood. Immediately worried, Greg had asked himself, *what kind of pollution will this thing bring? My God! What will happen to my family's health?!* His next thoughts were equally concerning. *My home value will drop like a rock!* Soon realizing the answers only contained bad news, Greg soon set out to talk to his neighbors and bring it to everyone's attention.

My wife opened the front door. Since I was sitting in the room near the entrance I heard Greg ask, "Hey, have you guys heard anything about a proposed biomass, gasification pyrolysis facility coming to the area?" Waving a red piece of paper in his hand he said, "I got this red flyer about it."

My ears perked up. I got off my duff and migrated to the front door. After living in Ashwaubenon for 10 years, and having been an attorney for nearly 18 years, I wasn't used to missing news of this kind coming to our area. Bewildered, I shook my head and replied, "No, what is that?"

Greg was obviously was more up to speed on the matter. "It's some sort of facility that'll haul in trash for gasification processing, but something just doesn't add up right. They keep saying there won't be any pollution, but that they're also going to haul out tons of ash. That's just not possible — to burn all that trash without creating a big stink."

I couldn't help but agree, thinking *the trusty old smell test was at play here, but in both a figurative and literal sense.* If something doesn't smell quite right about what was being claimed, then upon closer inspection something generally is not right.

As our conversation continued, Greg mentioned that he planned to meet with an official from the nearby Village of Hobart who could provide some background on the project, because this matter would likely have already come to their attention.

"Can I come along? I have a vacation day tomorrow anyway," I asked.

"That'd be great. Two sets of ears will be better than one."

Just then my wife reappeared, holding a red flyer. She compared it to the one Greg held and confirmed that they were a match. She had been about to toss it in the recycling bin.

After Greg left, I glanced at the morning newspaper and there on the front page of the *Green Bay Press-Gazette* was the headline, 'Dispute over Oneida gasification plant festers.' The opening paragraph describing a fight by Hobart and Ashwaubenon officials against a waste-to-energy plant prefaced a very concerning article. It seems that the developer had already broken ground, calling the project both a 'gasification plant' and a 'biomass facility', which the paper said had infuriated neighboring communities who note the plant is at cross purposes with the area's zoning.

As I scanned the lengthy article, my attention zeroed in on the statement of Ashwaubenon village president, Mike Aubinger. "We don't hate the Oneidas. We don't hate the project. We just think it doesn't belong there."

My first thought upon reading was, *That's odd. I wonder how the questions to Mike were being framed to elicit a response articulated in that way?*

The article noted Ashwaubenon's concern that the proposed facility would decrease property values and bring in a large volume of truck traffic. It also stated that the Village of Hobart had already passed a resolution supporting Ashwaubenon's objections.

I wonder how long this brouhaha will last? I questioned as I suddenly realized something important. For me, this unpleasant discovery meant *today is effectively Zero Day and the clock is already running.* As I came to this conclusion, I also thought, *Time was already running out before I even got off the bench to get in a game I didn't even know was going on. I gotta get in there and make a play — and do it fast!* My concern had sky-rocketed so fast that I had difficulty sleeping that night, worrying about the health of my family, and the likely impact on our home value.

The next morning's meeting imparted some very alarming information. From this day forward, I tracked each event, using Zero Day as the beginning to help you, the reader, get a feel for how long these battles can last.

CHAPTER 2

The Band Starts to Come Together

"If you're going through hell, keep going."

— Winston Churchill

Monday morning dawned cold and gray with featureless low hanging cloud cover and dim daylight. This grim setting reflected the dark news Greg and I were about to receive.

When Greg pulled into my driveway, I quickly piled into his car for the short drive to the Hobart municipal offices. The Village of Hobart office is located to the west of Austin Straubel International Airport (now renamed Green Bay–Austin Straubel International Airport). Hobart's municipal offices are in a small building; the kind which encourages a smaller government footprint through lack of physical space. We were soon ushered into the office of Elaine Willman, the village's Director of Community Development and Tribal Affairs. Elaine, a white-haired woman in her mid-sixties with a deep, smoky voice, had, in a prior life, been a tribal communications coordinator in the state of Washington on the Yakima Indian Reservation. Having been hired by the Village of

5

Hobart after a Hobart elected official had read her book, *Going to Pieces: The Dismantling of the United States of America,* she was likely hired for her expertise on Federal Indian policy.

After introductions, our following discussion was illuminating. Elaine brought us up to speed on the foreign company behind the incinerator. That company was the Oneida Seven Generations Corporation (OSGC).

OSGC was asserting that the municipal zoning ordinances of Ashwaubenon were inapplicable to the latest project site on Packerland Drive in Ashwaubenon. Elaine explained, "OSGC is owned by the business arm of the Oneida Nation. The original reservation boundaries overlap parts of western Ashwaubenon, all of Hobart and some of the western parts of the City of Green Bay. For the past few decades, the Oneida have been buying lands to reclaim ownership of those lands, and at first the local officials didn't know enough to oppose allowing the land to be put into federal trust. Land held in federal trust isn't subject to local ordinances due to federal preemption, nor do they pay any local taxes to the communities anymore. Meanwhile, those communities are required by state law to 'provide' community services to the trust lands, so those services are provided at a fiscal loss to the communities."

Perplexed, I shook my head. "Indian reservation law isn't in my wheelhouse, so if I follow you correctly here they're not paying local taxes anymore, and getting community subsidized services by paying below market rates for them?"

Elaine nodded. "Exactly! The local officials don't like to talk about that and how it forces the residents in their communities to pay higher taxes to make up for the loss, but that's the reality of the situation. Federal law first requires agreement from the local community *before* they can be placed in trust. The trust lands, which went into trust before the local communities figured out it was not in their best interests, now include the latest proposed site of the new project."

Greg and I exchanged worried looks before I asked, "Latest?"

"Well," Elaine responded, "this project had originally been proposed in Hobart, then it migrated all the way over to the Town of Oneida sometime last summer. No explanation was given by OSGC for that change of venue. Then suddenly a few months ago, there was an announcement OSGC had executed a power purchase agreement with Wisconsin Public Service and was moving the site of the facility from Oneida to Ashwaubenon. This latest move to Ashwaubenon was reportedly 'after factoring in community concerns about the project's site in Oneida'." Elaine made air quotes with her hands as she said that last bit.

Greg looked at me, and both of us spoke simultaneously. "I've never even heard of OSGC." Although we accidentally blurted out the same thing at the same time, the situation was too serious to see who could then say "Jinx" first.

Elaine nodded her understanding about how new this information was to me and Greg. "Six weeks ago, the *Ashwaubenon Press* ran an article titled, 'Village Learns of Bio-Mass Plant on Packerland'. In this article, the Ashwaubenon Village President 'asked if there was another facility like this somewhere else, so the Village could compare this proposal to the experience of others.'" As Elaine explained the background to us, she rifled through her desk drawer.

"Aha, here it is! This article both helpfully and alarmingly states that the answer from the developer's public relations department is: 'No, this the first plant of its kind.'" Elaine read as she again made the air quotes.

Glancing meaningfully at Greg and I, Elaine continued. "Two weeks before this morning's meeting, WLUK TV ran a report where Mike Aubinger acknowledged the proposed site was on federally held trust land located in Ashwaubenon, which was zoned in conflict with the surrounding zoning by the village."

Picking up another piece of paper from her desk Elaine said, "This a transcription of the WLUK television report, and this is what Mike said: 'For neighbors to get along, you have to be considerate of one another and in our view, this is not a considerate thing to do to a place where we spent hundreds of thousands of dollars to make it into a business park.'

"A resident living near the proposed site, Joanne Choudoir, was also interviewed and I can put the two of you in touch with her. She's in Hobart, living on the border with Ashwaubenon. Joanne has been very involved but hasn't been able to find much help yet. This transcription even quotes Joanne saying, 'It's the wrong thing in the wrong place. The citizens aren't against building a facility, we're concerned mainly with our health and our environment, which are interconnected.'"

Greg and I shook our heads in amazement. "We were totally unaware of those reports or the budding controversy," I replied. "Looks like we need to scramble to catch up. We definitely need to reach out to Joanne." Greg nodded in agreement, his face looking grim.

How could I have missed all this? I'm feeling pretty out of touch here, I wondered. Also contributing to the growing *out of touch* feeling was Elaine's statement noting that this project had already been the subject of a standing room-only governing board meeting in Hobart and a public works board meeting in Ashwaubenon, just in the last few weeks!

Elaine broke into my thoughts. "OSGC is going to host a public open house at the Ashwaubenon village hall in a few weeks, so there is a little time for concerned citizens to gather and talk things over."

"I still can't believe I hadn't heard anything about all this before," Greg said. "John, did you catch anything on it?"

I shook my head ruefully. "Man, I got nothing. With the past couple months of girls swimming and boy's football taking up most of our spare time, I've obviously been living in a cone of silence. Elaine, any thoughts on our next steps here?"

Elaine definitely had a few thoughts. Thanks to the chain of events set in motion by Joanne appearing on TV and her distribution of that red flyer to raise awareness, talking things over and figuring out next steps was exactly what we did.

Later that day, Greg and I contacted Joanne, who immediately told us, "My husband and I were out distributing the red flyers. We did three different batches in different colors and we were running out of them again. The last two we gave out were to your homes. We received no response from the hundreds of other recipients. Can you imagine the odds — that the final two went to you guys?"

"Sometimes, it just takes a couple of people to decide to get the ball rolling," I said. For Greg and I, zero day plus one was a long one, made longer by the worries that the day had brought.

CHAPTER 3

Genesis

"Big things have small beginnings."

— T.E. Lawrence, Lawrence of Arabia

The next few days were a blur of activity with late night and ad hoc weekend planning sessions. Elaine attended the meetings on her own time, as did Ashwaubenon president Mike Aubinger, and Hobart president Rich Heidel. Rich was in his third term as president of Hobart and served as a potential candidate scout for Brown County's Republican Party. An engineer, he is a kind and charismatic man in his late fifties, often seen wearing a dark brown hat that said 'ARMY' and clenching an unlit stogie in his teeth below an impressive handlebar mustache.

Mike Aubinger is a slightly different animal. Born of an Ashwaubenon family that had been there for generations, he is in his mid-sixties and often wears a loosened tie. Mike also sports an equally impressive mustache. His family owns the *Ashwaubenon Press*.

Following the necessary protocols, all three made it clear that they were not present in any sort of official capacity. Expecting this but enor-

9

mously grateful for their presence, I responded, "Message understood." And so our motley little group of residents organized itself accordingly.

The first group meeting occurred the evening of zero day plus 5 in a Ashwaubenon village hall meeting room. It had been a chilly, gray cloudy day with temperatures hovering around 25 degrees by nightfall. Elaine and Rich were there from Hobart, as was Joanne Choudoir and several other Hobart residents who had helped her in printing the flyers and getting the word out, as well as another dozen Ashwaubenon residents. Joanne is a petite woman in her fifties with a head of snowy-white hair and boundless energy. She worked at a local clothing boutique in Ashwaubenon, and her husband is a retired engineer.

After the greetings, I got the meeting started and spoke over the hubbub. "All right, everybody, we have a lot of ground to cover tonight. But first I'm giving the floor to Rich and Elaine, who have a lot to say about the project developer, OSGC, and the unique situation that we all need to be aware of."

Elaine took the floor first. "One thing you should all remember is OSGC is a situationally powerful company that has a stranglehold on internal support and friends who have protected it from all dissent for years. That company is ruthless and will not hesitate to say some pretty nasty things about you for daring to step up and oppose it."

Rich, his Army baseball cap at a jaunty tilt and motioning with an unlit cigar in his hands for emphasis, chimed in. "That's right. We've been dealing with OSGC for a number of years now, since the tribe started reacquiring properties. OSGC has gotten its way for a long time on everything. There hasn't been anyone in a position to tell them 'no' for years and years, so expect OSGC to adamantly refuse to accept being told it's wrong, or unqualified, and doesn't know what it's doing."

Mike listened to Elaine and Rich's quick briefing, and added, "I was sitting in my office a couple of week ago when an OSGC representative stopped by to see me. This person strolls in and immediately announced, 'We've got a clean energy solution to disposing solid waste.'"

Mike shrugged as he told the group how it played out, his thick, salt and pepper eyebrows going up while his matching mustache curled down. "This person claimed they had some fantastic new technology called pyrolysis that was going to process solid waste and save the land-fills. There would be no emissions, and they thought the facility was a perfect fit in the Ashwaubenon business park adjoining Packerland Drive.

"That's when I asked him, 'Your facility will bring loads of trash into a corporate business park designed for company headquarters and simi-lar facilities? I don't think that's an appropriate activity for the surround-ing area, and its adjacent to some nice residential neighborhoods.' This guy curtly responded by saying he wasn't asking the village's permission. He said OSGC was placing the facility on Indian reservation trust land over which the village has no control; they were just being a good neigh-bor by letting Ashwaubenon know about the project.

"After hearing that, I asked if he thought the huge office building across the street from the project site would appreciate having a trash processing facility next to their corporate headquarters. There are hun-dreds of people who work there.

"His response was, 'They'll be fine. There's no emissions or smoke-stacks. Everything will be self-contained in a large building that looks like a warehouse. If the village has any questions, let us know. We'd like to host an informational session to get the proper information out.'"

Looked around at the group, Mike noted, "There was no thought given by OSGC to appropriately siting the facility. Ashwaubenon spent a lot of time and money developing that corporate park. We'd love to see more headquarters and things like that move in, but a heavy indus-trial trash facility that normally would be kept out due to Ashwauben-on's zoning has no business in a corporate park with nearby residential neighborhoods. Even if the thing works like they say it will, which I have serious doubts because it sounds way too good to be true, it'll drive away businesses."

Mike nodded toward Joanne, who was seated at the other end of the table. "So, when Joanne came into my office a while back to talk about this project, I could have kissed her when she came armed with informa-tion about the health effects!"

With that, I couldn't wait any longer and exclaimed in surprise, "They said no emissions? How can that possibly be true? Joanne, how does that square with your research?"

All eyes turned to Joanne. Her voice quivering slightly at first due to her discomfort of speaking before groups of people, she replied, "I have spent a lot of time the past few weeks looking up pyrolysis, and melting plastics and baking trash and other related topics, and all of the various methods which have been tried produced emissions at some point in the processing. The emissions were always filthy, because the fuel being used was itself filthy, and there was no way to avoid the filth."

Based on his own experience in the corrugated machinery and paper cutting industry, Greg asked, "How far will the emissions disperse? Do we know? That's a scary question, because the prevailing winds will blow particles for miles, which would often bring them to our neighborhood. One thing I do know from working with plastics is that melting or burning plastics, or anything else for that matter, will always produce emissions at some point in the process. It's unavoidable. Any outfit that says there won't be any is either lying or telling half-truths."

That prompted me to nod and respond to Greg. "Well, a half truth is equivalent to being wholly untrue according to the Supreme Court. It's a well-known legal precedent, so it seems this might be applicable to this situation."

Most of the group viewed my statement with surprise. "How do you know that?" asked Mike.

"Oh. Ah, I've been an attorney for the past eighteen plus years and have litigated quite a few fraud and misrepresentation claims. But it's not something I typically mention unless there's a reason to because normally people's eyes just glaze over."

Rich wanted to know, "Where did you go to law school?"

"University of South Dakota. I ended up in Wisconsin when I was being transferred to Chicago with my prior company, and a head-hunter cold-called for a gig. Once I got the job offer, my boss at the time described it as a 'no brainer' because he was also being transferred to Chicago, and neither of us wanted to relocate there," I quickly summarized for everyone.

Turning back to the agenda I had created for the evening I began with the setting of goals for our little group. Calling them the 3F's for the moment, I stated, "The initial goals as I see them are to identify the weak spots of this project, giving us a place to start. My thoughts are to uncover what we can about the project's Fuel, Funding and Friends. Joanne, we need to know more about what to expect from using trash as a fuel so we can get that word out to everyone. Then, where is the money coming from and can we interrupt that funding? And who or what are the friends of this beastie? Can we find a way to apply pressure on them as an indirect way to apply pressure on the facility to move elsewhere?"

Joanne agreed that she and her neighbors would continue with the fuel research, while Elaine and Rich had insight on the friends and funding since they had heard multiple rumors that this was funded by the federal or state government. They agreed also to work with Mike to identify the project's allies.

Next on the agenda was the list of tasks.

I shared a high-level overview of the task list before diving in deeper. "Alright, we need to touch on some of the topics before hashing out who does what for now. The larger action topics I could identify at this point are legal action, political action, and research actions."

"If there's a possibility of legal action I would think it would be taken up by the village's legal team first if the village identifies harm to its residents or properties," Mike suggested.

I nodded. "I agree, and at this point potential legal issues likely wouldn't be ripened enough for the village or its residents to file a suit. We wouldn't even know what they would claim. So, legal is a back-burner topic until we hear otherwise.

"Next topic is political action. This seems like the most potentially fruitful area at the moment. Elaine, Greg and I had been discussing how this whole thing will play out in the political arena due to the media and need for advocacy pressure on bureaucrats. First thing is to develop messaging points for the group based on what the research has turned up thus far, like this being unproven technology with no track record, the various impossibilities of the project, plus it's wasteful and a biohazard with some known risks. Any other thoughts here?"

The next half hour was filled with a productive buffing and polishing of the early messaging, before the group moved on.

"Communication is the next step to messaging. How do we go about that?" I asked the group. "Letters from the villages to state and federal officials? Publicity? Activism with boycotts, flyers, picketing and media? Any other ideas to give cameras something to point at?"

Rich nodded in agreement. "Those will all be effective. Just remember to keep everyone on the messaging you settle on."

"You betcha," I replied. "Everyone has to stick to the same overall points, which I'll collate and distribute for the next meeting. Now, how about optics? We could possibly use a video and web campaign, aerial impact photos, even prevailing wind maps. What do you guys think would be effective?"

"We can get the aerial map photos from the county website or satellite pictures from the web," Greg suggested. "That should work well for a flyer."

Elaine added that the group should "have a crowd of protesters marching, with colorful signs. TV loves a good protest". That sounded like a good idea to all folks at the meeting, so we quickly approved of the marching, aerial and flyer approach based on available resources.

"Last big topic is research. We need to develop a body of scientific research to counter unsubstantiated safety claims, and to collect data on vulnerable populations in the particulate fallout zone. Anybody know any engineering firms or consultants?"

Unfortunately, no one in the group had an environmental engineer on speed dial but Joanne offered, "There's a lot of searching we can do on the internet. I'll keep working on it and have more ready for the next meeting." That would have to do for now.

As a final housekeeping item, Greg and I agreed to continue taking lead as co-chairs, recognizing there likely would be times when only one of us would be available because life has a way of getting in the way. We had no idea how fortuitous the utilization of co-chairs would be at the time, but it would become a necessity when things got hectic and one of us wasn't available when needed.

As with any ad hoc team, the various talents, passion for the cause and dedicated interest of the participants quickly began to sort themselves out as the team members settled into roles dictated by the needs of the day. Over time, the core team would sift itself out from the at-large membership, but in these early days tasks and talents hadn't been established to such an extent yet.

The wise advice volunteered by Elaine, Rich and Mike proved instrumental in forming the foundation of our group's conduct throughout this adventure. As our still-anonymous group was about to engage in a battle of contested credibility in a very public setting, the sad reality was we were starting with no authority of our own while the opposition had preemptively anointed itself as the only experts in existence.

After the majority of the meeting attendees dispersed, Elaine gave the remaining handful of us some solid advice — to learn the rules of this game, very quickly. "Since you folks are getting a late start, Lesson #1 is how to be a credible opposition.

"Learning to become a credible opposition due to the late start means following certain rules. Never overstate your case, make up information, or lie. And don't sound overly emotional, because that just distracts from the message. Other things to always remember: (1) always assume the opposition has planted an informant or two in your larger meetings, so don't call the developers nasty names even if you have a couple of doozies floating around in the back of your head, and (2) always be a straight shooter, especially with the media and don't shy away from giving the media what they're looking for, within reason."

As he listened to Elaine's words I thought, *Of course, all these rules are tempered by remaining within the boundaries of remaining civil.*"

Elaine also shared something that struck me as perceptive and very true — the importance of being a voice for those without a voice in the proceedings. "Keep in mind public officials and regulators have only been hearing one side of the story for these incinerators, and it's a very rosy story indeed. When you give voice to those who've been unseen and unheard for so long, it might be a bit of a shock to these public officials or regulators who didn't know the whole story. Just remember to sound reasonable as sometimes they'll be dealing with the surprise of learning what they were initially told isn't true."

After taking a short break, the remaining team of Greg, Joanne and I reconvened for Elaine's Lesson #2. "Figure out a strategy to offset the lack of pertinent legal authorities to protect residents from incinerators."

I couldn't help but immediately connect Lesson #2 with the need for political action.

Elaine continued. "Our contacts in other cities that encountered projects like these had the same observations. Developers of these fake green energy projects will constantly promise to meet or exceed 'federal' standards. The sad reality is there typically aren't any meaningful standards, or that a permit monitored by some government agency somewhere will keep people safe. You need to keep in mind that the environmental pollution must already have occurred before a permit violation can even become a thing. By the time awareness of the inevitable problem spreads, the damage is ALREADY done." Elaine's wisdom was most helpful in giving our group a heads up of some occurrences we might expect to encounter.

Man, this thrill ride is going to suck, I thought. Too bad my ticket to ride can't be refunded.

Critically, the collective wisdom clearly told me our new movement must gain favorable media coverage by cultivating a relationship with a press. Unfortunately, in an era of rapidly declining advertising revenues, local media is likely predisposed to favor both OSGC and the tribal owner's due to the simple fact their advertising dollars tend to generate favorable press. Methodical cultivation meant our group had to become a solid source of reliable information and also by giving the cameras something to focus on.

Knowing all of these lessons were about to be put to use, I was worried. I wasn't sure how well we could put those lessons to use, and even if we played the game well, there was no guarantee of success.

CHAPTER 4

DAY 17

The Open House

"By failing to prepare, you are preparing to fail."

— Benjamin Franklin

Oneida Seven Generations Corporation (OSGC) held their open house at the Ashwaubenon village hall in the evening of Day 17. The third and now current home of the village offices, located a few blocks from the stadium, is an attractive, modern building built in 1994 and outfitted with all the technology needed to carry on village business. By now winter had arrived with a blanket of ankle-deep snow and frosty air that would stay with us for the next few months. Our still unnamed opposition group was in attendance, including the core membership of Greg, Joanne and me. We had arrived with hope in our hearts, but all of us took heed of the wisdom and advice from Elaine, Rich, and Mike. Especially the part about staying on message and giving the cameras something to focus upon.

And that we did. Joanne and I had already given local news stations advance notice that there would indeed be something to point their cameras at. Prior to the open house, dozens of citizens, many with children in tow, marched around in front of the village hall holding protest signs and chanting. My lanky young son was excited to later watch himself on television, marching with the others. In some cities, protest signs aren't particularly remarkable, but this was a protest in Ashwaubenon — a quiet, orderly, mostly middle-class village populated with numerous educated professionals who go about their daily lives without participating in messy protests and agitation. Protests normally happened elsewhere, while Ashwaubenon and Hobart residents only read about them or watched them on television. But this evening was different.

One other bit of wisdom Rich had shared with our group in the hopes of preparing for the evening was the prevailing attitude of folks in northeast Wisconsin and the Upper Midwest; one of reluctance to appear on television in a protest march. Rich had privately told me we would just have to overcome our natural reticence and discomfort with that sort of activity if we wanted to start making a difference.

Local TV news stations filmed our marchers walking in a long line up and down the sidewalk in front of the main entrance of the village hall, repeating various chants that included, 'Don't burn trash for cash' and the timeless classic, 'Give a hoot, don't pollute'. The film crews also interviewed individual marchers. Multiple local papers duly reported on it as well. It appeared that our group effectively managed to communicate the local resident's feelings about this project. But the night was young and the open house had not yet officially begun.

Mike, in his role as Ashwaubenon village president, was clearly no fan of the incinerator project but was obliged to stay officially neutral. He was quoted by the *Green Bay Press-Gazette* saying, "I just don't think the information that the people were looking for was answered. I think they felt they had questions that either weren't or couldn't be answered."

Meanwhile, apparently confusing itself with the State Farm jingle, OSGC managed to offer empty platitudes, with its spokesman muttering something about OSGC and the Oneida Nation having always been a good neighbor and only wanting to do what's best for the neighborhood. OSGC seemed not to grasp the jarring juxtaposition between inanities like wanting to be a good neighbor, while proposing to plop down a dirty trash incinerator next door to those neighbors.

Inside the village hall was aswarm with Ashwaubenon residents, plus a fair number from Hobart as well. The place was crowded.

The spectacle presented by OSGC was filled with solemnly delivered empty promises and assurances, and low on meaningful substance. OSGC's presentation was ridiculously vague and filled with techno-babble, setting off a cascade of red warning lights in my internal bulls!*t detector like a Christmas tree. After I walked in and observed the spectacle for a few moments, I tuned into an OSGC representative speaking to a crowd that had gathered round him.

This rep was going about how OSGC just wanted to continue being a good neighbor by keeping everyone informed, and that they believed this first-of-its-kind pyrolysis biomass plant was a good fit for the area. This guy went on to claim that there was a lot of misinformation out there, and that they were here today to answer everyone's' questions. He kept claiming this was a proven, closed-loop technology with no emissions and that there are many of these facilities operating in Europe today — look them up. And that people living there love them and have no problems living near them.

Just then, despite her discomfort with public speaking, Joanne interrupted the OSGC guy. "But that's not true! None of that is true!" she called out loudly, her voice quaking.

The representative looked way, way down at Joanne (because of their relative height difference) and responded with, "It is true, ma'am. All the information is out there. Just go look it up."

"I already did, and like I said, none of that is true."

The representative, not wanting to look bad on the television cameras that were now turning his way, replied, "Well then leave us with your written questions, and we'll be more than happy to respond to them."

A future core group member who goes by the *nom de plume* Alette Foster, watched this spectacle. In her mid-thirties, Alette is a mother of two small children and an elementary schoolteacher in nearby Green Bay. She lives in close proximity to the offensive proposed incinerator site.

Striking up a conversation with her as we watched the show, I shared that, "We're planning a counter-presentation in a few days right here at the village hall. Why don't you come and see if you want to get more involved in fighting this project?"

Alette nodded with a lot of interest. "Thank you! I'll definitely come and see the show." Alette spoke with me again later that evening. "I went to fetch the mail and found a notice on red paper detailing the incinerator project, filled with details of its devastation to health. Listed was an upcoming town hall hosted by OSGC at the Ashwaubenon village hall. After attending tonight, I'm absolutely horrified, but also relieved to learn of your upcoming counter presentation."

I was entertained later that night when the television reports on the evening's festivities took all of eight seconds to show a map marking the proposed location of the proposed 'incinerator' on south Packerland Drive in Ashwaubenon. One citizen said to WLUK-TV, "I am scared to death for this to be in our neighborhood." Videos of our signs were shown that said, "We Don't want the Biomass Facility in Our Neighborhood", "Why Our Backyard? Why Not Yours?", "Biomass to OSGC, Biomess to Us", "We Want Clean Air for Our Seven Generations" and more, all carried by our obviously large group of peaceful protesters. Another Ashwaubenon resident was interviewed saying, "My main concern is definitely the health problem, plus the fact our property values are probably going to go down. Plus, the added truck traffic, the smells, and we don't know what it's going to do to the land."

The reporter on the piece then said, "Pollution is a main concern for John Filcher." After seething from what I had overheard during the presentation at the open house, I had been surprised when the reporter wanted me to talk with her on camera. But I was game because this was a scary situation. I recall asking on camera, "How are you going to prevent pollution? What is their training? Who's going to sort out toxic materials from the trash?" Still good questions, I thought as I watched it on TV later. After flashing back to some guy with a flat-lined personality portraying himself as some sort of expert and mumbling something vague about the "project has all the necessary safety systems," the reporter cut back to me by saying, "But OSGC's presentation certainly didn't convince some residents, including Filcher."

Again, I clearly recall what I said. "Actually, I feel worse about it. You know, to be honest, this doesn't help anybody. Doesn't give out the proper information."

As I watched the news on DVR later that evening I was relieved to merely have appeared highly concerned and only somewhat annoyed instead of some wild-eyed, crazy man. Mulling it over afterwards made me think about our strategy. *OSGC's 'experts' are obviously nothing of the sort. In fact, the vague platitudes muttered by OSGC clearly signal a shocking skills mismatch between a construction campaign following the 'baffle 'em with bullshit' model, and the poor communication skills of the same folks trying to do the baffling.*

Watching the TV reports a second time, I now also realized, *OSGC actually hasn't figured out deploying word salads of semantical techno-babble is so unpersuasive it will turn even the most open minded against the project. We can turn that weakness against them.* It also made me realize our group's game face needed to improve as the rhetorical sparring matches would likely increase in intensity.

After a fitful night of worried sleep, I was pleased to learn the next day that many of our neighbors had likewise become alarmed — seemingly overnight — due to the fact that OSGC's open house messaging was such a fiasco. As I pondered what my neighbors said to me while taking a winter stroll through the neighborhood, I vowed, *we need to capitalize on their clumsy tone deafness and inability to communicate in simple terms.* This was a hard-won lesson in the game of persuasion from my own past experience (learned mainly from making my own mistakes) — that inability to articulate a position in simple terms will doom any players suffering from that disadvantage.

The next night our still nameless group of concerned citizens gathered in a conference room at the Ashwaubenon village hall (where many of our group's meetings would occur over the next few years) to discuss and plan out a counter presentation to be held over the upcoming weekend. It was an unusual start as Joanne immediately said, "Geez, I can't believe we actually protested like that."

I nodded. "Yeah, that was kinda fun. Has anyone marched and protested like that in the past?" Heads shook in response. Nobody had marched in protest or been interviewed by TV news before.

Just then Elaine arrived and filled the group in on the immediate effects of the protest and how the open house was received.

"I want to tell you all you performed wonderfully at the open house. OSGC couldn't answer any specific questions and came across like an outfit with something to hide. But there's more. OSGC and its own-ers, the tribe, were absolutely stunned by the protest. They pay a lot to ensure favorable representation in the local media and in one night their image was ruined by being associated with this biomass project. They aren't used to ANY unfavorable media, especially in a quiet 'burb like Ashwaubenon and the greater Green Bay media market, and all of a sudden they're blindsided by a highly publicized protest that they never saw coming. It was a real bombshell for them."

To my mind, the open house bombed because it was clearly a poorly executed attempt to mollify Ashwaubenon with misdirection and word salads of techno-babble and empty rhetoric. That being said, it definitely WAS news to the group that the OSGC leadership was 'stunned' over the protest and remarkably unfavorable media from just one act of pub-lic resistance.

Newfound awareness and word of the danger to Ashwaubenon was quickly spreading quickly and already affecting intergovernmental rela-tions. I shook my head slightly with a small laugh before saying, "It's about to get dicier with the counter-presentation this weekend, as OSGC isn't the only outfit that can throw around $10 words like 'pyrolysis' to show everyone who went to college this week." The group laughed a bit at my articulation of our shared determination to show that OSGC had brought the wrong ball to the game.

Day 19's counter presentation at the village hall went even better than I had hoped, thanks to the diligent research efforts of the group, especially by Joanne and her next-door neighbor. Working inde-pendently, they had spent several dozen hours researching the proposed type of incineration process for this facility, plus pages of material on the types and patterns of many of the untruths told by previous project developers. Joanne also found emissions data and trash composition data — all so the group would know what to expect in advance. And, planning ahead, Joanne and her neighbor wisely emailed their indispensable research to the rest of us in advance of the meeting so we had time to get up to speed.

Greg and I had plenty to present on an overhead slide presentation which I cobbled together. In front of a packed house, we methodically went through the expected fallout zone from the vent stacks the facility had to have.

Greg spoke first, introducing those at the head table before stating (as best I can recall), "Thank you all for coming. Please find a seat if you can. Overflow will have to stand in back behind the seating. Our citizen's group seated here at the podium are those who attended OSGC's open house the other night, and they have spent a lot of time researching the proposed facility. So, let's get right into it.

"For those of you who attended the open house, you heard OSGC repeatedly suggesting it was a proven, 'closed loop system' that somehow contains all wastewater and gases. In the research we conducted into the proposed method of processing biomass we were unable to locate any commercially operational pyrolysis facility anywhere, nor could we locate any form of pyrolysis that did not involve the creation of significant amounts of wastewater discharge, exhaust and venting of the exhaust."

After the grumbling crowd died down, it was my turn. "At the current proposed site, the area could expect to receive particulates from this facility. Schools, homes, senior centers, daycare's, hospitals, playgrounds, churches, and commercial buildings could expect to receive trash fallout thanks to the good neighbor emissions discharged by OSGC's incinerator. As you can see from the slide we've put up onto the screen, that, ladies and gentlemen, is a very conservatively drawn 4-mile diameter fallout zone of the particulates in that exhaust. Most actual experts on venting indicate the particles can fly as far as 20 miles, but for today's purposes, 4 miles was more than sufficient to give you all a good picture of the zone."

The crowd was stunned, as the zone included all of Ashwaubenon, most of Green Bay to the north, and a large chunk of Hobart to the west. I clicked to the next slide, before continuing.

"Using online mapping, we've now highlighted those facilities on the map so you can see their proximity to the incinerator. These areas to the north and northeast of the facility are currently residential, while the south and southwest are lighter residential. East is the Ashwaubenon industrial park."

More inconvenient truths were shown and discussed by both Greg and I. The facility was expected to be funded by a hefty $23 million in public money and create less than two dozen jobs. That's a cost of over $1 million per job! Further information on what was in the particulates was shared. And we nailed it. Sulfur dioxide, nitrogen oxide, hydrochloric acid, carbon monoxide, mercury, nickel, chromium, lead, cadmium, arsenic, dioxins and furans. Just the kind of yummy chemicals growing families need!

Already, we had found some of the soft spots in OSGC's claims of being a green recycling facility with no pollution or other nasty emissions. OSGC never seemed able to figure out the irreconcilable differences between people generally knowing the contents of municipal solid waste (trash) and trying to convincingly pretend trash feedstock wouldn't also be contained in the incinerator's emissions. Literally, the GIGO principle (Garbage In, Garbage Out) was inexorable in its application to the miraculous claims of OSGC merely two nights before.

Our presentation continued to drill down on putting all of this incinerated trash into context. This facility was supposed to incinerate 150 tons of trash per day. The charcoal-like fly ash waste product would contain thousands of pounds of leached heavy metal contaminants from the trash, and it would take up to 40 inbound and 40 correspondingly outbound trucks per day to haul in the trash and haul out the fly ash through the area. Presumably rats would take up residence as well because of the presence of trash.

After concluding the presentation, commentary by the residents showed that they were clearly alarmed. Oh sure, there were a few who refused to believe any company would be so callous as to recklessly risk the health of a large number of residents. But there were many more who were outraged — and a number of those who were simply disheartened but unwilling to fight for their right to live in peace.

While a broad range of reactions were expected by Mike as he moderated the meeting, he was shocked when Jim Schmitt, the mayor of neighboring City of Green Bay, stood up and indicated his city might be willing to take a look at a facility like this for placement in a more appropriate area. Discussion continued for quite a while until the Q&A wrapped up.

Once the village hall had cleared, our small core group gathered round the front table to discuss what we had seen and heard. Rich also remained behind to participate in the discussion. What confounded everyone was the inexplicable interest the mayor of Green Bay had in the OSGC facility.

"I can't believe the mayor of Green Bay would ever want this thing," said Greg.

I shrugged and replied, "Not that I would want to stop this thing from moving a few more miles away from our places. I didn't know who he was even after he said his name. It wasn't until he said he was the mayor of Green Bay when his title gave me some context around his identity. Why was he here, anyway? A weekend citizens meeting in a nearby community seems like an odd place for him to pop up."

Mike nodded. "Well, he probably has reasons that only make sense to himself."

Greg and I had no idea it wouldn't be until much later that Schmitt's presence today, and his intentions would become clear.

Another plus arose from the Day 19 meeting as the final core group member, Alette Foster, had also attended the counter presentation meeting a few minutes earlier. Day 19 was what prompted Alette to decide it was time to become involved. Later she told me and Joanne, "I sat next to Joanne, who had written the red flyer with notice of the town hall and afterwards decided to sit at the head table next to Joanne, yourself, Greg, Rich, Elaine and Mike. I was so impressed by Mike's high level of respect for us as citizens and impartial views, and his reminding us to seek the facts and the truth and never waiver from a 3-bullet point view of the issue. I remember scanning the variety of interested citizens. Some had taken steps to be more involved already; all were welcomed and despite some obvious diversity, the group was very united. I decided it was time to join and become involved."

Joanne smiled broadly and said, "You are so welcome to the group! We need all the help we can get here."

Also smiling, I said "Yes, definitely! You are most welcome to the team. Based on the advice we've received so far, there's going to be plenty to do and we'll be doing it for a long time."

Alette nodded, and replied, "That's what I'm afraid of."

The *Ashwaubenon Press* ran a headline on Day 20 under a picture of Greg and I that read, 'Citizens Oppose Biomass Plant'. It was a long article describing Ashwaubenon's efforts to hire a legal expert and an environmental expert to help with filing objections with the proposed facility. The *Press* quoted Mike, who indicated Ashwaubenon first objected to the site because it conflicts with the corporate business park setting. Mike also noted our residents objected to the placement of the facility because of strong ecological and health concerns. I was gratified to see the *Press* raise concerns about the lack of candor about the project in the context of the residents' concerns. "Several residents who have done some research on the issue brought up concerns from emissions that could come from the plant. They pointed out that the tribes claim that there are no smokestacks so there are no emissions is not true." The *Press* also quoted Joanne pointing out that, contrary to OSGC's claims suggesting this is a proven technology, the OSGC project is a one of a kind prototype. "How can they claim that when there isn't one other plant like this they can find, according to what they said?"

The next day, Greg called me up. "I think our group's core has finally come together. At the next meeting, more steps forward need to be taken."

"Yes," I quickly agreed. "And presumably, OSGC won't be sitting still while we get up to speed."

Neither Greg nor I were very surprised when OSGC decided to keep up its momentum by sending a letter to the affected neighborhoods in Ashwaubenon on Day 30, thanking them for their interest and stating,

"There is no incinerator. There will be no smokestacks (like those associated with coal-fired plants)." It also claimed, "The gasification technology to be used is not new nor is it an experimental prototype."

When I read those brazen claims, I just thought to myself, *I wonder what OSGC's next claims will be after these get shot down?*

CHAPTER 5

DAY 22

Biomass Opposition Committee (BOC)

"The most difficult thing is the decision to act, the rest is merely tenacity."

— Amelia Earhart

Throughout the week, Alette and Joanne continued their research. When next the group met, I noted as I entered the meeting room 20 minutes late, *our group size is already down to a more manageable number of fewer than 20 regulars.* I had forewarned the group that I couldn't manage to arrive at the Day 22 meeting on time; I would be running late because my daughter and I were at an indoor softball skills workout.

As I sat down, Greg looked over and said, "Since we knew you were going to be late, we moved ahead on a few of the agenda items. We've decided on the name, Biomass Opposition Committee, or BOC, for short. You and I will continue on as co-chairs, and additional research will be conducted by Alette and Joanne in addition to anyone else assigned a topic."

28

I nodded. "Outstanding. Where are we on the agenda? OK, next is the Survey Team."

Surveying had been conducted by an Ashwaubenon resident who lived very near the proposed site on Packerland Drive. He was polling the corporate business park establishments for their thoughts about the proposed trash facility which they were willing to share. This resident stated, "This effort is hampered by OSGC being the landlord of several of these businesses, as there was fear of summarily being evicted for saying something OSGC disapproves of. For those who don't have OSGC as a landlord, I couldn't help but notice there were no such qualms. Excluding the businesses which couldn't respond as OSGC or the tribe were their landlords, over 90% were opposed to this facility. The remainder were unsure and wanted more information, or a couple of them did not care."

"OK. Thanks," I said, and continued moving down the long agenda.

Input from Elaine, Rich and Mike was always welcomed, especially when much of it pertained to dealing with OSGC. Elaine made it clear to everyone when she stated, "BOC should expect to be the subject of various unsavory insinuations and to always remember nothing said by the project developers can be trusted. Expect them to mischaracterize anything BOC says or does, and to flat out lie about you all. Because it's owned by an entity that owes no allegiance to you, OSGC will be hostile and rely on the sovereign immunity of the company's owners to protect them from bad press and lawsuits."

As I listened, I couldn't help but mull over the situation. *Ironically, the one thing BOC actually can rely on is expecting OSGC's story to change. A lot.*

After the Biomass Opposition Committee took care of some housekeeping matters, I then announced, "Alright everyone, before this meeting I seeded a new bank account with $100, which was the minimum required to get an account open. We expect a long fight, and that costs money, so if anyone can donate anything to the cause, it will be both helping yourselves, and helping the cause." The account immediately received a generous $5,000 from a concerned Ashwaubenon business owner who attended several of the meetings.

Greg then brought up another issue. "What do you guys think about putting up yard signs? They're relatively cheap and might help get the word out."

"I doubt they would be very effective in this instance," Mike responded. "The homes near the site are in low traffic areas, and project supporters might just steal them if they find them on Packerland Drive." We all grumbled a bit but had to acknowledge Mike was right.

Alette then asked, "Is the group still planning on a boycott or future picketing?"

I responded with, "Tentatively, yes. We haven't decided on when and where, figuring that decision could wait until after some upcoming community events to drive more news exposure."

Alette nodded. "That makes sense. No point in freezing if the cameras are busy filming other activities."

Knowing OSGC's story would change a lot and having experienced it already, BOC approached the situation in the only effective way I knew of. I advised the group of this approach. "I'm going to use the same approach I use when the other party's story is slippery and changes when they find it convenient. This is an 'old school way' of cobbling together a master timeline and keeping detailed copies and notes of everything OSGC says. That means I'll be making detailed files, along with copies of the source materials, including television reports, radio, and all media. Depending upon how many times we can get OSGC to talk to the news, this could become very detailed as time drags on. We'll need to goad OSGC into talking more to create a verbal record for us that can be turned against it."

Pulling his cigar out of his mouth and gesturing with it between his index and middle fingers, Rich replied, "That sounds like a lot of work! You sure you want to go there?"

"If someone has a better idea, I'm all ears. I'm pretty sure this outfit won't be too agreeable to me nailing down their story in a deposition that I could later use against them the next time they want to start singing a different tune, so hopefully this is the next best thing."

What I didn't expect was that this 'old school' timeline would eventually span 12 pages. Usually there are only 1 to 3 pages, but a lot was yet to happen that I couldn't have anticipated at the time. When some developer gets clever with the techno-babble surrounding a trash incinerator by dressing it up in green energy clothing, they should anticipate their opponents will factor the developer's blarney into their strategic goals. And as expected, BOC's strategic goals were generating wider media coverage and chipping away at the credibility of OSGC. BOC's tactical methods of utilizing protests, pressure, clearer messaging and devastating rebuttals also worked well to achieve our strategic goals. OSGC apparently didn't recognize the danger of inconsistent messaging, and it was an early blunder we were determined to ensure would be one from which OSGC would never recover. Many more blunders would follow over the next few years, starting with the BOC already receiving internal documents from entities, employees and community members who thought they would be useful to the BOC's effort to resist the incinerator.

For me, the early meetings had a consistent theme: the need for additional solid information and pressuring OSGC into talking. I was sure it would work to our advantage that the more ridiculous statements OSGC would make, the more BOC could box OSGC in.

It turns out the wheels were already in motion for OSGC talking trash because the *Press-Gazette* contained a notably understated headline indicating both sides disagree in the biomass controversy. Despite OSGC repeatedly suggesting the BOC was misinformed (OSGC seemed to think it was an effective message to imply anyone disagreeing with the sheer genius of the project was somehow misinformed), OSGC suddenly felt the need to contest whether there would be fallout zones because they have a magical 'closed loop' renewable energy biomass pyrolysis machine. I just wasn't sure why it took OSGC several weeks to react to our counter-presentation a few days after OSGC's open house.

At the Day 42 BOC meeting, our group discussed OSGC's latest messaging gambit. Taking a deep breath, Alette read aloud a long-winded report where OSGC dismissively addressed community concerns. When she looked up after reading she found BOC members chuckling derisively about the condescendingly smug tone of OSGC's comments in the paper.

After everyone finished, I semi-paraphrased a quip from a pirate movie, saying "That's a lot of long words, miss. We're naught but humble rebels here!"

Alette laughed. "How could anyone find this mashup of nonsensical words convincing? It's like they decided to use a BBQ grill owner's manual to write talking points."

"They also decided the telephone book was the appropriate style guide for their word games. Random sounding big words with nothing too meaningful behind them is going to be a hard sell for OSGC," I snorted in response over my chuckling.

"Our experience with OSGC, while often adversarial the past few years, is it isn't used to speaking to the little people," Rich added. "Having to speak to the media in more than a few canned sound-bites isn't OSGC's strong suit, especially when it has a weak technical understanding of its machine and can't just admit it's an incinerator."

Elaine agreed. "Well, they definitely can't just call it what it is, so they're putting lipstick on the pig and hoping nobody notices. That would give their game away in a heartbeat."

Importantly, Days 52 through 60 also brought new attention to the proposed project from other local environmental groups who would be key allies as the campaign grew, including from Charlene Lemoine of the Waukesha County Environmental League (WEAL). Charlene was a Board Member, and Waste Issues Representative for WEAL. She told me how she heard of this fight. "I learned of OSGC's plan to construct a pyrolysis project in Ashwaubenon and posted information about the plan on the Global Alliance for Incinerator Alternatives (GAIA) listserv. Bradley Angel from the Greenaction for Health and Environmental Justice responded to me and was put in touch with the Biomass Opposition Committee, which was soon to evolve into Incinerator Free Brown County. I was immediately impressed with the members and their dedication and knowledge. The group had clearly done a great deal of research."

During that week, WEAL and BOC members began an online discussion of the feasibility of hosting an environmental forum with Paul Connot and Bradley Angel, who are experts in trash incineration issues.

For some reason, circumstances around Day 52's BOC meeting at the village hall have remained strong in my memory. It was a clear evening. Midwestern winter had settled in with temperatures hovering near zero. Despite facing a long and packed agenda, most in our group were secretly hoping for a beer after a long day, but grudgingly had to settle for coffee and pastries. Alette and Joanne pitched the idea of picketing one of the proposed contractors.

"We found out the builder of the facility will be at the KI Center downtown for a presentation on another project," Alette shared. "Joanne and I were thinking that this would be an opportunity to picket and get some media attention."

Elaine's response threw cold water on that idea when she responded. "I'm not sure how effective it would be because OSGC isn't going to be there."

"Yeah. My thinking is we should try to stick to OSGC, because the news won't be too interested. Anybody have other thoughts on it?" I asked.

After a few moments of thought, nobody objected.

Next, the BOC Actuarial Team had prepared an estimate of predicted tax impact based on lowered property values. The actuarial team predicted a loss in residential property values in the range of 20-30%, plus other downstream affects like subsequently deteriorating property conditions as homeowners lose equity. Upon hearing that grim estimate I sighed, thinking, *Great, I'll lose all kinds of equity and so will everyone else. I wonder how people will react when they learn they'll be paying underwater mortgages because the home values dropped that far?*

Our group continued to the finalized results of the local business survey from the corporate business park in Ashwaubenon. "Unsurprisingly, about 80% were opposed to this facility before learning any more about the planned operations. When additional information about the proposed facility was discussed, the opposition number jumped to the high 90s," said the surveying team leader.

Next, I said that the group needed to talk about our upcoming forum that had been informally discussed prior to today's meeting. Alette reported that BOC's "Invitations to the experts were extended and accepted. Joanne and I are working on tentative dates for a forum and will get back with possible dates."

Joanne also mentioned working on a letter to the editor. "I'm awaiting publication on the letter I wrote, so hopefully that will be in the papers soon."

"I've finished writing a draft letter to affected residents about the upcoming forum. Mike had good advice on sending out invites to local officials to attend as well." Greg reported. He then looked at me and asked, "Didn't you get an invitation to talk to a local tax group?"

I nodded. "I would be speaking to the Brown County Taxpayers Association about the negative tax impacts as summarized by our Actuarial Team, but we don't yet have a date nailed down yet."

Significantly, BOC also reviewed the recent minutes of OSGC's oversight entity, the Oneida Business Committee, which were quietly delivered to us by some new allies within the tribe. Those minutes stated, "Now therefore be it resolved, the Oneida Business Committee enthusiastically supports this project and will work with Oneida Seven Generations Corporation and Oneida Energy to help them realize the opportunity and to locate the facility on a site that is most desirable."

The minutes also noted that someone was "opposing because there are too many unanswered questions. I want to know what we are putting up for collateral. We don't know and I need to know. I want to be assured that there are enough resources "garbage" to feed that generator because without enough garbage we will not be able to be successful. We have not seen any written agreements."

It didn't escape the attention of BOC members that the minutes definitely were talking about bringing garbage into Ashwaubenon to feed an incinerator.

Other comments captured in the minutes stated some "opposed the resolution because the Oneida Tribe's positive relationship with most all neighboring local governments and the Tribe's reputation as a good neighbor and environmental steward have been put at risk by the decision of the Oneida Seven Generations Corporation to construct and operate a waste-to-energy gasification plant on Packerland Drive in the Village of Ashwaubenon."

The minutes went on to express that, "Despite the opposition to locating the project on the Packerland Drive site, there seems still to be support for the Oneida Tribe's biomass energy project and I do support Oneida Seven Generations constructing and operating a biomass energy project, just not on the Packerland site. Many still hope that Oneida due to its mission to protect the environment will find a way to make alternative energy an option in Northeast Wisconsin that will help solve energy and environmental problems, improve our economy and create new jobs. This is one reason why Oneida cannot afford to fail and as one reason why I believe we need to enter into this project in collaboration and cooperation with our neighbors. This project has potential of putting the Oneida Tribe in an environmental leadership role positively impacting the Tribe's economy and positively helping the greater community in and around the Oneida Reservation."

Ironically, I thought, *the hopes that this project potentially puts Oneida in a nationwide environmental leadership role won't be the squeaky-clean energy version of that role as they imagined. Given the universal local opposition to building a trash incinerator in Ashwaubenon's neighborhoods, it's unclear how intentionally disregarding Ashwaubenon's wishes would somehow constitute collaboration with the 'neighbors'.*

What was most disturbing about the commentary in those minutes was a clear absence of concern for the health of the local community residents, or for contamination of Ashwaubenon and Hobart neighborhoods. Looking around at the aghast faces of the BOC core members, Alette asked, "So, Ashwaubenon and Hobart neighborhoods are supposed to be some kind of guinea pigs?"

"It seems so," I replied after a few quiet moments. "All for a grand corporate experiment in which our residents have to bear all the negative consequences. Unless we can stop it from happening."

While OSGC cooked up some new talking points it thought would contest the fallout zones, it also had filled out an application for a Conditional Use Permit (CUP) with the City of Green Bay. Important for future events, the CUP application and filed documentation were silent about stack heights. In fact, stacks were omitted altogether. In a coordinated effort, OSGC then took the extraordinary step of providing a document titled '*Myths v. Facts*' to the City of Green Bay which contained the whopper that the "proposed Pyrolysis system is a completely closed loop system so all gases and wastewater are contained."

As no one in BOC or Ashwaubenon was yet aware of the CUP application filing in Green Bay, on Day 71 Greg and I appeared before the Ashwaubenon Board of Trustees to update them on the status of the effort to oppose bringing the biomass facility into the village. The grave looks on their faces spoke volumes. This '*Myths v. Facts*' also appeared in the tribal paper, *the Kalihwisaks* a few days later, likely in response to the BOC's half a page ad which was placed right below it, asking, "Are you comfortable with no local control over a 'first of its kind' Biomass Gasification plant?"

By now I couldn't help but sarcastically think, *Weird that OSGC would get spooked over something like an ad — especially lengthy ads with maps of fallout zones and questioning the severe environmental, health and economic effects of a trash incinerator. We must've hit a soft spot of theirs and that can only mean one thing. Keep hitting that spot while we look for other soft spots.*

BOC's ad was fantastic and signaled to OSGC that there was no place it could hide from the truth, or consequences for untruths. OSGC was never able to answer what would happen with the tons of leftover toxic ash its incinerator would produce every day. It could not refute the fact such ash could be lethal and potentially cause cancer, heart attacks, strokes, birth defects, asthma, and pulmonary disease. OSGC could not refute the reality that the ash could enter the food chain or that particulates would threaten residents living within 20 miles. Nor could OSGC effectively rebut the reality that surrounding property values would plummet. OSGC couldn't even rebut the ad's statements about the current availability of greener, more cost-effective alternatives.

While OSGC was scrambling to prepare a defensive campaign, it was Day 82 when an official announcement was published naming the City of Green Bay as the new project site. Across the entire BOC team, all of us were relieved we had finally conquered the monster — but we felt the sadness of our friends in Green Bay who now faced it in our stead.

Within mere days, the CUP application was recommended for approval by the Green Bay Plan Commission, whose minutes indicated OSGC suggested, "there are no smokestacks..." In a bit of accurate prediction about the future, the *Kalihwisaks,* the official newspaper of the Oneida Tribe, quoted OSGC: "We expect a small group (of opposition) from folks who just don't support these types of technologies."

My own thoughts about this quote were, *Well DUH, of course opposition would continue! That plant's particulate dispersal still threatens the entire area depending on the winds of the day.*

As this incinerator was no longer in BOC's immediate neighborhood, a celebration was called for, plus a discussion as to BOC's future. That BOC soirée occurred on Day 83.

CHAPTER 6

Incinerator-Free Brown County

"You have enemies? Good. That means you've stood up for something, sometime in your life."

— Winston Churchill

On Day 83, the BOC invited Elaine and Rich (Mike was out of town and had to decline) to gather at Greg's home to celebrate over some food and brews. If nothing else, my sense was that BOC was starting to get a bit of a culinary reputation since food and beverages seemed to be ever-present at the meetings. Our small gang gathered over chocolate ice cream with bright sunlight shining into the Greg's living room. Elaine stood up in the middle and said she was "very proud of how this small group of regular folks stood up for themselves and their neighbors against OSGC and wouldn't back down."

After I selected a particularly tasty peanut butter nitro porter from a local brewer in Green Bay, Elaine continued, advising that she had new information given to her from some of her close friends in the tribal community.

"First of all, a huge congratulations for saving Hobart and Ash-waubenon from this monster." She then shared, "I have some very interesting information from my good friends who overheard what was said by OSGC informally to some members of the Business Committee. It was some nasty stuff about the members of BOC."

She dug into her purse for a notepad she had stashed. "Ah, found it. They said OSGC said such vile stuff I wanted to be sure I wrote it down correctly. OSGC said, and I quote, 'We are being opposed by a small group of non-natives. They do not want to see Oneida's succeed and the BOC just wants to prevent folks from developing jobs.'" Elaine looked up as she drew a breath before continuing. "Obviously none of that will be found in the official meeting minutes."

While I mentally processed the mind-boggling kind of stupid it would take to falsely say something that repellent about BOC members, Alette angrily said, "I have no tolerance for that kind of language. None!"

Looking over at Alette after her outburst, I was somewhat chagrined by the contrast between the caveman-like grunting noises which popped into my head and Alette's more civilized articulation, so I politely just nodded in response. Looking around the room, it was quickly apparent that Alette had vocalized what each of us had been thinking in response to such talk from OSGC.

In that moment, which to me seemed somewhat reminiscent of a scene from an old baseball movie where the manager informs the team that the owner wants to replace them with better personnel and then move the team to Miami, the issue of whether or not to continue the fight on neutral ground over in Green Bay had just been decided by nodding heads and determined looks. OSGC's false attack on the BOC membership was the sort of blunder that achieved exactly the opposite of OSGC's intention, because now the core team's resolve had truly hardened.

Glancing around at the faces in the room again, I asked, "So we're united in staying in the fight?" With nodding heads and murmurs of "uh huh" and "yep," the BOC core unanimously decided to take the fight to

OSGC and continue on indefinitely. "OK then, we'll keep on keepin' on!"

Happily, this wasn't the day's only blunder by OSGC. Because while the BOC already operated on a need-to-know basis and presuming the presence of informants in our large meetings that included more folks than the BOC operational core, OSGC was still unaware that the reverse was already happening. This meant BOC already possessed some interesting documents, copies of which were then handed out so our core members could look them over.

As I eyeballed the documents, I thought one of the most interesting was an internal update memorandum to the general manager from the Environmental, Health and Safety Division. *The amount of accurate inside information funneled to BOC is becoming astounding,* I mused. *Because of this inside intel, the BOC will often be prepared well in advance to counter OSGC's next moves.*

While perched on the arm of a living room chair, Alette raised the issue of the appropriateness of our group's current name. "Me and Joanne's research has clarified the use of the term 'biomass' is aligned with the incineration industry's objectives to misdirect attention away from the burning of trash."

Camped out in chair near the front window, I took a sip of my beer and replied, "I agree, what do you propose?"

Animated discussion quickly focused on what Alette said. "The need to reflect the reality of the situation in the group's name. Joanne and I found the name of a group in North Carolina which seems pretty appealing. They look like they have been in existence for a long time and it allows them to take on more than just trash incinerators. Using the word 'incinerator' in their name allows them to fight any type of incinerator if need be."

Nodding, Greg replied, "I like it. Something like that would give us more flexibility and geographic freedom."

I agreed. "Yeah, Incinerator Free Brown County has a nice ring to it. We'd have to either use all the words, or just the initials IFBC."

"IFBC is a good name and you can use that as a springboard to take the fight anywhere in the county. Its easily recognizable, and anybody can get behind a name like that because it excludes no one," Elaine approved.

BOC was re-branded by us that day as Incinerator Free Brown County. Eventually IFBC would also settle on a green leaf symbol as part of the evolving IFBC branding that represented the group's focus on a cleaner environment. Later on, the inclusion of the word 'incinerator' in IFBC's name would pay an unexpected and comical dividend when our IFBC billboards were put up around town — against OSGC's wishes.

A large part of IFBC's passion came from concern for the safety of our children. Most of the core steering team had young children at home, and parental interest in a healthy environment is extremely motivating. Accordingly, research and a healthy environment were issues close to everyone's hearts and in everyone's best interests. As the conversation touched on our similar motives for opposing the incinerator, Alette shared that her own upbringing mirrored the entire core groups collective backgrounds.

"I was raised by parents who always put health first, fed us carefully, stressed vitamins and clean living. Encouraged us to be outdoors, to play, wander, seek the beauty of nature. As a mother, my priority was the health and safety of my children, then 4 and 9 years old. The incinerator was going to be around, maybe 2000 feet from our home, our yard, and my most precious children. Well, not if I had anything to do about it." I could see Alette's strong feelings and motherly instincts plainly drove her commitment to getting the information needed to fight this incinerator.

"I was determined to find out everything I could about the project. With the internet, information was available and many hours and days of research proved profitable. The bottom line was, it was an incinerator and it would never generate a positive net in power. However, it could leave a path of nanoparticulate destruction in its shadow. I learned from the top scientists, nurses and researchers both in their written work and via email and phone. I called them... and they answered! The more I reached out, the more I found support and encouragement to fight. I joined email groups, connected with people around the country and world. We were one big team of concerned people with the same goal."

Alette's feelings were echoed by all in the IFBC. I knew that those feelings certainly mirrored my own. *I can't let this thing poison my family*, I thought. *I would have to find a way to sabotage the thing to keep it from ever operating if it comes to that.*

Branding issues now settled, serious discussion ensued over what were IFBC's next steps.

"You've had a huge victory, but, keep in mind to expect a long fight with highs and lows, and periods of time reflecting an ebb and flow to the action," cautioned Elaine.

In the IFBC, we also focused extensively on verbiage and not getting caught up using the developer's semantic techno-babble which was designed to obscure the facts and get opposition groups to waste time chasing red herrings. Sticking to just the facts would require constant vigilance on IFBC's part, which the core team executed perfectly.

Another semantics issue that came up again was how to refer to OSGC. "I'm so confused about all these sub-corporations and partnerships that we located, and so on. There's so many!" complained Joanne.

"These facilities play a rapidly changing shell game to hide who is doing what, and to keep opposition groups off balance," Rich added. "You're going to have to find some workaround for that problem."

"I was looking through the list of corporate sub-entities while I was cobbling together the whole timeline that we know of so far, and I noticed there is only one constant among them," I noted. "OSGC. It's the oldest, and it's used the same name the entire time. My thoughts are we keep it simple, and just collectively refer to all the entities as OSGC in our communications, while we merely monitor the rest in OSGC's murky web of sub-entities. My sense is OSGC represents the only stationary target here."

After some additional discussion, IFBC core members conclusively decided the only path forward was simply to continue to refer to OSGC as a standalone corporate entity. Elaine also shared that, "As you all know, my sources say a great many of the tribal membership are not in favor of the incinerator, nor do they have a favorable impression of OSGC itself due to its highly questionable past missteps that will soon be in the process of becoming exposed. There is a group on the inside working to bring down OSGC, but they will need time to get their chess pieces into place."

"These past OSGC missteps include squandering huge amounts of money, and stupidly planning to originally site the incinerator near the Town of Oneida," Rich added, "and near a daycare for Oneida children."

After the Day 83 meeting, IFBC's website went live, so I started a rapid-fire Google search for the terms 'Incinerator Free Brown County' and 'IFBC' to drive up the search results towards our group. Within days, people searching either of those terms quickly found IFBC's website. Alette and Joanne had populated our website with relevant information on emissions, fallout zones, how to contact IFBC, probable diminished property values, and a thorough debunking of OSGC's claims that I cobbled together that included the quoted claim, a link to the document it came from, and an explanation of why it was untrue along with relevant links to favorable documents.

Our newly branded and motivated group also decided to hold a large meeting to get the word out about the BOC's evolution into Incinerator Free Brown County. Hosted on the evening of Day 87 at a local corporation in the Ashwaubenon business park, IFBC previewed all the changes for the assembled crowd. This included our new email address, branding, website filled with important information, and transition to a more educational focus. IFBC also used this opportunity to cast a brighter light on IFBC's upcoming town hall and to invite everyone with interest in the subject to attend.

The crowd of about 100 snickered when Greg told them, "We also invited OSGC to appear and present their story tonight, but they declined." Also noted was the recent appearance of Greg and I in front of the village board to present a project update, and that Ashwaubenon high school would be the site of the next educational forum.

CHAPTER 7

DAY 93

Hubbub on Hurlbut Street

"We can't solve problems by using the same kind of thinking we used when we created them."

— Albert Einstein

The *Press-Gazette* published an article reporting that the 'Gasification' plant on Hurlbut Street received the go ahead from the Green Bay council. The article helpfully quoted OSGC saying, "There are no smokestacks." Bizarrely, OSGC and industry personnel were still spinning half-baked fictions in the media — like incinerators not needing stacks or pretending there is no incineration because the feed stock is merely heated up until it's ash instead of being burned in an open flame. Ironically, the literal definition of incineration can also merely mean to reduce to ash without specifying any particular method.

Meanwhile, we continued to carefully collect copies of all media and statements as preparation for our next event. We were finally going on the offense! Part of our game plan was to speak out against incinerators by actively promoting viable methods of recycling, with the realization that it's always easier to attract interest by standing *for* something rather than fighting *against* something.

The IFBC agenda for Day 94 contained some potent points. Reading the agenda items to the group, I shared, "Greg and I discussed strategy in advance for tonight's meeting. First, we will be 'educating everybody everywhere' on incinerators. We will not advocate — at any time — moving the facility again. The reason is that there is no upside in doing so, plus we believe the value of us adopting a purely educational position will be of benefit to our growing list of Oneida Nation members who are becoming emboldened to speak out. Remember, we are here to educate, and also to assist our silent but fast becoming more vocal partners from the Nation, as well as those right here in our own surrounding communities."

With that, we dove into the planning and logistics for our upcoming educational forum. As a major part of our instructive outreach, IFBC was planning a recycling and anti-incineration public forum with Dr. Paul Connot, Ph.D., an expert at educating the public on the dangers of incineration emissions and toxicity, and Bradley Angel with Green-action for Health and Environmental Justice. Alette and Joanne had learned of both men during their deep research dive and had taken the lead in arranging travel plans for both Dr. Connot and Mr. Angel.

Alette told the group that, "Bradley Angel will get us his schedule so we can shuttle him to the hotel. He doesn't know yet, but I'm going to ask him to dinner! He arrives 6:20 pm on the 9th. Anyone want to meet and greet him? Who's willing to pick him up at the airport?"

Joanne noted, "I'll pick up Dr. Connot whenever he arrives, although he's tentatively scheduled for 12:00 noon at the moment. I'll find him lunch if he needs it and then show him the Ashwaubenon site and new site in Green Bay, then drive him to his hotel. That should give him some down time until about 4:15 when I pick him up for dinner. I hope some of you will join us in welcoming our guests."

Joanne added that she and Alette were going to put gift baskets in their guests' hotel rooms as a special welcome from our group.

"I like that. Nice touch!" Greg enthused. Once everyone confirmed that they had each reached out to their assigned media contacts, the group double-checked all of their preparations for the up-coming forum. To publicize the event, IFBC members had sent out fliers and even posted videos introducing their 'expert' speakers on YouTube. Judging by how dismissive the incineration industry was towards these longtime adversaries, it was obvious that IFBC had drawn another bead on the industry's weaknesses.

Day 101 would be the big day of our meticulously planned recycling and anti-incineration public forum at the Ashwaubenon high school.

The evening before the big event I joined the others of the IFBC core group at a bar and grill in Ashwaubenon for the welcome dinner, which turned out to be an enlightening prelude to next day's forum.

Bradley and Paul shared some of their most interesting and persuasive insights into incinerator companies. When comparing types of pollution from windmills to incinerators, Paul mentioned, "When a windmill goes away, the pollution generally goes along with it as it is noise pollution. Contamination stays in the ground and in the water, even after the incinerator goes away. And eventually, incinerators will always go away because the money runs out."

When I heard Paul say that, I sought some clarification. "It almost sounds like incinerators are an industrial version of a locust, and when a spot is played out they migrate on to whatever new feeding grounds they can take over for a while."

Paul smiled and nodded. "Yes, I hadn't heard it phrased quite like that before but that describes the pattern pretty well. They make all these ridiculous promises that are too good to be true, but local officials believe them anyway because they want to have some nice 'green' credentials to flash about. They'll vacuum up all the money they can for a few years until the government money spigot is turned off, then shutter the facility and sub-corporation because they're bankrupt, and then they move on simply because the things can never financially sustain themselves for long. But the mess stays behind for everyone left to sort out."

Bradley was highly approving of IFBC's core concepts about messaging and credibility, and then shared his desire to maintain Greenaction's excellent prior working relationship with the Oneida Nation. He cautioned IFBC about working with certain individuals or outfits who had failed to heed this lesson, or who had 'screwed' him over in the past. This was duly noted and taken to heart by the steering committee because we sure didn't want to look like the bad guys! But, IFBC was definitely even more intent on figuring out what the unwritten rules of the game were and then use them to our advantage.

Bradley was very concerned about was the possibility this incinerator previously was to be on the Oneida Indian Nation reservation, making it the first solid waste incinerator sited on '*sovereign*' lands. As things had developed — and after Bradley's plans to come to Ashwaubenon were in place — the incinerator site was moved to Green Bay, but Bradley was still game for helping educate with the truth, sharing that he had been in meetings with Oneida leadership prior to coming to Ashwaubenon. Bradley stated, with the current situation where IFBC was combating where a permit had actually already been issued, Greenaction was very concerned about the troubling combination of development companies and incineration sites on all '*sovereign*' lands since it appeared that the incineration industry thought that was a way to force its way into the U.S.

As a practical matter, IFBC was already aware that once a permit is issued, it's extremely unlikely that project can be stopped. That said, IFBC was also informed enough to know that permits can, at times, be rescinded for misrepresentations or omissions, particularly if the community handles the process right. This knowledge about the standard to rescind a permit was already guiding my thinking in determining what sort of information was needed. As a 'lawyer', I was well aware by now that stopping this thing would initially have to be done politically rather than legally.

The remainder of the evening's discussion centered around the economics of incineration. Bradley said something that that really perked up my ears. "Trash burners can't stay in business because it costs too much to burn the trash, and the landfill tipping fees which are redirected to the incinerators aren't enough to cover the deficits. They have to burn something that other communities want to get out of their towns so badly they're willing to pay a lot to ship it to the incineration site."

With a sinking feeling, I asked, "Burn something? Like what? Chemical waste or something?"

"No, it's usually something more plentiful with much higher tipping fees, like tires and medical waste." Bradley shared a story about his uncle, who works in the medical waste industry, and the massive amounts of money being paid to dispose of the medical waste anywhere they could, just to get rid of it.

The big day dawned sunny and bright as people filed into the high school auditorium expectantly. When the program began, the audience was immediately spellbound by the charismatic Dr. Connot. It was hard to tell which was most intoxicating for attendees, his engaging British accent or the fact that, as he stated, he does all this work *pro bono*.

Dr. Connot told the audience that he had been educating the public about the dangers of incineration for 26 years, ever since a developer tried to build an incinerator very near his own home. "When I first heard about the incinerator, I thought it was a good idea. You get rid of those landfills. We have 32 leaking landfills. We would generate energy to boot. And we would have one facility to be totally monitored. That's what I thought.

"Then I started to read about the issue and discovered to my amazement as a professor of chemistry that simply by burning household trash we actually generate the most toxic substance that we've ever made in a chemical laboratory. THAT got my attention."

It certainly captured IFBC's attention as well. Dr. Connot noted that the easy job is to defeat the incinerator. The more difficult part is to push through an alternative to landfills and incineration. And so, he shared, his mission was to generate excitement about a genuine alternative that promised to be better for our health and local economy, and also better for the planet. Paul centered his concern on three categories: (1) sustainability, (2) the argument against incineration and additional concerns about gasifying incineration (Paul also noted the audience will hear more on this topic from Bradley as this is his specialty), and (3) the Zero Waste Strategy.

Alette, who was sitting in the audience next to Rich, whispered, "The sustainability portion of Dr. Connot's presentation is *very* educational!"

Rich nodded. "Comparing the amount of waste being produced by Americans, Europeans, India and China is enlightening. I really loved it when he mentioned our societies are 'linear societies' where every single one of us makes waste every day."

Paul had shown a chart on the screen that clearly displayed this concept of a 'linear society'. It begins with extraction of virgin materials, which he explained is a process that itself creates solid waste, air and water pollution, and carbon dioxide. From there the materials are shipped halfway around the world for manufacturing processing, again creating the same forms of waste in even greater amounts while also using the highest amount of energy at this stage. The final two stages are consumption and discarding.

Dr. Connot then addressed what the various ways of handling waste does to this picture. What does landfilling do to this picture, he asked rhetorically. "Nothing! You bury something in the ground, now you've got to go all the way back to the beginning to extract more virgin materials." He then brought up the comparison to incineration. "Incineration — the same thing. There's no change. You burn something, you have to go all the way back to the beginning to replace it whether you burn it in a conventional incinerator or whether you destroy it in a pyrolysing plant."

As we listened, I glanced around the room and noticed that nearly every head in the audience was nodding in agreement. Greg was sitting next to me and grinned as he glanced over before whispering, "This is AWESOME! I've never heard the process explained this clearly."

"Yeah, wow. Really good stuff! Best lecture I've attended in years!" I agreed. Clearly, neither landfilling nor pyrolysis incinerating were sustainable. Although, as Dr. Connot pointed out, incinerators will always claim they are superior to landfilling by comparing them as a dirty, messy landfill versus a shiny new incinerator.

Dr. Connot methodically debunked even more of the arguments put forth by trash incinerator developers. He established that the economics just do not work despite rosy claims to the contrary. Incineration is actually the second most expensive form of electricity production because there is a sliding scale correlation between the cleanliness of the underlying fuel and the cost of the resulting electricity. The dirtier the fuel, the higher the cost of generating power from it. Accordingly, natural gas is both clean and efficient, then clean oil, dirty oil, clean coal, and dirty coal. And then comes trash, which is the dirtiest fuel! And it costs a fortune to incinerate because half the cost of a modern incinerator goes into pollution control devices to capture the toxic air and wastewater emissions. Plus, the cost of dealing with the obviously toxic ash must be factored in because it certainly can't be used for roadbeds since the ash inevitably leaches into the groundwater.

Other economic failings were pointedly debunked. Paul noted that trash incinerators create very few jobs for a huge capital investment, causing a 25-year freezing in place of new development in respectable recycling programs because of the payback period required to pay for the incinerators. Particularly entertaining was Dr. Connot's comparison of the pitiful amount of energy to be generated by the incinerator (six megawatts, or about the equivalent of merely two wind turbines) compared to the huge amount of toxic ash being created. And creating toxic ash does not get rid of landfills, it merely fills them with toxic ash that can then leach contamination into the groundwater. He advised the audience that one ton of ash is created for every four tons of trash, before stating that we could do the math for the project proposed in Green Bay. With that calculation, OSGC's project proposes to create 37.5 tons (yes, that's TONS) of unwanted toxic ash and char each and every day!

While this information was disturbing enough, the pictures Paul shared of hazardous waste ash landfills were shocking. The ash actually covered up road signs, formed clouds of blowing ash-residue, and formed ash mountains the size of recently plowed Ashwaubenon parking lots after a particularly nasty winter storm.

Now that Dr. Connot had everyone's attention with the deleterious environmental effects the incinerator would produce in Green Bay, he discussed the health effects of toxic nano-particulates. Particulate pollution is an already troublesome issue for our metro area because of the relatively high amount of pollution in the air due to the existing factories. In fact, The *Press-Gazette* would later run an article noting how air quality in the area received a poor grade by government regulators. Dr.

Connot additionally discussed the remaining deficiencies of the project, OSGC's complete lack of relevant experience, the industry's inadequacies and the need to develop products and packaging that do not need to be destroyed — pursuant to the Zero Waste strategy.

After Dr. Connot concluded his passionate remarks, IFBC co-chair Greg Kujawa took the podium. Greg noted that the IFBC's invitation to OSGC to attend tonight's educational forum was respectfully declined, which prompted a wave of chuckles in the audience. Greg thanked the government officials who were present, stating how very much we respect and appreciate their attendance for this important issue. Next Greg welcomed Bradley as an Executive Director from Greenaction for Health and Environmental Justice located near San Francisco. After summarizing Bradley's impressive background, Greg turned the podium over to him.

Bradley was as riveting as Dr. Connot. After thanking IFBC for the invitation to speak he noted that he had also met with the Oneida Indian Nation's leadership prior to traveling to Wisconsin. As part of his work over the years, and because he worked with numerous individuals, Bradley was very concerned when he heard about this incineration project. Sharing what Greenaction had learned about the unclear nature of this proposed project, he said that John Filcher had obtained a copy of the permit application just the day before.

Bradley indicated that each time he looked at a filed document associated with this project, he noticed that they, "Leave out information — contradict each other — there's something new — it's not backed up. So really, they need a detective agency here." In fact, Bradley continued, this *detective agency* should start looking into the brand-new companies who want to build this thing. Weeks or months old, they likely have zero experience in building or operating an incinerator. In his opinion, more mysteries remain to be investigated.

Bradley identified many of the fantastical claims made about this incinerator: it's a closed loop (meaning nothing comes out), the using of allegedly proven technology, and that is can generate electricity that's renewable. There's just one problem with that, he said, pausing for effect. It doesn't exist!

And it gets even "worse." Bradley said he had worked with hundreds of communities that have been dumped on and polluted, and only in very rare circumstances does the government come to people's aid. This is exactly why groups like Greenaction exist.

As he read excerpts from the permit application, I thought it was fascinating to listen to Bradley hammering on the document's own internal inconsistencies. While it was suggested on page one that it was only intended to incinerate solid waste, suddenly on page two there appears a list that also includes food waste, tires, and an open-ended reference to 'any other material of BTU value.'

Pausing to stare at the audience, Bradley suddenly asked, "How's industrial hazardous waste for you? How's certain medical waste for you?"

Greg and I had found the open-ended reference when I had received the materials the day before. When Bradley discussed this reference, we looked at each other and I whispered, "I suspect the audience will certainly agree those are very worrisome." Greg nodded.

Bradley asked a few more tough questions. I agreed, and also wondered, *why is it nobody in the Green Bay government flagged the open-ended waste category? Did they even review this?* Then he simply asked, "What did they approve?" He then observed that one page claimed that OSGC would only process organic matter, while a following page indicated it would be both organic **and** synthetic waste material. We shook our heads in bewilderment.

It certainly was not to generate power. Echoing Dr. Connot, Bradley said, "There is no pyrolysis plant doing what they propose to do here, in the United States. There is none. And we wanna know — what's your model to back up these claims that you could generate all this electricity? So, what did they come back and do?" They claimed there are 87 of these plants generating power, a claim which fell apart when Bradley pointed out to the EPA official working with the Nation, there are zero plants like this one dealing with solid waste. And yet Green Bay accepted a permit application claiming there are 87 facilities. "Just one problem. None of 'em, are this. For all I know, Seven Generations Corporation folks might not even be aware that they've been told this misinformation from the other companies involved."

Bradley then comically shredded OSGC's closed loop system claims. "Now one of their main claims is that it's 'closed loop'. We've all heard that." I leaned forward as Bradley said this. "But it can't STAY closed, because what happens when you heat it, a gas is created. They call it syn-gas. Now it would be closed loop legitimately if, in its entire life you'd only put one load in. Because once you put that load in and increase the gas, if you wanna put more in, you've got to let the gas out. But that's the part they don't like talking about. What this would do is then vent the gas, and then burn it. Incinerate it. Combust it. In a turbine or internal combustion engine. I think an accurate term would be a second stage, a two-stage incineration process. And that's where you do get pollutants to come out."

Whether it was intentional or accidental, the uncertainty over the precise composition of the future emissions was because no one knows exactly what's going in due to the open-ended permit application. Bradley also said the applicant's using the Romoland pyrolysis plant as a potential model is especially rich. Romoland, which wasn't even the same model or technology as what OSGC was proposing, was never able to get beyond the test permit stage. Several other points worried Bradley, like being loose with the facts about other referenced facilities that either failed or had significant contamination emissions.

After the forum concluded, Charlene Lemoine from WEAL shared her thoughts with me on how she thought the information had been received by the audience. "I felt there was a strong sense of empow-erment from people who attended the presentations. They now have a clear understanding of what is at stake, and why having well docu-mented, factual information is so important. It's also very good for the audience to get a feel for the various bogus claims and misstatements that were made by the developers of these types of incinerators. They try to hide what they're doing until it's too late in the legal process to stop them."

One of their rules of the game meant IFBC members were free to move about and spread the truth. Prior to Dr. Connot's departure,

Alette, Joanne, Paul and I scouted out the new proposed site on Hurlbut Street during a cool, but sunny day with sparkling blue skies and only a few wispy clouds. In close proximity to the site was a botanical garden, the Fox River which feeds into the bay, and numerous neighborhoods. Immediately next door to the site was the office of a large construction contractor.

While we were nosing about in the vicinity, the four of us stopped to take that contractor's temperature about the proposed incinerator. Joanne volunteered to go in while Alette, Paul and myself stayed in the car and discussed how these uninvited incinerators try to impose themselves on a neighborhood with all sorts of wild claims about recycling and jobs.

Time passed, and just when I thought to myself, *I sure wouldn't want to be the guys inside the building getting a talking-to by Joanne*, Alette piped up with, "Oh, I REALLY wouldn't want to be those guys right now! Can you imagine these burly contractors on the receiving end from petite little Joanne?" The three of us burst out laughing at the visual.

Arriving back at the car Joanne told us, "Those men in there agreed, and told me they don't want an incinerator next door and had already come to that conclusion on their own."

CHAPTER 8

DAY 133

Oneida Nation, General Tribal Council Presentation

"Information's pretty thin stuff unless mixed with experience."

— Clarence Day

On Day 133 OSGC gave a detailed presentation about its project at the General Tribal Council (GTC). OSGC had invited an individual to talk about the waste-to-energy project. As I listened to the audio recording of the meeting, this guy claimed to be the inventor of the pyrolysis technology that would be used for the proposed incinerator in Green Bay. (His company would later lose an eight-figure judgment for negligent misrepresentation in federal court!)

The 'inventor' of this simultaneously proven and first of its kind technology approached the front of the meeting, was handed a microphone, and began speaking. The majority of the presentation is contained here to provide a sense of how ridiculous we believe it was.

"Good Evening. Um. Number one, I'm honored to be here in front of you. I've been in front of classes of, ah, about 200 or 250 students, but this is outstanding.

This is amazing. Hee hee. Um, I'm a mechanical and chemical engineer. Ah, I've a doctorate degree in chemical engineering. Been working in the environmental, um, ah, area for many years. I set the, ah, low emission rules Los Angeles, California, and I'm kind of proud of it. Ah, in 1990, I wrote the 1146 that required, the emissions, air emissions to go down and since I was able to bring it down four times more. And right as we present this presents most stringent emission on Earth. It requires below 9 ppm dioxin emissions and below 50 ppm carbon monoxide emissions. And as a result, California is a better place.

"Ah, I've been working on, ah, basically cleaning the environment in, um, all of my professional life. Because that's one of the things that I live for. For me the most beautiful thing is that when I look at that analyzer and I see 8 ppm nitrogen dioxide emissions I get mesmerized. And I keep looking at it till somebody says stop looking at it and I gotta change. So today I am in front of you here to answer all of your questions about the technology that we're presenting here. It is, um, called the thermal conversion of waste to energy. And what we will do is we take the waste, your garbage, normal waste that you have at home, and turn it in to gaseous or liquid energy that is presentable and acceptable by environment.

And we have already in California have two certificates that says that our technology is sound. We have the only certificate in California to, to change medical waste into energy. We are the only company that is allowed in California to change medical waste to energy inside California. Otherwise all the medical waste goes outside California. So being California as the most stringent on Earth, we're kind of proud to be here today to present you something that really you deserve. Which would be cleaning your environment and, at the same time, give you energy that you can put in use.

"Um, I have to do this and I'm, since I am, um, normally when I lecture I don't even look at things like that. But, um, that's the gasification system or one of the units. And unfortunately it right now doesn't show much. Um, the unit is, it consists of a retort. And if you stay with me, a retort is like a, like a tube inside the box. And it goes many, ah, passes, depending on how long you want the material to stay there. And we feed the material through this retort. And you can see it a little bit, the, two valves on top, and they're called the gate valves because we do not wanna oxygen to go in there. If the oxygen or air goes in there then it turns it into carbon dioxide which is kind of combustion and we don't want that to happen.

We want to produce energy. So those valves will prevent the air to go in, and then the material is fed into the retort and only stays in the retort. On the outside of the retort is a flame that heats it up like a pressure cooker. And it heats it up. Once it heats it up, it's called an en-do-thermic process. And the material goes through a point where it changes to exothermic. And the material, it going to disintegrate into its components, original components, which would be carbon components and hydrogen components. So, as a result we end up with hydrogen, carbon monoxide, methane, ethane, propane, butane, all the fuels, and maybe a little bit of nitrogen which is originally with the material."

As I listened to the recording I found myself shaking my head in disbelief.

"So as the gas travels through, it comes out at the bottom. We capture the carbon and the ash. And the carbon is still a very good product, and marketable product. There's a four billion dollar market for carbon, and the carbon is a very marketable product. And then the gas is put through, um, what we call is a venturi wash. It goes right there. We wash the gas. And to wash this, we use water. And we wanna wash chlorine, or maybe some sulfur out of it and also dirt and dust from the, from the ah, gas, so the gas would not, would be clean. And then it will go through the demister, which where we take the water out. And we condense it down a little more. It goes up through another demister. And then eventually end up inside that tank.

From that tank, we take, we can take the gas and further de-sulfurize it. We bring it down to zero sulfur. And then we can use the gas for producing electricity or making liquid fuel from it or turn it into hydrogen for hydrogen cell. And if you turn it into Fischer–Tropschs we reform it into carbon monoxide and hydrogen. Use carbon monoxide and hydrogen to make diesel, gasoline, jet fuel, wax, and these are a whole area, other area of, ah, of ah, business where you can even produce, ah, ah, cosmetics from it. You know wax is the mother of everything.

And if you wanna produce electricity, we use the gas, we take the gas, we pressurize it, we put it into a gen-set, and the gen-set will produce electricity. Now, let me emphasize that this gas is very, very clean. This gas has no, the people are looking for furans or toxic gas in it, there is no such thing in this gas because the gas has a not been in a combustion. It has been just cooked so the gas is only methane, ethane, propane, butane so it's nothing, nothing out of ordinary. You don't look for furans and toxic gas in this because it doesn't have, ah, any of that. And it is also created in a very controlled atmosphere. If you look there is nothing, nowhere that this gas go but that tank.

We will not allow it to get out. It goes into that tank and from that tank we take it and pressurize it into a larger tank or a set of larger tanks where, um, from where it's going to be used to make, uh, electricity. Now, I'm not gonna talk too much because the more I talk the more confused you become, so, um, if you have any questions, any concerns, I'm right here and I'll be more'n happy to answer.

About 200 concerns, OK. The fuel is transported via compressors. So, what you do is pressurize the gas, and then the gas is, is transported through the, through pipes, is transported to the um, to the, uh, generator, and it's going to make the electricity. The fuel is not practically moved from one place to another but it's like inside a pipe."

After the 'inventor' finished, there was an extensive question and answer period. I just thought to myself, *it seems the most accurate thing this guy said was, the more he talks, the more confused everybody becomes. Could be the understatement of the day.*

First was a remark from a pipe fitter who explained that he worked to dismantle the multi-million-dollar incinerators at a resort in the south that only ran for six months. The 'inventor' replied,

"Um, thank you very much. We have sixteen units that are in operation right now and to address your concern, actually in a more general basis, yeah there are bad units there, I agree with you. If you go to Japan, there are about seven, eight hundred of, not my technology but other people's technology, that have been in operation for ten years. And this is really not a hard technology. For me, reducing nitrogen dioxide from a flame is much more difficult than this. This is very, very easy technology."

Notably the 'inventor' stated,

> "You have to know chemical engineering. You have to know reaction, you have to know the resident time of the material, um, turning into chemicals, and then you're OK. If you, um, do this in your garage, I don't recommend that you use it anywhere."

As I listened to the condescending claim about needing to "know chemical engineering," I rolled my eyes and thought, *Then why did you just BS the audience with all that blather about being able to make all these chemically different fuels from a variable feedstock that might never contain the necessary elements?*

The next question came from an engineer who asked about the "carbon, marketable product" the presenter was talking about and also about the sulfur. The speaker responded,

> "Very good question. Sulfur comes out as h2s mostly, or mercaptans. We catch the sulfur two, three different ways. One way is amin wash, the one that we're suggesting here is going to be with iron, um, iron ore. We catch the sulfur, hydrogen sulfide, and we regenerate it with air. When we regenerate it with air, the elemental sulfur falls out and then we wash the elemental sulfur, capture it and its marketable."

Again, I rolled my eyes as I listened. *Soooo, you don't want to talk about purportedly carbon marketable product because… you can't transmogrify the non-carbon elements already in the trash to a form of carbon merely because you threw them into an oven? Shocking,* I thought sarcastically.

The third questioner asked where the plants the inventor had created were located within the United States. The speaker replied,

"There is one at a very, very, ah, important place that you will not miss. It's at the, um, Los Angeles Sanitation Department. Has been running for two and a half years. We have been turning human waste into diesel fuel. And you're more than welcome to come and visit and I'll be more than happy to take you there." Strangely, the lack of permitted incinerators in California seemed to be portrayed by the speaker as a triumph of the technology instead of trash incinerators simply failing to meet the state's air quality standards.

Later, another speaker responded to some questions on the project's funding. "There was an insinuation, actually it was not an insinuation it was just plainly said, that we shouldn't get one more dime or we shouldn't invest any money in this, so what the funding, the sources, the amount of money that we're getting from the Oneida Tribe is zero. Um, we have not received money from the Oneida Tribe since 2004. So, for this project, we're getting no money to do this project." The speaker then immediately contradicted that claim about not getting any funding from Oneida by detailing up to $24 million in grants and loan guarantees to fund the incinerator.

This meandering presentation suggesting an overgrown Easy-Bake oven somehow solved the age-old fable of transmogrifying elements made me wonder, *why didn't anyone press the question to this guy to see how he responded?* Curiously, I had always questioned why the developers only advocated changing trash into gas composed of different elements than was originally in the trash. Whenever I pondered this, I also wound up thinking, *Maybe the rhetorical device of an intermediate step sounded more believable than proceeding directly to converting directly into gold bars or something?*

I couldn't help but be riveted by the audio recording, especially when another unidentified speaker referenced the OSGC open house debacle in Ashwaubenon back on Day 17. "I attended both the, the, meetings too, the both the one here at the Radisson for tribal members, and the next night, the one at Ashwaubenon," the speaker stated. "And I, too, felt that, that racism was, and it was ah, ah, it was pretty blatant. We were there, and there was maybe 15, 20 Oneidas there, and the rest of the, you know 150 or so, you know, were non-tribal of course. And all the people that were there, ah, as part of the presentation, no matter how much information you could give these people, they still were in your face, pointing fingers and pretty much yelling at you! You know. Why you doing this? You know, you know, I don't. I had one person come up and say, you know, I don't have a problem with Oneidas doing this project. It looks like a good project. Um. And that was one person. All the rest of 'em, you know, just, it was, it was, it was blatant. And it was kind of scary! Being out there, being strong by all these people pointing their fingers at you and telling you that this is, this is, it doesn't matter how, what type of technology it is and, and the information that you give 'em cause they weren't even gonna listen. They weren't even gonna listen. They didn't even have an open mind to even hear the facts that the, the technical team that was there to share that information with them. They pretty much didn't want to hear anything. Anything about it. And, you know, that, so it was, it was kinda disheartening cause, you know I, too thought that we had good relationships with our local, um, people around the area here, and, and, and that really showed to differ that one, it was time for our, our other community people to step up and support Oneida. They weren't willing to do it. Even though, you know, we try to support other communities around the area and, and they weren't willing to return the favor."

By this point I was risking permanent eye injury due to my tremendous eye-rolling. *Kind of 'scary'*, I thought derisively. *You try having an incinerator built near your home and family, then tell me about scary!*

Slandering the citizens of Ashwaubenon in a rant certainly spoke volumes. Clearly OSGC was destined for disqualification from any Good Neighbor of the Year nomination. As more citizen groups continued to join the fray, the spurious narrative from this speaker's rant rapidly collapsed.

CHAPTER 9

Department of Energy Hearing

*"When everything seems to be going against you, remember that
the airplane takes off against the wind, not with it."*

— Henry Ford

In the afternoon following a morning filled with bright sunlight
and singing birds, the federal Department of Energy (DOE) held a
scoping hearing in Green Bay, soliciting comments from concerned
parties so that the DOE could later write a response. Day 134 proved
to be remarkable and thought-provoking to the IFBC members as we
appeared in force. It also marked the first time we were actually able to
meet in person with Charlene from WEAL's board of directors, who had
sent the group (back on Day 75 when we were still operating under the
name Biomass Opposition Committee) a letter of support. Our core
members had been looking forward to meeting with this influential
group.

Notably, WEAL had also sent OSGC a letter back on the same date
clearly indicating WEAL's opposition to any solid waste incinerators and

urging the company to abandon its plan. Unsurprisingly, OSGC failed to respond.

In what was becoming a regular occurrence, a quote by IFBC was featured in the news the next day. I remember saying, "We have concerns about the potential countywide impact of this project." I was satisfied, because at least we got in a dig against the project into the article.

Far more importantly, the *Press-Gazette* article about the 'Biomass' plant coming under criticism stated, "Oneida officials have assured Green Bay city leaders that the 60,000 square foot plant would not pollute the environment." The *Press-Gazette* reporter even went the extra mile, noting that the local DNR air management supervisor stated OSGC has not yet applied for state permits and, "his agency cannot find a similar biomass plant anywhere in Wisconsin and possibly anywhere in the country." It would take time for officials and the media to drop the term 'biomass', but this article already made it clear our IFBC position was slowly beginning to dominate in the media.

As part of its preparations for the scoping hearing in Green Bay, IFBC and other environmental groups had cobbled together extensive written comments and submitted them to the DOE.

An informal discussion that occurred after the DOE hearing was eye opening. A resident struck up a conversation with me and Joanne about the viability of the proposed incinerator. The topic was whether the proposed development could actually convert the base elements contained in trash (including lead, mercury vapor from bulbs, and so on) into carbon like the developers had been suggesting. The man stated, "Yes, but what IF this actually could work? It would be a miracle that solves all sorts of environmental problems."

This guy clearly did not expect me to quickly agree. "Yes, it would be quite a miracle to change elements into other elements, but as far as I am aware humanity has yet to solve the riddle of how to turn lead into gold. Changing elements from one element into another just doesn't happen just because someone baked it for a while."

Joanne, who was standing next to me, chuckled softly and agreed. "Baking elements doesn't change them from one into another. It just makes the same element a little warmer!"

Undeterred, the guy shook his head, and with a dreamy smile responded, "Yes, but what if it DOES work? We would be the leaders of a whole new industry and way of life!"

I glanced at Joanne before looking back at this dreamer and asked, "Will OSGC offer to restore the health and property values of the residents who live here? And if OSGC's is wrong, who pays the price for its gamble? The residents near the incinerator, or the residents way over in Oneida?"

The man shook his head. "No, they will be fine. OSGC has already said there's no danger because there's no emissions. Haven't you been paying attention to the education they've been providing about the project?"

Arching my eyebrows, I couldn't help myself. "Yes, telling me fairy tales about science projects that can't possibly be true are exactly why I've been paying attention. Especially when they're told to us using a 'shut up, they explained' kind of vibe to try to keep anyone from asking awkward questions about what they're really doing."

The man just shook his head. "I'll keep faith that OSGC is right."

"Well, believe what you want. It's fair to say we'll just agree to disagree." I watched as the man walked over to other eco-group representatives. I couldn't help but reflect about how the fairy-dust-magical thinking of the incinerator proponents was truly astounding, and now they were spreading their fairy dust on other groups.

IFBC continued daily to refine our campaign based on information uncovered by the dynamic research duo Alette and Joanne. But research wasn't the only method we used as we drilled down into the issues. We had questions about every aspect of the OSGC project and the group spent a great deal of time chasing down every lead.

On Day 160, Rich, Mike and I met together at Titletown Brewing Company downtown in Green Bay for a lunch meeting with the Brown County Taxpayers Association. Due to the enormous amount of information about the OSGC project that IFBC had amassed, I still hadn't mastered the art of speaking succinctly when conveying information to the taxpayer's association. Thankfully, Rich bailed me out with effective comments highlighting the important parts.

Afterwards, Mike shared some invaluable advice with me on public speaking. "When you speak to a group about something highly complex, just talk about three main bullet points. People's attention will start to wander after three. Plus, it's easier on you to only have to remember three. With all you know on the topic, three is enough to fill an hour's discussion."

I immediately wondered, *Why the heck didn't they teach THAT nugget of wisdom back in law school?'* Annoyed with myself, I vowed then and there never to let myself get bogged down by the overload of facts and developments in the future. Mike and his three-bullet point advice made an immediate impact on my messaging and I used it heavily from that day forward.

CHAPTER 10

DAY 164

Distinctions Without Differences

"Always stand on principle...even if you stand alone."

— John Adams

On Day 164, OSGC filed its Proposed Plan of Operation with the Wisconsin Department of Natural Resources (DNR). In it, OSGC stated, "[O]dors and contaminant dispersion issues may be alleviated through increasing stack heights..." Upon reading that claim, I was immediately thankful IFBC had studiously been collecting OSGC's prior statements which suggested that there would be no stacks!

At our next core meeting I exclaimed, "We've been waiting for this moment! It's so great that our group has been diligently collecting everything OSGC says and publishes so we might find something to use to derail them."

"Good thing Elaine warned us to remain alert for the sudden appearance of OSGC documentation," Greg added.

With bright white hair bouncing and a look of satisfaction on her face, Joanne enthused, "It's finally time to start throwing OSGC's words right back at them!"

Elaine arrived late, just before the meeting was wrapping up, in time to hear me say, "By now, you guys are well versed in seeing through rhetorical distinctions without differences and none of us are too interested in playing along with OSGC's word games."

"I hear one of IFBC's fan favorites is when OSGC or industry promoters wax poetic about exothermic and endothermic reactions, and multiple chambers for processing stages to bleed off gas, blah blah blah," Elaine remarked, causing the group to roar with laughter.

"Yeah," Greg said, finishing everyone's thought. "It's painfully apparent to everyone that none of their rhetorical distinctions carry any meaningful real-world differences when nearby homes still become contaminated anyway."

CHAPTER 11

DNR Says, Come Again?

"I always wondered why somebody didn't do something about that and then I realized I am somebody."

— Lily Tomlin

Apparently underwhelmed by the Day 164 filing, DNR issued OSGC a Notice of Incompleteness for a Waste to Energy Facility with surprising swiftness. Also occurring with surprising speed was the *Press-Gazette* reporting soon after that this Notice of Incompleteness contained DNR's concern that in "its current form, the information submitted does not provide us with a confidence level that would ensure a reasonable expectation of success."

As we gathered at the Day 175 IFBC meeting, I couldn't help but see our IFBC folk were understandably delighted at this face plant by OSGC. "Wow, that was a pretty public screw up by OSGC for the DNR to say that," noted Greg. "I wonder what they're going to do?"

Alette nodded in response. "I don't think they'll let some regulator get in their way. OSGC will throw something together and file it to get the DNR off its back."

69

Elaine heard this and remarked, "The state regulator doesn't have the power to shut down a proposed project it doesn't believe will work. It can only determine whether the permit application requirements are satisfied."

Now it was my turn to nod. "My sense is that we adopt a wait and see posture. It'll give us a chance to look over OSGC's responsive filing to see what bubbles up. Maybe there will be some details in there they didn't want to let out into the wild."

IFBC wouldn't have to wait long. An amended Permit to Construct Application based on OSGC's submitted information to DNR identified ten stacks. Three stretching up to 60 feet high, one at 45 feet, three at 40 feet, and the remainder at 7.5 feet. Elated, I thought, *Jackpot! This was just the sort of revelation we can use to burn OSGC.*

IFBC's core group gathered again to discuss what to do with all this new information. We held the meeting outside on my patio since it was a lovely warm day. After serving beverages and the inevitable snacks, I opened the meeting by quickly covering the new stack height documents, and asked, "Anyone have a preference on how we approach this? We need to do something to push the information out there for all to see."

Alette nodded emphatically. "I agree. This is too important not to. Is there a TV report in the works where we can try to get them to discuss these stacks?"

I shook his head. "There's nothing I'm aware of."

Elaine had decided to drop in to see the IFBC gang since we were all in one place. Her well-informed participation was always welcome. "I'm hearing from my tribal friends that they would like to see some of these important details get out into their local community too. Maybe you all could make your own news by taking out an ad?"

"The rates in the *Kalihwisaks* are a lot more affordable than over at the *Press-Gazette*," Greg noted, "and it would get the information directly to the Oneida community. I love that idea, Elaine. Why not place an ad with the Kalihwisaks?" The group quickly agreed, and to keep everyone informed of OSGC's antics, IFBC took out another paid advertisement in the *Kalihwisaks* to inform Oneida members of what happened. The ad read:

Incinerator Free Brown County ("IFBC") would like to provide an update on the status of Oneida Nation Seven Generation Corporation's ("OSGC") controversial incinerator on Hurlbut Street in Green Bay. In April, the United States Department of Energy ("DOE") held a hearing as required by the National Environmental Policy Act ("NEPA"). The DOE must investigate and answer all questions submitted to it. Incinerator Free Brown County and its members submitted over 400 scoping issues to the DOE in addition to hundreds more submitted by concerned environmental groups such as the Sierra Club, Midwest Environmental Advocates, Physicians for Social Responsibility, and the Waukesha County Environmental Action League. The next day's headlines to EVERYONE in Brown County noted OSGC's biomass plant plan came under fire again.

> Recently, the Wisconsin Department of Natural Resources issued a Notice of Incompleteness to OSGC because it filed incomplete or irrelevant information pertaining to unrelated technologies. In response, OSGC avoided speaking to the media and instead issued written statements claiming DNR's notice was expected and an anticipated part of the approval and permitting process. If OSGC did actually expect DNR's response, then either: OSGC lacked the minimum technical knowledge to file accurate and relevant information, or it knowingly filed a deficient project plan. The corresponding media headlines proclaimed OSGC's incinerator may not be viable and prompted significant regulator concerns because no successful pyrolysis plant exists on a commercial scale.
>
> OSGC continued to generate ill will and bad press by bungling public relations with a neighborhood association near the incinerator site when OSGC refused to meet with that association and its members to answer their questions or concerns. You read that last sentence

correctly, OSGC outright refused to meet with concerned neighbors. Imagine what such refusal by a prominent Oneida corporation did for public perception and opinion, especially when they learned the incinerator is also 'ready' to burn medical and hazardous waste (according to OSGC's filing with the DNR).

We're pretty sure OSGC hasn't figured out how to turn lead into gold any more than how to make matter completely disappear by merely heating and incinerating it into a more dangerous form of matter. In fact, OSGC cannot save any landfill space by incinerating otherwise recyclable material that is already illegal to put into landfills. Why not help create up to 500 jobs by joining with local governments in an effort to recycle 100% of the county's trash instead of simply proposing to make toxic ash out of it? As we move forward together through this summer, please keep in mind OSGC's previous accomplishments and ask whether it's worth enduring more of the same.

Elaine and Rich found the advertisement totally entertaining. At the next IFBC meeting Elaine advised, "My friends in Oneida are telling us OSGC was highly irritated by IFBC's efforts to keep the Oneida updated with truthful information."

We all got a laugh from Alette's response. "Imagine how upset OSGC would be to learn they've been blissfully unaware of the number of IFBC members who were also members of the Oneida Nation?" By now, over 150 had secretly joined IFBC and many had donated money to help fund the operation.

Then things began heating up. By Day 220, the *Press-Gazette* ran a devastating (for OSGC) article under the amusing headline "Biomass facility feeling the heat". The various opposition groups had been discovered by the *Press-Gazette* via a Freedom of Information Act (FOIA) request to the Department of Energy. This included filed opposition from IFBC, concerned residents and environmental groups including the Sierra Club, Door County Environmental Council, WEAL, and several others. By this time these disparate groups had also reached out to one another and were mapping out how to work together. IFBC, WEAL and the Clean Water Action Council (CWAC) became a powerful partnership as the battle continued. Significantly, the *Press-Gazette* remarked that *none* of the fifteen groups filing comments were in favor of the project and quoted a physician in a telephone interview memorably saying, "It's like having a gigantic cigarette in the neighborhood."

CWAC is an interesting organization. Funded by membership dues and donations, it was founded in 1985 as a result of a week-long Greenpeace publicity campaign in Green Bay, which was part of their "Waters for Life" tour around the Great Lakes. At the conclusion of the week, Greenpeace held a public meeting at the Neville Public Museum where about 200 people showed up on one day's notice and decided to form a local group to follow-up on the serious toxic pollution issues highlighted that week. CWAC has an impressive outreach program to educate members and the public about current issues affecting our area and provides information on actions the organization is taking and how members and the public can become involved. The sheer number of issues CWAC has been closely involved in is almost overwhelming, and their work includes protecting wildlife habitat, promoting solid waste recycling programs and working to reduce water pollution in its many forms, important for everyone in Northeast Wisconsin. CWAC President and Executive Director Dean Hoegger retired from 30 years of public-school teaching and earned a paralegal degree in order to pursue his interest in environmental issues. Dean and his wife Julie live in Southern Door County on the base of the peninsula where they enjoy organic gardening, country living, and the waters of Green Bay.

Waukesha County Environmental League (WEAL) is also a longstanding protector of the environment. Since 1978 WEAL has undertaken and promoted thorough local actions, public programs, newsletters, and up-to-date information on environmental issues to the general public, teachers, county, city, and village officials and state legislators. WEAL was formed in 1978 by citizens alarmed by development threatening Waukesha County's natural resources. Since then, many

WEAL members have become active in local and county government, greatly influencing the environmental well-being of Waukesha County just west of Milwaukee, Wisconsin. WEAL board member Charlene Lemoine would be instrumental in bringing IFBC up to speed on the issues surrounding incinerators. WEAL stays on top of many issues, include clean water, waste/zero waste, gasification/incineration, and so on. Both CWAC and WEAL have been involved in litigation over the decades.

On Day 225, DNR issued a preliminary determination identifying those ten towering stacks. And then, in yet another blunder, OSGC deliberately mailed an Open Letter to Brown County residents on Day 240 that intentionally omitted the stack emissions from the letter's detailed rendering. That letter also charmingly stated, "We believe the small but vocal number who oppose this project either do not under-stand (or want to understand) that this is not an incinerator (which would require the actual burning of material) or have other renewable energy agendas (such as zero waste or wind energy). Some may simply oppose it because it is an Oneida business project."

After those two events, Greg stopped by to see me. As we settled down in my home office in the basement Greg could overhear my beloved Texas style blues softly streaming from the speakers, and we cracked open a couple of cold ones.

"You see that letter from OSGC?" I asked Greg after a sip of frothy nitro porter. "It says we're too stupid to understand the technology of their facility."

"Yeah. Came in the mail. Telling everyone that they're stupid if they oppose the magic machine seems a bit tone deaf."

I chuckled and took another sip. "Right out of the handbook on 'How to Win Friends and Influence the Public'."

Greg shifted topics to the DNR's preliminary determination. "Stacks. No stacks. Simultaneously already proven yet somehow still new cutting-edge technology. Do you think these guys are starting to panic?" Greg said, pausing to take a sip of his honey ale while the raspy singing of Stevie Ray Vaughan could barely be heard in the background. "They can't seem to get their story straight!"

I chuckled. "Ha! No kidding. Sometimes I think OSGC is rattled, other times I think OSGC is just not competent. Or maybe both." By now, IFBC routinely questioned the engineering acumen of OSGC. And engineering wasn't the only area IFBC had been questioning.

The pressure was building on OSGC. The Day 227 edition of the *Kalihwisaks* featured a long letter to the editor by a tribal member who easily refuted many OSGC claims and then posed some tough questions. The writer pointed out that, despite hearing a representation suggesting the plant was complete, it was not, and he questioned the need for a $19 million loan as it obviously was an untrue representation. He also noted OSGC was unable to provide complete parameters of the facility to Wisconsin DNR, or even basic supporting information such as laboratory tests or existing operatives. The writer also revealed his deep displeasure at being told at a General Tribal Council meeting about whether there were other units like this one, and urged this facility be approved by the people instead of like a prior debacle where the "directors enriched themselves on Big Bonuses and 'Finders Fees' and Christmas Bonuses."

The writer posed some very intriguing questions. "At the GTC meeting, we were told 7 Gen would pay back the $19 million in five years. They would have to earn over $3.8 million a year or $316,000 a month to do so. At 20 working days a month that would be $15,800 a day. If this business is that good, why isn't anyone else doing it?

"Even John Gilcher [sic], Co-Chair of a group called Incinerator Free Brown County, said, 'The DNR has confirmed what skeptics long suspected: a project like this has never been allowed anywhere else in the country. Why make Brown County a guinea pig?' Let the people decide."

The original letter apparently misspelled Filcher as Gilcher. If not, then whoever this Gilcher guy was, he was both a real pain in OSGC's hinder and a world champion at being elusive because no one had seen him before. Alette and Joanne were entertained and spent months randomly blaming all sorts of nefarious things on Gilcher.

CHAPTER 12

Economics

"The difference between the right word and the almost right
word is the difference between lightning and a lightningbug."

— Mark Twain

One of the real-world weaknesses of trash incinerators is the industry's campaign to paper over the unfavorable economics of these monsters. Never has a trash burner produced more energy than it requires to burn the trash, for the simple fact that municipal solid waste is a negative net energy fuel. As Bradley Angel had advised, it was time to start looking into the economics of the OSGC incinerator.

By now, IFBC had consistently been hearing that this thing was funded by taxpayer dollars but there seemed to be a deliberate cloud obscuring whether it was federal or state funding. OSGC also managed to get a puff piece article in the *Press-Gazette* with a headline vaguely proclaiming the "Biomass plant safe, report says." Notably, OSGC did not correct the article's conflation of biomass with trash, although OSGC

76

officials hilariously kept trying to portray the unwashed rabble opposing OSGC as a *small* but vocal group of opponents.

Shaking my head as I read that article, I thought, *you'd think OSGC's public relations firm would finally come up with better stuff, but they never do. Stuck on stupid by default.*

"Can you guys believe the tone deafness of OSGC claiming this latest development should answer their critics. Ridiculous. And it sounded so evasive!" exclaimed Alette at the next meeting. "All they did was create more questions."

"Ha! Saw that!" I snorted. "Sounded like another of OSGC's condescending 'shut up, they explained' replies that avoids explaining anything at all."

Elaine was also in attendance, and declared, "No one buys a ridiculous article that mimics a sleazy politician claiming it's time to have a conversation about something when they really mean they just want to yap about their position to friendly media while unhindered by any opposition being present." As all the environmental groups were well aware, none of our incinerator criticisms were rebutted.

Soon after, on Day 266 I spoke to the Brown County Planning, Development & Transportation Committee about the adverse impacts of the incinerator. I could hardly contain my excitement. I knew this presentation was going to ruffle some feathers. I tried to suppress a smile because everyone who knows me well knew that lawyers live to ruffle feathers.

After trying to be patient while waiting my turn, I was finally able to address the dozen committee members. Afterward, in an off-the-record, non-official discussion off the premises, I shared what IFBC had uncovered about the economics of the proposed OSGC trash incinerator. Remembering to mention that the proposed incinerator would divert approximately 150 tons of solid waste from the landfill, I added, "That's true from a certain point of view. What's important is to understand that in context, and what that fully means. The county's solid waste program is heavily funded by tipping fees, and the county told me the gate rate at the BOW landfill in Outagamie County is $33 a ton. This project would then remove $4,950 a day of income from the recycling program's ledger. Add that up, and it's $1.7 million a year, for which OSGC certainly is not offering to reimburse the county."

I paused to assess their surprised reactions, then continued. "Can the recycling program, which depends upon economies of scale, continue its operations after such a loss? It would take a decent sized tax increase to make up for that. And it gets better, because for every ton of trash that is incinerated, one ton of toxic ash and char is produced. That ash contains what was already present in the solid waste, but now it's in a form susceptible to leaching. Is the county landfill capable of accepting that sort of material? Does the landfill have the necessary lining to prevent groundwater contamination? Judging from the looks I saw, these sound like questions needing answers.

"We also suspect the landfill lacks the capacity to prevent all that fly ash from blowing around. And it will blow around, especially as the tons start to add up. You can see in this picture what happened with the ash from another old incinerator on the east coast prior to the EPA shutting it down. And by the way, those aren't blades of grass in front of a huge mound in the picture, those are telephone poles — which are dwarfed by the mountain of ash right behind them. No doubt OSGC isn't willing to pay much, if anything, for tipping fees to dump tons of ash." As I said this, I showed the picture I was referencing.

"None of this even touches upon the optics of the public uproar if any of that ash is allowed to escape or leach, nor the optics of poorly tarped tractor-trailers of ash being hauled through the local communities to the landfill."

It was apparent to me by the reactions I saw that there hadn't yet been consideration of the financial impact that diverting waste to incineration posed to the county's solid waste disposal and recycling programs.

By Day 288, DNR issued its Conditional Plan of Operation Approval. In response, a joint Press Release entitled "Don't Let Oneida Seven Generation Corporation's Risky Garbage Combustion Project Become Wisconsin's Solyndra" was issued on Day 303 by the IFBC, the Sierra Club, and WEAL. The release stated there were serious concerns about the technical and economic viability of the proposed facility, estimated to cost $23 million taxpayer dollars, and claiming to be capable of generating 5 MW of electricity under best-case scenario conditions. The release also bluntly stated that this proposed pyrolysis technology intended to create and burn syngas in a way that has never been successfully put into commercial operation for solid waste anywhere in the world.

It appeared that IFBC's growing focus on the incinerator's economics was beginning to yield results. On Day 304, the *Press-Gazette* reported that OSGC abruptly ceased talks with Brown County officials, who were expected to act on a proposed modification to Brown County's solid waste agreement to divert trash to the incinerator. While we can only speculate what happened during the talks, we decided to score another one for IFBC and friends!

Seeing such positive results of IFBC's agenda to scrutinize the economics of the issue, I did some more research — it's what the cats at IFBC do — and figured out the process for obtaining public documents under Wisconsin's Open Records Law. *Time to start poking around some more*, I decided.

CHAPTER 13

Ask and Ye Shall Receive

"The cat is let out of the bag, so to speak."

— *Falise v. American Tobacco Co.*, 193 F.R.D. 73 (ED NY 2000)
citing in *re von Bulow*, 828 F.2d 94, 103 (2d Cir. 1987)

By now, I had submitted open records requests to Brown County, DNR, and Green Bay. While those were percolating through the system, On Day 337 Greg and I were able to address the Green Bay Common Council about the city's need to obtain indemnity. This indemnity was for environmental remediation and to restart Brown County's trash disposal program at the landfill — due to the high risk of failure for the incinerator. IFBC demonstrated that the economic model for the proposed incineration scheme had not been shown to differ from the failed Harrisburg, PA, incinerator, which had forced Harrisburg into bankruptcy.

This appearance in front of the Common Council was the first of several by members of IFBC. Thanks to a phone call from Elaine giving Greg and I advance notice about the interpersonal dynamics between several Common Council members and the mayor, IFBC's posture going in was mapped out in advance. IFBC would be respectfully polite during almost every appearance. Greg and I recognized that it would be difficult for OSGC to portray IFBC as an unruly mob of radical lunatics when we create a reputation for acting with respect, restraint and decorum.

It's one thing to get a heads up about some hostility betwixt the mayor, the Common Council and individual Common Council members, but it's was quite another to see the combative spectacle in person. Rather than getting caught up in putting even more of the 'fun' in dysfunctional, Greg and I decided it was a prudent game plan to keep it simple and command attention with respectful tact and restraint, which should prove both effective and entertaining. Putting our plan into practice was rather fascinating, though, because the mayor repeatedly had to break from pointedly ignoring me by responding in kind to my deferentially respectful presence.

Two weeks later, on Day 349, I wrote the mayor a follow up letter from IFBC discussing the sketchy economics of the proposed incineration scheme, with copies to the entire Common Council. I wrote:

> From a liability standpoint, the City is being asked to assume a risk that should solely be borne by the entities proposing this incinerator. The economic model for this proposed incinerator has not been demonstrated to the Green Bay Common Council to differ meaningfully from the failed Harrisburg, Pennsylvania MSW incinerator (forcing Harrisburg to close the incinerator and declare bankruptcy). Having been pre-warned about the predictable possibility of failure, your voters will demand City government protect them by requiring indemnity from the project supporters. Such indemnity would need to include costs necessary to clean up any environmental contamination after operations cease and to restart landfill access, especially if MSW cannot be removed from resident's homes while new tri-county landfill access is negotiated for Green Bay.
>
> In the interim period between the beginning of incineration operations and incinerator closure, council

members will likely need to address several other issues. These issues include explaining to voters why county taxes increased corresponding to a budgetary shell game that will remove about $250,000 from the city's MSW budget, and adds twice that to Brown County's MSW budget because the county will lose efficiencies of scale in landfill rates due to the City's diversion of MSW to the incinerator.

As voters in Green Bay are approximately 40% of Brown County's population, these voters will then pay Brown County's increased MSW landfill costs in addition to the City's incineration costs instead of only paying for one as they do today. Due to the seriousness of these issues, the City may wish to consider delaying entry into any agreement involving the proposed incinerator for a year so it can study them further and reach the best possible decision for its residents. Again, the citizens of IFBC thank you for your time and attention.

My reference of financial failure and the need for indemnity would be prescient for the class action litigants of another incinerator, who were forced to seek contamination indemnity when an incinerator in Sioux City got shut down by government authorities.

CHAPTER 14

DAY 367

Proper Decorum
for a Public Forum

"Abuse of words has been the great instrument of sophistry and
chicanery, of party, faction, and division of society."

— John Adams

D ay 367 was quite a day for IFBC. The main event was a public informational forum located in the Brown County central
library in downtown Green Bay, hosted by OSGC. Although
pointedly not invited, several members of IFBC were delighted to crash
the party. Many members of the general public joined Joanne outside
the venue entrance to picket with colorful signs saying, "No! to Toxins",
"No Oneida Incinerator Here", "Woodsy Says Give a Hoot Don't Pollute" (the 'Woodsy' sign was my personal favorite), "Pollution no Solution", and "The Oneidas are Burning Public Money for Dirty Energy"
along with a host of others. With typical Midwestern politeness, the
picketers gave OSGC nothing but trouble by maintaining well-man-
nered decorum.

Of course, since media awareness of the controversial nature of this facility had been elevated over the months, the media was there to see it all. To make sure they wouldn't miss the show, IFBC had again given our contacts in the news media advance notice there would be something of interest to point their cameras at. The front-page *Press-Gazette* headline "Biomass protesters keep the heat on" and pictures of the marchers did OSGC no favors, while Joanne carried top pictorial billing on the front page. A lady from Green Bay was quoted in the paper as saying, "Burning this garbage just cannot be safe." Hilariously, the paper noted that the supporters of the incinerator were "significantly outnumbered" by the opponents, and quoted Elaine calling the plant a "beast" that "has to be stopped" because it was unproven technology that would be dangerous to the environment. Elaine was happy to repeat that to me and the others when our gang got together afterwards for a bite to eat, a few drinks and an entertaining chinwag about how it all went from each of our various perspectives since we all saw and heard different remarks and visuals from our different locations.

Meanwhile, other members of IFBC and our new friends from the Clean Water Action Council (CWAC) and WEAL were inside the forum doing what we all do best — stirring up trouble for OSGC by asking awkward questions and making truthful statements. As representatives from various subcontractors and 'experts' hired by OSGC explained their point of view to onlookers, they did their best to either ignore or minimize the issues raised by our three groups. I noticed one person was talking with a small crowd in a corner out in the hallway. "As you can see, this is a closed loop process with no emissions. It's very safe and quiet," said the representative from an industry interest group. "It won't even have smokestacks," he had been saying when he was rudely interrupted by me.

"What about the 60-foot stacks OSGC admitted the facility required to the DNR? Are you saying OSGC was mistaken about whether their facility needs these tall stacks, or are you mistaken? You both can't be right."

Glaring at me, the guy responded. "Well, you are correct. There would be 60-foot stacks on the facility and those are included in the filed plans with the regulator, but there is no need for tall smokestacks like at a power plant. They're different."

The assembled onlookers shared questioning glances among themselves as I retorted, "Sounds like you're trying to draw distinctions without differences to me. If OSGC's process is closed loop, why need ANY stacks? Or are you just being cute by only referring to the first stage of your process, which is closed, and pretending the second stage where it has to vent the gas doesn't exist?"

The rep raised his hands in a gesture to *please listen* before nodding. "It's true there is gas vented after it is combusted in the generators, but it is closed loop for the pyrolysing stage. It's relatively clean when it is combusted in the generators and vented."

By now, I was quite enjoying the man's discomfort, and interrupted him once again to ask, "So where did all the harmful contaminants go? Do they just disappear because the gas was piped from one stage to the other? Or are you suggesting the act of running it through your jet engine caused them to cease to exist?"

When the rep tried to suggest the combusting process greatly reduced the contaminants to very safe levels, one of the onlookers shook his head and loudly called out, "Oh man! You guys are so full of crap. Particles don't disappear when you run them through an engine. Why aren't you being honest about this? Do you think we're stupid?"

The other onlookers, many shaking their heads and frowning in disgust, quickly dispersed. I frowned. *They just keep saying the same old BS over and over. I wonder when they'll come up with something new?*

That was not the only troublesome efforts IFBC, CWAC and WEAL had planned.

CHAPTER 15

"Scary" Threats of Litigation

"Broadly speaking short words are best and the old words when short, are best of all."

— Winston Churchill

Frustrated with the intransigence of OSGC and the Green Bay political machine, Dean Hoegger and I had been working on putting up a billboard to gain even more attention. Soon after we submitted the specs to a local billboard operator, that operator brought it to the attention of OSGC as other billboards run by the operator contain a lot of ads for Oneida enterprises.

Day 367 was also the date of a threat letter sent by OSGC's hired law firm to IFBC and CWAC, which I received after the events earlier in the day in Chapter 14. The letter pompously intoned that the proposed billboard "implies a false statement of fact" and ominously warned against implying that the proposed trash machine involved incineration. The letter closed with a rather cheeky demand to replace the billboard with one describing the incinerator in a way that would meet with their approval. I was pretty sure the OSGC lawyer's idea of a suitable replacement message did not resemble IFBC's. Just as I was reading the letter that evening, Dean called from CWAC's local office to talk it over.

"Did you see the letter we received from OSGC's lawyers? What do you think of it? The sign company already reached out and said they won't run it as proposed."

I blurted out, "Yeah. It came to my house. What a stupid letter. This is good opportunity to give these guys a black eye."

Dean wasn't clear on how this could be a good thing. "Um, what do you mean by that?" Dean's tone was that of a sane person attempting to placate a madman. Dean was probably not far off in his assessment of the weirdo on the other end of the phone.

I laughed. After a sip of milk stout craft beer, I described this particular letter as toothless. "That's because the commonly understood dictionary definition of incineration merely means to reduce to ash without referencing a particular method of doing so. We even have a screenshot of the dictionary definition which says just that. It doesn't only mean open flames burning something to ash, and they would be swimming upstream by filing a lawsuit that's contrary to the commonly understood meaning of common words. Then there's the optics of it. OSGC's lawyers should be bright enough to realize they don't want OSGC to be publicly perceived as bullies. They for darn sure don't want to sue IFBC and CWAC because we certainly would use the opportunity to obtain and publish all of OSGC's internal documents that we could get our grubby paws on during pretrial Discovery. That could be devastating. And for some reason, these guys still haven't figured out they can't defend the indefensible with a word salad of techno-babble. Seems like they're allergic to the KISS method and prefer to vomit jargon all the time, which is a poor way of trying to convince both courts and ordinary people of the righteousness of some cause."

Even though I went to law school way back in the paleolithic era, I knew every law student is still taught to know that truth is an absolute defense to claims of libel and slander, so literally relying upon a commonly understood dictionary definition will win the day. And, as a bonus, now IFBC can say they're being threatened from these scary, menacing lawyers. Trying to bully IFBC would not look good for OSGC in the publics' eyes, especially when IFBC could easily and very simply articulate our position while OSGC would inevitably continue to get bogged down in vague sounding technical jargon.

Dean agreed. "OK, you've convinced me. So now, how do we work around the sign company's reluctance to use the billboard?"

After a bit of discussion, a solution suggested by Dean ended up being even better than the original plan. The remaining billboards that went up carried a compelling picture of Deans niece and nephews in gas masks with the message "'Tell City Council and Mayor Schmitt "No Gasification Plant!" over IFBC's website address.

Both Dean and I liked how the revision's use of IFBC's website name still got the word 'incinerator' into the billboard (because the website at the time spelled the word out as part of the address). Greg thought it was hilarious how we still managed to feature the word 'incinerator' on the billboards anyway. Greg and Dean agreed during separate calls it was appropriate to send a response letter to OSGC's lawyers appearing open to a reasonable discussion, while at the same time suggesting they buzz off unless they have something meaningful to discuss. That letter, which was sent to the same lawyer who later appeared for OSGC at a Green Bay Common Council hearing, read [With the Date and Links Omitted For Purposes of this Reproduction]:

We received your letter suggesting you believe there is some sort of improper use of the word 'incinerators'. While your letter lacks any legal and scientific authorities to substantiate your semantic assertion OSGC's proposed trash incinerator is something else, it is unclear why you object to the common meaning of such a commonly used term. In the interests of engaging in productive dialogue with you, IFBC would note:

1. The word "incinerator" commonly means an "apparatus for incinerating something, especially refuse".

2. The word "incinerate" commonly means to "reduce to ashes".

3. Materials filed by your client contain references to incineration for its proposed processes. The OSGC process is two-staged,

heating followed by incineration of the syngas to produce power. The ash is to be hauled away afterwards.

Before IFBC or CWAC could agree to semantic modification, we ask you to please explain why you believe the common meaning of common words is impermissible. Should you fail to substantiate why using common terms that clearly appear to accurately describe your client's proposed processes is somehow unlawful, we will be left with no alternative but to consider your personal representations to be a knowingly false, affirmative statement of law to a third party pursuant to Wis. SCR 20:4.1.

We await your reply. Thank you for your help.

In practice parlance, cobbling together a letter noting someone's flawed premise is 'unclear' was my way of stating it was unpersuasive for reasons like being a non sequitur, failing to see the bigger picture or was just otherwise unpersuasive because no one was smart enough to understand its genius. I even thought, *Probably all three applied to their letter.* Unsurprisingly, there was no response.

The four billboards were all live by Day 373. They were all located in high traffic areas, especially the one next to the stadium. Days 375 and 376 featured some fantastic television news reporting about the ridiculous litigation threat and the billboards. Greg did a great job for the news interviews where he quite reasonably stated we don't want to offend anybody, but our group was merely trying to raise awareness of this untested and unproven process. IFBC and CWAC were left to speculate whether the news cameras closeup lingering on the word 'incinerator' in IFBC's web address on the billboard was a subtle message.

Afterwards, the *Press-Gazette* reporter called me at home. When I noted during our discussion that the mayor's televised griping about not having been contacted by IFBC before the billboards went up was patently untrue, he agreed because he was present at IFBC's appearance in front of the Green Bay Common Council last month.

The reporter was referring to the Day 337 Council meeting where we first met. The reporter also said that, "It's interesting that IFBC submitted a follow up letter to the mayor a few weeks afterwards. I didn't know that."

Responding to his comment about being unaware of the follow up letter, I said, "Oh. Well then, how about I start copying you on other correspondence going forward so you can stay in the loop?"

"That would be helpful," the reporter replied. "If I have questions when something comes up, all I have to do is give you a ring then, okay?"

I assured him "Absolutely welcome to. Anytime you want!"

Reflecting on the events of the past few days I mused, *Media reporting that OSGC is trying to bully us with high paid lawyers, and accidentally improving our billboard messaging. OSGC's blunders and unintended consequences are certainly starting to pay dividends. Too bad everyone's still deathly afraid this thing will still get built. You almost can't live far enough away from one.*

CHAPTER 16

DAY 412

Upping the Pressure

"But the police are not allowed to proceed on the theory that
'ignorance is bliss'."

— *United States v. Dearing*, 9 F.3d 1428 (9th Cir. 1993)

While I was awaiting delivery of the documents related to my open records requests, Dean called from CWAC and said they were organizing a boycott of Oneida businesses. The eye-catching, two-tone red and white yard signs said:

TELL THE ONEIDA TRIBE
NO GASIFICATION INCINERATOR
GET THE TRUTH
[NOTE: WEBSITE ADDRESS OMITTED]

These signs appeared all around the Brown County by Day 412. Given a heads-up about the new push, the local NBC station featured Dean handing out the signs and gathering petition signatures in a story about the growing opposition to the plant. Dean said, "We're out here to share information because many people in Green Bay have not heard about the incinerator." Dean also said later in the report "This is not just unproven technology, but this is technology that has been proven not to work in many instances across the United States."

In a clear sign of frustration, OSGC's comments to the media continued to be condescending while totally ignoring the truth. OSGC defaulted to its standard position it was sad that a small, vocal opposition group continues to try and mislead the public about what this proposed facility is and what it will do.

As far as I'm concerned, clearly OSGC continues to follow its 'often wrong, but never in doubt' model, I chuckled to myself when I saw the comments.

CBS also reported on Dean's statement that the plants that have tried to get their operating permits have been unsuccessful because they always end up exceeding their pollution-to-permit limit.

CHAPTER 17

DAY 445

Information as a Weapon

"The greatest enemy of knowledge is not ignorance, it is the illusion of knowledge."

— Stephen Hawking

For about thirteen months, IFBC had been digging deep — researching anything and everything they could find on the issue. We searched the sub-corporation filings with the state regulator to trace the mysterious web of relationships between the different entities trying to build the incinerator. IFBC had quite a time tracking the numerous and rapid name changes of these outfits. We were also building up an 'early warning' network of deliberately anonymous persons who could pass along confidential information to IFBC and our allies from right under OSGC's nose.

Unfortunately for OSGC, a mother lode of information was delivered to me from our Open Records requests beginning on Day 445. This voluminous information from DNR was eye-opening and answered many of IFBC's long-standing questions about the economics of the issue, and also detailed the levels of pollution that could be expected in Brown County.

Precisely as predicted by Bradley Angel, I noted the filings clearly stated the incinerator could process tires and medical waste. While poring through the documentation, my mind recalled what Bradley had so memorably stated at dinner before the IFBC forum. "Those are two odious forms of waste that are so undesirable, other communities will pay top dollar to haul them to other States." Ominously, the filings also identified a massive amount of "highly contaminated" wastewater which would gush out into the bay — every day! And OSGC had filed no plans for the prevention of bay water contamination. This trash incinerator was poised to produce a grotesquerie of toxic contamination.

Information regarding the government financing delivered through the state was also obtained from the Wisconsin Economic Development Corporation. There were a pair of loan contracts; one made out to OSGC and another to one of its myriad sub-entities. The first contract for $2 million required creation of less than two dozen jobs in Brown County, slated to begin in a couple of years. The second contract for $2 million required annual payments of $1 million, for which "The Oneida Tribe will set aside 50 for the project."

As I read this, I immediately wondered, *Where the rest of the project funding supposed to come from? That's still unclear here.*

On Day 450, the IFBC core group was joined by Elaine as we gathered in Ashwaubenon to discuss the documents that had been obtained via the Open Records requests. Copies had been duly distributed for review a few days prior.

It was time for me to start the meeting. "Alright, first I have a few thoughts about all these documents. Yes, they confirmed what we previously found about tires and medical waste as potential feedstock. By now, that's no surprise. They also confirmed the pollution levels that we've been warning about since the beginning, so major kudos to Joanne and Alette for nailing the research way back then! The docs also confirmed our suspicions about contaminated wastewater discharge into the bay, although the sheer volume of it was an unpleasant discovery." There was a chorus of disapproving sounds from around the table as they all eyed the numbers. "I assume you all agree that we now have a new pressure point to poke with the state finance contracts, even though it's only a piece of the total financial puzzle?"

Alette responded, "Yes, although I don't see what we can do with that information at the moment."

"Maybe nothing, at the moment. The time might come at some later point when that information will be useful though."

I then asked, "Did everyone have enough time to review the docs?" Seeing the heads nod, I followed by asking, "Any other thoughts about what these revealed?"

Greg spoke up immediately. "You're right. Bradley totally predicted this months ago when he was here for our forum. I wish I could say I'm surprised to see tires and medical waste among the feedstock, but by now nothing is too shocking. Really disappointing to have our worst fears confirmed though."

"We really need to find a more effective way to get this information out. People will get pretty outraged over the idea of tires and medical waste potentially being hauled in from elsewhere to OSGC's incinerator." Joanne stated.

Elaine added some discouraging words. "While all this is just as Bradley predicted, the DNR still doesn't have authority to decline the permit just because of tires and medical waste. OSGC buried the potential feedstock under a murky cloud of uncertainty as to what will be used for fuel. They made it so they can always say they planned on using something else."

After the internal kerfuffle settled down over the additional confirmation of our suspicions, I spoke again. "OK gang. Let's not get bogged down by arguing what else OSGC can possibly use for fuel. We should stick to what we know. And what we know is precisely what's in their documents. We know the fuel potentially may include tires and medical waste. OSGC's own documents say so. That's bad, and they said it, and now OSGC is stuck with it. They can't say we're wrong, because all we have to do is distribute OSGC's own paperwork. Ironically, this time we're not even using our own words, we're using theirs. OSGC shouldn't be heard to complain when we adopt their own articulation."

Greg agreed. "Yeah, and now we can simply circulate OSGC's own paperwork in our messaging. That'll hurt." Sounds of agreement were made around the table.

Elaine got a look on her face indicating that some unexplained dots had been just been connected. "Well, all that explains a little of what my friends in the tribe suspected. Suddenly OSGC was scarce as far as they were concerned, and then everything was focused on trash inciner-ation after that — never responding to inquiries. No one knew what was going on with OSGC anymore. It's like it went off to do its own thing while still using Oneida's resources. My friends will be very interested to learn what we've been discussing here."

After the meeting IFBC was more determined than ever to get the word out.

CHAPTER 18

DAY 455

Strategy and Tactics;
They Start a-Changing

"Therefore, the clever combatant imposes his will on the enemy,
but does not allow the enemy's will to be imposed on him."

— Sun Tzu, *The Art of War*

Day 455 brought some encouraging inside information. Elaine's
sources were reporting that many in the Oneida Tribe were
growing extremely upset over the increasingly negative image
of the OSGC incinerator. Quite understandably, they did not appreciate
being associated with a polluting dirty energy project, nor the increasingly negative trajectory of the media reporting. And the potential economic impact on Oneida was still unclear.

During a short meeting in the Ashwaubenon business park that evening, Elaine spoke to IFBC. "My friends have said everyone has had
enough of OSGC and its antics. They're still gathering the information
they need to make the case to stop the incinerator and maybe do away
with OSGC, but they need more time."

"Do we have a sense of how much time they need?" I asked.

Elaine shook her head. "No. It's a slow process and they have to be quiet about it because OSGC has powerful friends."

"Well, that's fine. We'll just keep doing what we're doing as it helps their efforts and the residents near Hurlbut Street at the same time. For now, we are all following parallel tracks towards a similar goal and it sounds as if they'll let IFBC know if they need anything or what their next steps will be."

IFBC's sources inside Green Bay were also making progress. IFBC had learned much of the true political power structure in Green Bay actually resides with the neighborhood associations, and IFBC's strategy needed to evolve to incorporate an associations influence on the City Council. Tactically, this meant stepping up educational efforts for those neighborhoods and involving them in protests. Several of the associations somewhat adjacent to the proposed incinerator site on Hurlbut Street invited IFBC representatives to speak with them and bring them up to date.

IFBC representatives also spoke to the local chapter of the Audubon Society and several birding clubs that meet near that the wildlife preserves which would be contaminated by the incinerator. On a sunny warm day I found myself scrambling to get to the monthly meeting of the Mather Heights neighborhood association after helping coach my daughter's softball team during its annual home tournament. I was relieved to arrive just in time, managing to hit a succession of green lights as I raced through Ashwaubenon and Green Bay praying not to be late.

Once there I was quickly introduced to the association residents by their president. "Alright everybody, we're turning to the issue of the proposed waste-to-energy facility on Hurlbut Street. Now just so you all know, the association also invited the developer, OSGC, to come as well. But OSGC declined for now. The main local opposition group is Incinerator Free Brown County, and I'd like to introduce its co-chairman, attorney John Filcher from Ashwaubenon. Please give him a big welcome."

I stood up in the front where everyone could see, since most were seated at picnic tables in the park. From there I enlightened the group about the incinerator's unhealthy emissions, our group's new discoveries, and OSGC's flawed permit approval. It was obvious the association was intent on presenting an unbiased forum for both sides to speak about the incinerator, so they were clearly uncomfortable about the news I brought and unsure whether to believe me. Accordingly, I didn't press the issue too hard, but did openly invite them to ask questions, and helpfully suggested some they might ask if or when OSGC would make its case. After answering their questions during the Q&A portion of the show, I also invited one and all to reach out to IFBC with additional questions and we would answer as best we could. After I finished and was driving back to the softball tournament I wondered whether IFBC might be able to leverage OSGC's refusal to speak to the association. *Judging by looks I saw on the faces this afternoon, it was apparent that they were outraged and shocked by what is coming into the area. I'll have to mention that when the time is right*, I decided.

Importantly, IFBC also worked to follow up on new feelers put out by OSGC about possibly moving the incinerator yet again. The next new spot was to be the Village of Suamico, located in the northwest of the Green Bay metro along the west side of the bay. Ashwaubenon and Hobart are several miles to the south of Suamico. During our next IFBC meeting we discussed how best to reach out to Suamico leadership. Elaine provided some insight about the reputation of the village leadership. I was given the impression they wouldn't be too interested in hearing from nobodies like IFBC.

Greg and I decided that, as our solution to skirting around this sort of gatekeeper, we would send a letter to the entire Suamico leadership warning of the matter and asking for a meetup. Then we would see what played out.

Elaine laughed at us. "The village leader is liable to bite your heads off for going around her office like that!"

I just shrugged. "Hmpff. Wouldn't even be the first time this week I stepped on someone's toes. A few years of carefully supervised therapy, and I'll manage to get over it. Be as good as new."

"That therapy come with some good drugs?" Greg laughed.

I thought about it a moment. "It better, or the whole process must be really overrated!"

A few days later, we met with the village leadership at a small restaurant in Suamico along Main Street. Though willing to have a sit down with Greg and I, the leader didn't hesitate to vent displeasure about IFBC's way of forcing the issue out into the open. Sufficiently warned in advance to expect an icy reception, Greg and I wore our 'A-Game' faces and brushed it off while nonetheless doing our best to look contrite for breaching some sort of protocol. Obviously Greg and I were not particular students of protocol. The remainder of the sit down was productive as Greg and I discussed the uncertain incinerator economics, the Harrisburg bankruptcy from their failed incinerator, the tire and medical waste capability of OSGC's incinerator, stack heights, and the expected pollution emissions. Greg also mentioned some of the other identified problems like the sheer increase in truck traffic, fly ash, and the fact the filed plans called for one person — just one! — to hand sort over 150 tons of trash daily without any training or safety gear.

"Wait! You said this project can process tires and medical waste? Do you have any proof of that? We were told this project was only anticipated to process solid waste," said the skeptical village leader. Considering the tale we had been telling, she was right to sound skeptical. I would have been too.

Greg and I looked at each other, and Greg replied "We're sure. And just in case you didn't want to believe us, we highlighted that fact on this copy of OSGC's own filing with DNR." He slid a copy of the filed page over.

While reading the document, the leader's face darkened with anger. "Well, just because it's capable of incinerating tires and medical waste doesn't necessarily mean they're going to."

"Maybe," I said. "But please recall that we mentioned the uncertain economics of these things. Solid waste is a net negative fuel source, which costs even more to incinerate. They would also be producing one ton of char and ash for every tons of waste incinerated. It costs money to haul and dispose of all that ash, further impacting their finances. The feedstock is quite dirty, which would mean lots of downtime for the incinerator because they break down due to lack of clean burning fuel, costing additional money. None has ever remained economically viable over the long term; they only last as long as the government money does. So, how does an incinerator project stretch out this timeline? By incinerating the kind of waste that brings in higher fees than does solid waste. Top of that list are tires and medical waste."

Nodding reluctantly, the leader had to agree. "Oh, I hate to say it, but you're probably right. Your information gives me a much more a complete picture than they have painted. OSGC never mentioned any of that to us in the first few meetings."

Greg nodded in return. "Well, if you're trying to put lipstick on a pig for sales purposes, would you want to start pointing out all the warts and blemishes?"

The leader laughed ruefully. "Nope. Just nope. It all just seems so disreputable. Like dirty tactics for a dirty project."

That statement prompted Greg and I to look at each other with raised eyebrows and matching expressions before Greg remarked, "That's a really good way of saying it. I wish we would have thought of that!"

The village leader was decidedly unhappy to hear about all this 'dirty business' because it had certainly not been imparted by OSGC during their preliminary discussions. However, the leader was quick to see the big picture now that we had helped provide more context. OSGC had again characterized its incinerator as an amazing green energy gasification plant that solves all sorts of problems but doesn't cause any. All upside, and no downside.

As Greg and I prepared to depart, the leader again expressed her displeasure about IFBC's chosen method of reaching out, but noted there was much more to be upset about regarding OSGC's misleading presentation.

Greg and I left, quite satisfied that Suamico now knew not to make a play for the incinerator.

IFBC was be now getting a good feel for the impact our messaging was having, but more surprises were coming.

On Day 470, the *Wisconsin Reporter* ran an article in an annual American Society of Newspaper Editors series called "Sunshine Week" covering how well local governments responded to the open records laws (aka the Open Records Law, or Sunshine Acts). Reporter Kirsten Adshead wrote that the group, Incinerator Free Brown County, hoped to kill the OSGC incinerator with a public information campaign. Reporting from Madison, Adshead wrote, "And key to that campaign, Filcher said, is information he's received from state and local government offices about the project, much of it obtained through open records requests." Adshead also quoted me saying, "The documents speak for themselves and they're absolutely essential in getting true and accurate information out there, as opposed to what was represented to the public."

CHAPTER 19

DAY 477

Rally Time!

"I alone cannot change the world, but I can cast a stone across the water to create many ripples."

— Mother Teresa

On Day 477 many concerned residents rallied with CWAC and IFBC, attending a Green Bay Common Council meeting to request the Conditional Use Permit (CUP) either be rescinded or enforced as it had been represented. The large crowd squeezed into a conference room at the downtown library.

"Thank you all for coming. Clean air and water for our families and environment are a crucial issue for each of us here this afternoon. Before we all head over to the city council meeting as a group, myself and Mr. Filcher here," said Dean, gesturing to me as I stood next to him, "will talk about some aspects of the proposed incinerator, and how we as a group will conduct ourselves in the gallery of the council chamber."

As I spoke to the crowd about tires and medical waste, stack heights and nondisclosure (eliciting some angry mutters) and other glaring omissions by OSGC, I was struck by the plainly visible shock and anger on their faces that seemed to grow more severe with each passing minute.

Afterwards, Dean and I discussed the rally. "I thought that went well," I said to Dean. "These folks are very, very angry, but they were receptive to playing their role when we get to the council chambers. Hopefully the council will listen to what is said and take action on that permit." Dean thought they would.

Nodding as the two of us crossed the street to city hall, Dean said, "The Common Council seems to be under the mayor's influence, and he really wants this project, so I wouldn't get our hopes up too high tonight. But they need to see how angry the voters are." Getting a laugh from Dean, I quipped in reply, "Normally when a crowd gets this angry and riled up, it's directed at me instead of at someone else. This is refreshingly different!"

At the Common Council meeting, Dean and the president of the Mather Heights association appeared together by request. Dean passed out copies of the petition to the Council members. When they were ready, Dean began by stating, "We're here tonight because we believe there's cause to revisit the Conditional Use Permit. We feel there are a number of misrepresentations made by OSGC and that's what we're here to share with you tonight."

The association president's comments included, "The neighborhood association really got involved at our last annual meeting." He noted that it was "when one of our neighborhood members suggested that we come out officially and oppose this." He added that the association board decided to randomly survey the neighborhood and ask whether the residents favored or opposed the project after each had reviewed literature provided by the OSGC public relations department and also information put out by IFBC. "We tried to be fair and balanced. The responses that came back were opposed two to one."

"It's not a small group of people who oppose this," said Dean, with the president noting over 1000 opposing the project. "We believe that the Oneida Seven Generations Corporation, or OSGC, misrepresented the true nature of its incinerator project by presenting false and misleading information to the public and the City of Green Bay for the duel purposes of gaining public acceptance of the project and obtaining a Conditional Use Permit from the City." The duo continued detailing each exhibit containing misrepresentations to Ashwaubenon and Hobart residents, to the Green Bay Common Council, to the Mather Heights Association, and to Brown County residents. It was an extensive list. After they finished, the association president asked the city to take steps to revoke the permit.

Later in the evening it was IFBC's turn at the podium. Mr. Schmitt, the mayor, introduced me. After putting on some reading glasses, my comments were as follows:

> Thank you Mr. Mayor.
>
> I'm John Filcher, co-chair of Incinerator Free Brown County. I'm not going to beat a dead horse because the hour is late, but there are a couple of points that should be raised. One, there's a lot of semantics being made here tonight. And really, whether we call it an incinerator or pyrolysis, which if you look at it means fire, which I think is kind of funny, really it's just distinctions without a difference.
>
> If you're burning trash, incineration by definition doesn't even refer to what method you're burning, it's just the fact that eventually it's reduced to ash. Fine, it's an incinerator. Great, moving on. I believe it was this evening Alderman Wery said, 'Whatever happened to being responsible for your actions?' Yes, let's revisit that. That's why we're here.
>
> Certain representations were made to this council. Turns out they probably weren't accurate. How much intent you want to assign to whether or not they were accurate deliberately or accidentally, that's up to you folks. But at the end of the day, if it wasn't accurate does the City of Green Bay want to bless approval of something when it was given incorrect information?
>
> That's the question here tonight, folks. If there's a large gap between rhetoric and reality this time, what's

next? What is the next thing coming down the road that won't face a prosecution, a lawsuit or some other action?

Even Mr. Ackerman, who I'm imagining was probably in favor of this thing, says the thing is "risky", his word, and may have been misrepresented. That's the best the pro-incinerator side can come up with is it may have been misrepresented and it's risky? And we still want to bless approval of that?

I don't see why we can't unwind and require Seven Generations to come back in here and explain why things were portrayed one way to the Council, and may have been portrayed in an entirely and vastly different way to a different regulator. It's certainly a question worth asking here.

Another question. Siting. It would probably be useful for everyone to stop and ask themselves a simple question. Would you want this incinerator in your neighborhood, near your particular house? If you don't want your family to be a guinea pig to something that's never been tried, there's no management expertise, there's no experience expertise, no educational expertise of the people trying to build this, there's nothing, if you don't want your family to be a guinea pig under this hypothetical, look at all these people.

They don't want it either. These are mad people. Their families are at stake. Their homes are at stake. Their properties. Their livelihoods. That's why we're here tonight. The last thing was something about 'it's going to cost the city'. Really? The City's not the one that made the misrepresentation according to what's been presented to you tonight.

So, are we discussing phantom fears? How's it going to cost the City to say 'hey, you need to come back in and explain this to us, folks'? Fine. If they don't want to

do it, well that's on them. But that's definitely questions
to ask yourselves.

Thank you."

Thanking the audience for listening, I stepped down from the
podium. This was the talk that I had been saying over and over to myself,
and to anyone that would listen. Tonight, as I had witnessed the shock
and horror on people's faces, I realized the impact of asking anyone's
family to be a guinea pig in a hypothetical science experiment had finally
resonated. When I looked back into their faces as I spoke to the council
and referenced the people behind me, I nearly lost track of what I had
been saying because of the depth of visible emotion on those faces.

Joanne took to the podium a few minutes later. Her presentation
below has been slightly modified regarding reference to a particular
date):

> You'll have to excuse my notes. They're kind of ran-
> dom. I didn't know I'd be speaking tonight, and these
> are just some thoughts I had.
>
> I want everybody to keep in mind there are no
> full-scale commercially permitted gasification pyrol-
> ysis plants using MSW only as the sole feed in the
> whole world. None. So, also in all the documents from
> the DNR, EPA or whatever, time and time again the
> word — estimates. We estimate. We guess. We assume.
> Because they have no long-term history to base this one.
>
> Those words are used again, and again, and again.
> Are estimates and guesstimates — are we to assume good
> enough? We have to keep in mind two major points.
> This company has no experience with this type of facil-
> ity. None. And every bit of safety depends on experience.
> There is no long-term history of effects, either. Medical
> or environmental. Which scientist could say takes about
> ten years.
>
> So, we need due diligence done before something
> like this is built. Why are we letting this company with

no experience do something like this when they don't even know how many megawatts of power they're going to produce, and on and on.

I was told to my face that there would be no stacks of any kind. No stacks. Now there's ten. And that's just one instance.

As far as our agencies protecting us, the EPA is going to announce when they're coming. Boy, how convenient that is. They can simply burn a safe load. They will know when they're coming to be tested.

As far as other plants in the world existing, there was a plant in Germany which was plagued by startup and close down problems. Ran and run. Ran and run. But it was a type of pyrolysis gasification. It closed in 2004 and it was like $500 million in debt.

There was one in Australia. Closed in 2004. $500,000 US dollars in debt. Ran, didn't run. Ran for a little while, didn't run. Didn't do at all what they said.

There was a full scale pyrolysis in Germany. It closed in 1998 due to an explosion of the pyrolysis gas into the neighborhood and the whole neighborhood had to be evacuated. Siemen's withdrew from this market after that.

Japan does have a similar type of incinerator and it had the power grid. But after six years, it has failed to produce any power, or supply any power at all to the grid.

As far as getting rid of landfills. This doesn't get rid of landfills. Seven Gens told us after the open house they're going to put the ash into these plastic containers, sealed tight containers, and haul them to the landfill. Or, they're going to dump the ash on top of existing landfills. Well, how long will it be before we have these plastic, airtight cartons stacked up?

It does not get rid of landfills. I don't know if anyone ever saw pictures of Covanta's landfills from single feed streams out east or anyplace. They're as high as telephone poles. As far as spreading the ash on top of landfills, well that's a good idea! Now we've chemically altered the ash so it contains unburned metals and we're going to let it blow away in the wind.

The DNR told me while that won't be a problem because they tarp their landfills very securely at night. And their trucks. So, I said to them, 'Well gee, you mean the wind doesn't blow during the day?' And they admit that the fly ash is toxic, especially if the temperature is not kept at a certain consistent degree. There are unburned metals in the gas, and it is toxic.

Once they take out all the plastics and all the papers, because those are supposed to be recycled, what are they going to have for caloric or heat value? They're going to be left burning sewage, grass, mud, wet papers. Then they're going to need to burn something that creates heat, like tires, medical waste and hazardous waste to get the caloric value to keep the heat temperature up.

Once the temperature goes down or waivers, we have toxic pollutants produced, so no, this does not get rid of landfills. Not at all. Only now, supplying it on top of the landfill, allows it to blow freely in the wind over the cultural land, over the bay where fish ingest it, animals eat it, and therefore like the places in Europe we get dioxins in our meat, milk, fish, eggs, cheese. Animals graze on the land. Fish consume it."

In response to the applause for Joanne's spot-on comments, the mayor reminded the crowd that they really don't allow applause in the Common Council chamber.

The Day 477 edition of the *Kalihwisaks* reported on the rally, stating CWAC and other community members rallied in the streets outside the Green Bay City Hall in an effort to stop the OSGC incinerator on the city's north side. The report indicated CWAC President Dean Hoegger said OSGC had misled the public and the common council to obtain the CUP. "We all feel like we have been misled. We all attended meetings where they told us there would be no smokestacks, no emissions. I felt like I was lied to. Not only was the public misrepresented, so was the city council." A OSGC official was even quoted as saying OSGC has always said there will be no smokestacks like those associated with power plants or paper mills. There will be exhaust pipes, which are referred to as stacks in DNR permitting, that are common to many industries.

OSGC's techno-babble verbiage continued to strongly remind me of the immortal words of Humpty Dumpty in Lewis Carroll's work, *Through the Looking-Glass*. "'When I use a word,' Humpty Dumpty said, in rather a scornful tone, 'it means just what I choose it to mean—neither more nor less.'"

One Day 483, the *Press-Gazette* reported that the Mather Heights Neighborhood Association had joined CWAC and IFBC in an effort to stop the plant. The article further noted that plant opponents protested before City Hall, gathered numerous signatures on a petition, and threatened a boycott. Accordingly, the petition was presented to the Council and the opposition asked them to rescind the CUP. OSGC's tone deaf messaging was described in the article as 'dismissing' these concerns. My own statement about not making the people of Green Bay the guinea pigs test this untested technology followed additional comments from local residents asking why this wasn't being placed near the residences of the folks who want to build the thing.

After all these exciting events, IFBC met on Day 490. I excitedly observed that this was the "first news article to actually mention that the proposed facility was able to incinerate tires according to OSGC's own filings."

Elaine nodded. "OSGC's grip on local media is clearly slipping. News of the regulatory filings confirms exactly what IFBC has been warning about and adds to your credibility and ruins what little credibility OSGC has left."

Greg slowly nodded. "Yeah, it sure seems like media is getting more and more negative about OSGC's incinerator. Sure seems like the more the media looks into what was originally said about the thing, the less they believe OSGC."

Greg's comment made me chuckle and called to mind Winston Churchill's quote about a lie getting halfway around the world before the truth has time to fall out of bed and put its pants on.

CHAPTER 20

DAY 490

Media Loves a Good Controversy

"The adage surely applies that if it looks like a duck, acts like a
duck and quacks like a duck, it should be considered a duck."
— *Ainsworth v. State Farm Mut. Ins. Co.*, 284 N.J. Super. 117, 663
A.2d 1365 (NJ Ct. App. 1995)

Things were moving right along. Early on Day 490 Dean appeared on the Jerry Bader Show, a local conservative talk radio broadcast for the area. During the show opening, Jerry mentioned that both CWAC and IFBC were fighting the incinerator project, also stating that OSGC did not want its project to be referred to as an incinerator. This broadcast sparked a series of informal and off-the-record email and telephone discussions between me and Jerry, all of which were informative and thought-provoking.

I was as helpful as I could be in providing Jerry with OSGC's filed and withheld information, giving him a much clearer picture of how the application process was playing out. Jerry said that the proposed plant had received most of the needed approvals from the various regulators, but CWAC and IFBC wanted the permit rescinded due to the misrepresentations stated in their filings. Interestingly, Jerry also said that he would be reaching out to OSGC for their response; however, Dean, Jerry and I already knew OSGC wasn't willing to participate in a forum of media where it would not be able to control the narrative.

The radio interview began with Jerry asking Dean about the definitions and whether or not this was an actual incinerator. Dean deftly responded that the facility is both a gasification plant like OSGC calls it, and also a two-stage incinerator. Dean also stated we are not in agreement with OSGC's use of the term "biomass" since trash is not biomass because it should have nothing to do with gas, oil or plastics.

Jerry and Dean discussed the contents of municipal solid waste, both noting that it contains considerable amounts of plastics and other non-biological material. Various misrepresentations about the lack of emissions and the fallout zone were also talked about, as well as the 18-month period this experimental facility would have to try to get its emissions under control once it began operations — despite the proximity to the Mather Heights neighborhood.

The two of them had an in depth and productive conversation, which I think served to keep the pressure on both the Common Council and OSGC. Dean offered great information about the lack of data provided by OSGC to the public and lack of notice provided to the public when the mayor invited this monstrosity into the neighborhood. Green Bay residents weren't the only ones justifiably upset about that lack of warning and respect about this 'gasification' project imposing itself on their neighborhoods.

While I listened to the broadcast, my eldest daughter asked whether it was that important if the word 'incinerator' or 'gasification' was used. "Well, while sometimes arguing about different terms amounts to little more than making distinctions without differences, in this issue it actually makes a huge difference because OSGC is deliberately choosing words whose meanings diminish the listener's sense of the true dangers this project poses. It's the difference between being a little bit accurate, and much more accurate."

"Sounds like the difference between a truth, and the whole truth," my daughter replied.

"Correct, grasshopper!" I replied with a huge smile.

"Grasshopper? Are you referring to ancient TV shows again, dad?"

Busted, I laughed and fessed up. "Yes, yes I am. It was a cheesy show from when I was a kid, but the show did spawn a great one liner."

On Day 498, many concerned residents accompanied CWAC and IFBC to another Green Bay Common Council meeting. After the local residents complained that OSGC materially misrepresented facts with regards to emissions and 'no smokestacks', the Council then voted to further investigate these representations during the run-up to the CUP approval.

There were many hard-hitting comments and heartfelt emotions expressed by the residents since the Common Council had failed to dil-igently take heed of their concerns earlier on Day 477. Interestingly, one of the Council members got into a heated debate with Dean over semantics and the word 'incinerator'.

And then things turned deadly serious when a resident named Laura spoke. "I live literally where this plant is going. I don't have vast edu-cation about what this pertains to, I don't know all the scientific stuff." She continued, pointing at the Mayor and Council members, her voice cracking with emotion. "But I'm a mother of five children. I don't want this in my yard. Don't you put this in my backyard. You put it in your backyard. Put it in your backyard." At this the onlookers all cheered and applauded.

Just then the same Council member who had tried to argue with Dean unwisely interrupted her. "It already is in my backyard."

"Bullshit! It's not, it's in my backyard." Laura exploded.

Mayor Schmitt attempted to regain control of the proceedings. "Look, ah, we have to keep just a level of civility here and even applause, and I understand it's an emotional subject it happens here all the time, we would just ask people to make the testimony. We record this all and that's what's in the record."

Somewhat subdued but still passionate, Laura continued, drawing a very serious comparison to the window of time between occurrence and finally learning something is unsafe by describing that when she was a young girl, Laura's father was a member of the United States Army who served in the Vietnam War. The military said that the Agent Orange defoliant they used to clear the jungle was safe. She noted they told our soldiers and their families it was safe to spray on our soldiers because the manufacturer had tested it. But now her father is slowly dying a horrible death from a diagnosis of Agent Orange-related cancer four or five decades later because there was no possible way to test how exposure would poison our people for the long term. Laura was devastating in comparing that same lack of certainty with this incinerator.

Pausing for a moment to compose herself and wipe the tears from her eyes, she cleared her throat and continued. "You can't tell me you know what's going to happen with this in 40 years. There's been people misspeaking, they've been telling half-truths, you can't get a straight answer from anybody no matter who you call and talk to. If this is such a great, fantastic, wonderful option, why isn't it on Oneida property in their backyard? Why not? Why is it in ours? Why is it being shoved down our throats? Why do we have to have it? I can't get an answer from anybody about that.

"I don't want it, and I don't know anybody, I defy one person from the west side here to say they want it. Nobody does. And I think the Oneidas brought this on themselves because they came out with mistruths, half-truths; you can't get a straight answer. I think people have had enough, and nobody wants this. And I will fight this to the death. And I'll tell you now, if my property values go down, those of you who vote this in — I'm going to sue you for it."

Greg shared that he was very concerned about what the contaminant dispersion rates would be at the new 35-foot stack height levels, asking whether DNR would have to re-look at the matter. Other residents voiced concerns about the changes in the plans between what was represented to the Council and what appeared later in other forums; changes in the story directly told to them when calling OSGC, and failures of due diligence. Still other residents spoke of their unease about the Council's lack of research and described the expected emissions. OSGC's attorney also spoke to the Council and did not formally object to a fact-finding hearing in an official capacity.

The Mather Heights Association President then said that he had reviewed what OSGC had stated before they later refused to meet with the association, only to learn that everything they had been told by OSGC was wrong.

Alderman Guy Zima gave an eloquent speech, culminating in a request that the matter be referred to the Planning Commission for further review. (In hindsight, Mr. Zima's comments were uncannily prescient and relevant for another trash incinerator debacle in another state some years later.)

The relationship between Mr. Zima and the mayor was adversarial and often resulted in a war of words. Despite this well-known combativeness, it was not on display when the mayor recognized Alderman Zima as wishing to speak that evening.

"You know I think I, as well as everybody else in the room, initially believed that the Oneidas initially thought they were doing something good. But, as time as gone on I think it's been kind of obvious to any neutral observer that they were just kind of feeling their way through this thing. At no time did the Oneidas come and promote this as an untried and previously unsuccessful project throughout the country and throughout the world. They were just were saying like this is the greatest thing since sliced bread, and this is going to be something great.

"You know, I've had a nasty habit of trying to follow the dollar bill throughout my career. And you know, is it interesting to anybody in this room that, as of today, the Oneidas have registered not one but three lobbyists with the City of Green Bay to promote this project? They don't come up and talk to us. They send up an attorney that basically has told us he doesn't really know about all of this. He's just here to guard their rights, I guess. But you know, I think there's something fundamentally wrong about a group of people that come to us and tell us there aren't going to be any stacks, aren't going to be any emissions, all self-contained. And then after they get it, they move on to the DNR and promoting the idea of having fifty to sixty-foot stacks when we're talking about none here.

"This was supposed to be like Mother Earth taking care of itself, that's really how it was presented to us. But you know I think we have to follow the trail of the dollar bill a little more now too. I think we have to watch where campaign contributions come and go from. I think we have to pay attention to who stands to gain, and who stands to lose. I mean, at this point in time the public, I think rightfully so, is more than suspicious about this.

"I received a lot of information from a lot of people that say hey, this project could end in bankruptcy and perhaps a big clean-up cost to the City of Green Bay. So whatever little bit you're going to save on your garbage over the years, may come back to haunt you big time. I think it's important that we really, for the, I think relatively insignificant amount of money that the City's going to save, not that it's nothing I never want to put down any dollar, but I think we have to ask ourselves and our conscience, is this what we really want to put, do we want to be a guinea pig, for the State of Wisconsin, for Green Bay, for maybe the United States of America, for a unfound, to date unsuccessful, process that may cause some harm to us?"

After pausing to pull out a sheet of paper, Zima continued, referring to a "letter from the Midwest Environmental Advocates" where he noted, "no request by the Oneida Seven Gens Corporation that the CUP authorized such stacks, chimneys, vents or structures was ever made. But they speak more firmly, they say moreover, affirmative representations were made that the operation would be entirely self-contained. That there would be no stacks, that there would be no emissions. People didn't only, now they're going to bring the stacks down to 35 feet. Well isn't that wonderful? It's kind of after the fact. They weren't even talking about stacks before. In fact, the picture they showed us didn't even show a tiny little finger of a stack. It showed a building that looked like a warehouse. And they have affirmatively made these kinds of statements to us."

Taking a breath, Mr. Zima continued. "Our city attorney has worked on this, and he's been very careful in his opinion to us. I read it thoroughly this afternoon. And he basically says, well, if we want to do something about this, we need to have a public hearing about it. And we need to, really get to the bottom and maybe do a further investigation of what was said in other places, in other venues. And, I don't know, it's my feeling that the very least we should do here tonight is not receive this opinion and place it in file but act upon what it says we can do. And it says we can have a public hearing. And we can gather information. And I think we should put the Oneidas on notice that any further moving forward on their project at this point could generate further financial problems for themselves if we discover something that might reverse our decision.

"So I would like to make a motion, your honor, that we hold public hearings, that we instruct our city attorney to gather all information and input using the folks who have done some of the work for him as well as the public records that exist and to bring it back here for a hearing. Cause I think is probably the biggest, most important decision we're going to have to make here in a long, long time."

After Zima's motion was seconded and passed, he concluded his comments. "Who's interested in making a big blunder? We're gonna take a chance at a big blunder without really investigating it? Everybody in this room knows that this thing was shoved through here in a very short period of time. Maybe 'shoved' is a little pejorative of a word. Just a kind of a horse and pony show was put about how great this thing was and that it was a no brainer. I think it was described as a no brainer. Well, I think we all know it's not exactly a no brainer. There needs to be a little brains put into this thing. And there's a lot of people out there who are smarter than I am, some of them spoke here tonight, that certainly raised doubts in my mind. And I think the very least we can do for the citizens of Green Bay and all of our constituents is to have a thorough investigation of this thing. And let's see just what, if anything, out there could prove us wrong in doubting what the Seven Generations want to do? I think it's clear that they've been kind of bobbing along. They maybe had good intentions, they think it's a green thing and all that that sort of thing. And maybe it is, but maybe it isn't. And this is something that could have a long-term effect, so that's my motion. Thank you."

The Day 500 article in the *Press-Gazette* included an outpouring of opposition from area residents. The Mather Heights Association president was quoted as saying, "The people are speaking, and the people do not want this."

Pursuant to additional calls between IFBC and Mr. Bader identifying the 35-foot stack height limit contained in the city's ordinances,
WTAQ published an article on its website on Day 501, reporting that
the waste-to-energy facility's DNR permit calls for 60-foot exhaust
stacks — which violate the city code. It was helpful that the article
added a statement by the DNR air management engineer clearly declar-
ing that OSGC would have to obtain DNR approval for 35-foot stack
heights. OSGC was now in a regulatory jam of its own making. At the
same time, OSGC was quoted in a particularly tone-deaf statement, as if
OSGC somehow thought anyone cared about OSGC's feelings enough
to call their opposition "appalling" and that OSGC was "offended".

At the next IFBC core meeting, the gang decided the angry sounding OSGC statements and pearl clutching were a sign of OSGC's growing desperation. We decided that IFBC would keep the pressure up, and
accordingly Greg sent a letter to the editor of the *Ashwaubenon Press* on
Day 506 after we had hashed out its contents. Greg's letter addressed
OSGC's new tact of calling the opposition a "misinformation campaign"
and called OSGC out for completely failing to identify exactly what the
misinformation had been that was supposedly presented by IFBC. Greg
also highlighted OSGC's revisionist history of falsely suggesting the filed
OSGC documentation magically now contained adequate information.
Tellingly, Greg's letter closed by noting that, if accurate information had
been originally disclosed, this project would have failed a long time ago,
and there would be no current need for residents to encourage reexam-
ination of OSGC's submissions, nor the need to possibly unwind the
permit.

As I read Greg's finalized letter before it was submitted, I thought
with amusement, *this is a nice twist. Now we're publicly demanding that
the DNR enforce the permits as written because OSGC created its very own
Damned If You Do and Damned If You Don't conflict between the city and
state's requirements. That ought to make OSGC's head spin.*

Despite past cautionary warnings from Elaine against allowing ourselves to become sidetracked by opposing more than one project at a
time, IFBC also agreed there was sufficient bandwidth to give an assist
to another local group of residents who had asked for our help the same

week as the Green Bay Common Council meeting. This time it was another company which was proposing to build a facility in a small neighborhood in Maribel, Wisconsin. These residents were organizing and looking for help on how to stand against this facility, which was being alternatively referred to by the developer as a digester or a gasification plant intended to process manure waste into methane and usable fertilizer. Their discovery of IFBC occurred the small-town word-of-mouth way common in our area. In this case, it was through one of the digester opposition leaders who happened to be a former resident of Ashwaubenon. The leader was introduced to IFBC's existence while discussing the digester over coffee with a friend who still lived in Ashwaubenon.

An Open House in Maribel was hosted by the digester project developers on Day 499. Located about 25 minutes away from the Green Bay area, Maribel is a small farming community that gave me the impression of having more bars than any other businesses. Maribel is less than a 10-minute drive west of the last known location of Teresa Halbach, the murder victim in the Netflix series *Making a Murderer*. Because IFBC was now quite used to speaking up, we no longer hesitated to upset project developers' apple carts. I was prepared for the uncomfortable stir of Maribel residents, as was typical when we employed IFBC's usual tactics. I was curious to see how the developers would handle the stress in an awkward and uncomfortable environment they could not fully control.

I waited for the perfect moment to make a move after the open house got underway. The moment came when I observed the crowd growing upset over the developer's evasiveness. I whipped out my smartphone, wanting to capture the reactions of the speaker to some tough questions.

I then began. "Alright, you mentioned earlier the facility will be producing compressed natural gas, which is petroleum based and impossible to get out of food stocks. You also said there would be no emissions stacks yet you're getting an air quality permit by YOUR own words from DNR. Why do you need an air quality permit if YOU don't have any stacks? And you're producing gas, from somewhere. Where is the compressed natural gas coming from, you got an oil well there or something?" I deliberately was using a very hostile and aggressive tone while I spoke from behind my smartphone as I recorded the exchange to see how this guy would react.

The project representative tried not to appear shocked. "Uh, no sir. Uh, natural gas is methane. It's 99% methane, which is what we're making. So, not all natural gas is petroleum based." Apparently 'natural gas' was this outfit's idea of a trendy euphemism for methane, but the speaker pointedly did not address why they needed a permit or stacks.

After that questionable level of candor, the public visibly became even more aggressive towards the speaker because his response clearly indicated a startling lack of engineering acumen.

A week and a half later, Greg, Alette, Joanne and I were highly entertained to read about OSGC's hurt feelings in a Day 507 article in the *Kalihwisaks*, where the company suggested IFBC was using untruthful tactics. "The goal is to stop the facility through a misinformation campaign. We find it appalling that the opposition steadfastly refuses to accept the facts and the findings and has chosen to misrepresent the project and its impacts." OSGC's statement continued with "OSGC, and those working on the project are offended by the continuing harassment of this business development."

I just laughed to myself, thinking, *it never ceases to amaze when a well-funded corporation thinks saying it is offended will get anyone to care about that outfit's feelings because everyone knows companies don't have feelings.*

This whining from an outfit with a Humpty Dumpty like record of malleable techno-babble to suit its motives managed to elicit a small reaction from the core IFBC members as we shared a few beers before leaving Greg's house. Joanne muttered, "Aw, the poor dears!" Her exaggeratedly insincere tone was Oscar worthy.

Alette laughed. "Sounds like OSGC needs a hug."

At the same meeting, Elaine was at first mildly surprised listening to IFBC's take on the article, viewing it as proof that OSGC was showing weakness and didn't know how to stand up to the truth. But she finally agreed that it did actually signal that OSGC was in a world of hurt. "You guys have really come a long way from the band of quiet, inexperienced residents you were when you started investigating this project. Now when OSGC says something offensive, instead of worrying about it you jump right in and take them to task!"

"Oh, come on, Elaine! We were COMPLETELY serious when we mumbled something sympathetic!" I responded, tongue in cheek. Joanne couldn't be the only one in Oscar contention for over-the-top insincerity today.

On a more serious note, Joanne observed, "Well, OSGC is such an easy target, especially when it tries to portray itself as a victim. And OSGC is the company that brought all this trouble to us in the first place."

Charlene from WEAL was also enjoying a beer with the gang at Greg's place. She described the slippery stories of incinerator developers she previously experienced first-hand. "Having been directly, and indirectly involved with various types of incineration proposals over the years, some projects dating back to the 1980s, I've learned not to trust *anything* said by an incinerator developer.

"We now hear gasification developers deliver presentations proclaiming their project will not generate emissions because they will have a 'closed loop' process, which is just the latest trendy term. Here, though, OSGC went beyond just saying their project wouldn't produce any emissions by omitting stacks in an artist's rendering on their website and not including the stacks in plans the company submitted to Green Bay for a permit."

CHAPTER 21

DAY 536

Tweaking

"Today, the trouble with common sense is
that it is no longer common."

— G.K. Chesterton (1874-1936)." *State v. Doss,*
2007 WI App 208, 740 N.W.2d 410 (WI Ct. App. 2007)

IFBC's questioning of OSGC wasn't the only tweaking that occurred. On Day 536 the *Press-Gazette* ran a front-page article under the headline, "Alternative Energy Plant Tweaked". The newspaper duly reported that instead of six stacks of up to 60 feet in height, there would now be only two 35-foot stacks. Hilariously, a later informal comment from a concerned Green Bay citizen that I overheard suggested the revised 35-foot stacks of the incinerator amount to a giant hair dryer because of the greater heat and incredible speed necessary to push the emissions higher up into the atmosphere to compensate for the shorter 35 foot stack heights.

As I read the newspaper and reflected on that guy's hair dryer comparison, I thought, *it was real world mathematical comparisons like this which help highlight the farcical "science" and desperate push to keep the proposed project alive.*

The same article also quoted me saying, "It sounds like a desperate move" as I called upon Green Bay officials to expedite the new review. The story also noted that earlier in the week IFBC had sent the mayor a letter asking for an expedited hearing, which I wryly noted was because I had begun copying the *Press-Gazette* on all of our letters to keep the paper in the loop like we previously had discussed.

Unfortunately for OSGC, being forced to change its plans due entirely to faults of its own was a major hit to the credibility of an outfit that had previously implied that it was infallible.

IFBC was once more in the press with a Day 537 article in the *Ashwaubenon Press*. According to the article IFBC would be receiving the Environmental Citizen of the Year award at the annual meeting of the Clean Water Action Council.

Dean called from CWAC to ask how the award should be titled; in our individual names or as a group. After a long day in the salt mines I called the core group together at a local coffee house to fill them in on the award and enjoy some much-needed camaraderie, coffee and a few laughs.

"OK, big news for IFBC, and a nice 'attaboy' pat on the back. Dean called me early today to ask how we should be listed on the award. Individually or as a group. Knowing us, I said probably as a group, but that we'd get back to him after I took everybody's temperature about it," I said when we got down to business.

"Well, one of the reasons we created IFBC was to give us a group identity, and to take the pressure off any of us as individuals," Alette chimed in. "I vote for as a group."

"Me too," said Joanne.

Greg nodded, "Ditto. We started as a team, and we play as a team."

"Those were exactly my thoughts, too," I agreed. "But it was nice to get together over a cup of Go-Juice to chat about it." As IFBC had always functioned as a team, accepting the award in the name of IFBC on behalf of our hundreds of members and not in the individual names of the leadership was entirely consistent with how we had agreed to function.

The CWAC annual soirée was lots of fun but also a bit of a surprise for the foursome. Held at the historic Riverside Ballroom in Green Bay, site of the final show from Buddy Holly, Ritchie Valens, and The Big Bopper, Greg was pleased to hear a band playing old favorites as he and I entered the ballroom at six pm. We went stag because our better halves were both busy herding kids between school activities. There was a silent auction of environmentally responsible items, an open bar, with several hundred guests milling about.

"Wow, this is a bigger shindig than I expected!" Greg grinned at me. "I had no idea it would be this big. This looks great!"

Spotting Dean talking to a couple near the bar, we headed over to say hello. "Greg, John! Good to see you. Let me introduce you to Leah Dodge of the *OneidaEye*."

Greg and I were delighted to finally meet Leah and her partner in person after our many correspondences in recent days.

"We came in for the soirée because Dean said we could finally meet the Fearsome Foursome all in one spot!" said Leah as a bar server took everybody's drink orders.

I laughed. "Yeah, pretty tricky of Dean to bait the trap like that and get us all into one place." Everybody chuckled.

Leah and her partner's reporting and relentless unearthing of documents had been nothing short of spectacular and thoroughly detailed, which had repeatedly impressed me. Although IFBC had only fairly recently learned of them, the *OneidaEye* would prove to be extremely influential and knowledgeable throughout the entire anti-incinerator fight. After about an hour of swapping stories, sharing drinks and getting to know one another, Dean excused himself because it was time for him to put his emcee hat on and get the evening's program underway.

"Good evening everyone, and welcome. Will you all please take your seats at the tables up front?" After the crowd was seated, Dean continued. "First thing, you all saw the silent auction at the back? Good, bid high and bid often. Proceeds go to help fund our operations. And those operations include quite a diverse set of maneuvers and processes again this year. Clean Water Action sued to help extend the cleanup of the Fox River from the industrial pollution of the early 20th century. The successor manufacturers wanted to wrap the contaminated riverbed cleanup two years early, but the court agreed with us that they weren't finished." At this the audience burst into applause.

Dean continued bringing the audience up to date on CWAC's actions over the past year, and they were many as CWAC is an active group. "Here in the northeastern Wisconsin area, this has been a very busy year due to the proposal to construct a trash incinerator by OSGC." He was interrupted by a boisterous wave of boos at the mention of the incinerator project. "Yes, and CWAC and other groups have been very vocal in opposing the thing. Tonight, the group of local folks who have been leading the charge against trash incineration in northeastern Wisconsin are here to accept the 'Environmental Citizen of the Year' award for their tireless and vocal work in raising awareness about the proposed incinerator. As a reflection of how their group functions, the four leaders of the group chose to accept this prestigious award in the name of their membership and not in their own names. Please welcome co-chairs John Filcher and Greg Kujawa, Alette Foster and Joanne Choudoir from Incinerator Free Brown County!"

The applause rolled while IFBC's leadership foursome walked up to accept the award. I had been 'elected' to make the short acceptance speech, which really meant that the others had outplayed me because I was outvoted 3 to 1. But I thought to myself that maybe it was due to just being by far the loudest. I had long been cursed (or blessed?) with a deep voice that always came across as way too loud, even when I was trying to be quiet. I've been getting into trouble for being too loud since I was a little boy in school, as the many notes on my report cards that I found one day at my dad's house verified. It wasn't until years later that I realized how handy a loud, booming voice could be during noisy fraternity parties while living in the Sigma Alpha Epsilon house or for teaching Tae Kwon Do at USD because everyone could hear you regardless of the ambient noise levels.

Nonetheless, I needed to remain careful in modulation, because my middle daughter once had to explain to the other softball players on her team that her dad wasn't angry when he yelled instructions from the dugout or across the practice field. That it was just so they could hear me over the traffic from the adjacent highway. She quipped "If my dad was actually mad at you, you wouldn't be guessing."

With a squinted glare at the majority voters of IFBC, I managed to stumble up to the microphone and introduce myself. "Good evening! I'm John Filcher. You'll all be very pleased to learn that I intend to keep the comments mercifully short. On behalf of the members of IFBC, we'd like to express how grateful we are to accept this award. We are also grateful to Clean Water Action and the board members for working with us in our efforts to stop the proposed incinerator. It has been quite a year for the incinerator saga, and it ain't over yet. The opposition has grown from one small group into multiple groups working together. So many local citizens have become involved that today that effort is better described as a movement. As we journey forward together we can expect to see and hear more about the incinerator's troubles. And also expect to hear about more opportunities to become involved in stopping this abomination. We do anticipate seeing this movement reach a conclusion in the near future, and with your continued support and involvement, we're hoping it's the right conclusion."

The soirée didn't conclude until well after midnight. *Good thing Greg drove,* I thought to myself the next morning, head pounding as I looked into the bathroom mirror. "Yikes! You look a bit rough, champ," I quipped at the bleary eyes looking back in the mirror. It was definitely time for the morning coffee.

Facing an increasing tempo of positive IFBC vibes, OSGC clearly had now decided it was time to gin up some publicity of its own. Recognizing that changing filed plans seriously damaged OSGC's already fragile credibility, IFBC members were rather amused by the OSGC letter to the editor on Day 552 which comically referred to "blatantly false rumors and innuendos."

The next IFBC meeting a few days later resembled the futility of trying to herd cats. "I was trying to think of a way we could incorporate the giant hairdryer …" Greg started saying, only to be interrupted by Alette loudly stating with an evil smile and glint in her eye, "Blatantly false!"

This was followed by Joanne laughing and stating, "Rumors and innuendo! How dare you say such stuff?"

I just rolled my eyes with a laugh. "Oh my God you guys, you're killing me!"

"He's lying! I can see it in his eyes," Greg replied, with an exaggeratedly suspicious squint at me. And the bad jokes rolled on.

Sometimes, no matter what kind of group it is, you are simply stuck in a meeting that has the collective attention span of squirrels. This was definitely one of those times.

CHAPTER 22

Re-education

"The problem is not the problem. The problem is your attitude
about the problem. Do you understand?"

— Captain Jack Sparrow

About a month later, on Day 597, the second public meeting regarding the proposed Maribel facility was held with DNR offi-cials. It was a beautiful day, with afternoon temperatures around 70°. The digester developers chose not to appear after the hostility and fiasco that had occurred at the first meeting back on Day 499. The local TV report on FOX11 showed many startling similarities between the OSGC and the Maribel projects.

I attended the Day 597 meeting of Maribel residents with the DNR and spoke to officials who were by now familiar with the escapades sur-rounding the proposed Green Bay incineration project. The meeting was a blur. At one point I stood to speak, and hopefully managed to mumble something reasonably eloquent and smart sounding, but likely was more akin to grunting, "Ugh, digester bad, me no like."

Fatefully, the follow-up TV report noted that the possible site would need to be rezoned.

The remainder of the summer brought little official action. The IFBC gang mostly focused on enjoying some downtime while still working on strategy and sharing new information with CWAC and the staff at the *OneidaEye*. That summer I was again was invited to update the Brown County Taxpayers Association during their lunch meeting downtown at the Titletown Brewing Company.

This time I was ready with three main points to discuss and could drill down as needed. Without need for notes, I spoke to a group of about twenty-five folks for nearly half an hour, then answered questions for another five or ten minutes. After the concluding remarks I returned to our table to finish a sandwich when one of the ladies seated with me complimented me on speaking "so well" on the topic.

I replied, "Thank you! I've had a lot of practice by now." Our conversation turned to more details over the proposed incinerator, and she asked what I thought the chances are the incinerator will get built.

"At this point, they're still all too good, and Green Bay has made a lot of blunders. We're intent on keeping OSGC stumbling until the clock runs out. Hopefully something will happen to change the situation."

She nodded, and said "Yes, hopefully. I can't believe anyone would ever think one of these things is ever a good idea or safe for the environment. Just ridiculous."

I returned home from a long day late on Day 622 to find an article written in the *Press-Gazette*. The article outlined the need for the county to work up a new landfill deal as the current contract was due to expire. It also mentioned there was some interest in the incinerator as an outlet due to increasing tipping fees to $40 a ton, but gave no details. I thought, *we need to squash any notion that 'interest' in a trash incinerator is a viable outlet.*

On Day 670, the *Press-Gazette* carried yet another article, this time a long one complete with large pictures. One of the neighborhood association presidents joined Joanne in the main picture under the headline "Oneida plant under microscope" with a caption stating that the neighborhood association president planned to deliver written testimony for

Green Bay's upcoming public hearing over the incinerator. The quote from him said, "There's so many different untruths about this. It just begs to be rescinded."

I thought, *the hearing will be in front of the Green Bay Plan Commission. It might prove particularly memorable on multiple levels according to the article's prediction it would be a 'showdown.'*

The purpose of another Plan Commission hearing was still murky due to the City's failures to explain the peculiar procedural posture in which this project now found itself. By now myself, Greg and Dean thought we might have an advance read on how this hearing likely would play out despite the lack of clarity regarding the overall purpose of the hearing, but we just couldn't be sure.

"Sending it back to the Plan Commission doesn't have any procedural basis in the municipal ordinances that the attorneys with Midwest Environmental Advocates could find," remarked Dean when the three of us discussed the matter over craft beers and a bite to eat. "All we know is that the city council sent it back for review, which seems to put the process into a procedural black hole."

Greg nodded. "Not like questionable political processes is anything unusual with this project and Green Bay." We fell silent for a few moments while the food arrived.

"Mmmm. Love this burger," Greg said, taking a bite of the hearty pub fare.

"How do the Midwest Environmental lawyers see this thing playing out?" asked Greg, still chewing.

Dean thought for a moment while he took a swig of his brew. "Well, best they can tell us is to make our case against the incinerator and highlight where OSGC provided misleading and incomplete information."

I chuckled and rolled my eyes. "Yeah, I think we managed to figure that out all by our lonesomes," I quipped before sipping a hazy IPA, getting a snicker out of Dean and Greg.

The day before the hearing Elaine suddenly called me to share her thoughts about how the somewhat mysterious Plan Commission hearing might play out. "I received some very interesting information from my sources over at Green Bay city hall. They're telling me the Plan Commission is going to try very hard to box you out from being heard at the hearing because they're the henchmen of the mayor."

I nodded to myself as I continued to drive my trusty old pickup down the highway during the call. "Why am I not shocked?" I responded.

Elaine continued, "No matter what happens, I'm hearing the Plan Commission will vote to uphold the permit because the fix is in."

"So why would we bother appearing at the Plan Commission's kabuki theater, then?"

Elaine then offered some VERY surprising advice in contrast to IFBC's past practices. "No one is too sure why this hearing is even happening because it's in a weird procedural place, but this time, Rich and I are thinking it's time you go be a little more aggressive, as only you know how to do. Don't go over the top, but that gravelly deep voice of yours will rattle some cages, particularly if you put your attorney hat on and sound like a prosecutor. CWAC is listed as a speaker, and I spoke with Dean. He said they can defer their time to IFBC, which will take 'em all by surprise."

At hearing that the leash was finally being removed from my attack dog collar, my response was to growl out something sounding like, "Ohhhh, with PLEASURE! Prosecutor Mode Activated."

Elaine just laughed at the demented excitement in my voice from the chance to torment OSGC once again. "I remember when you all were so hesitant about public speaking. What happened?"

"I have NO idea who you're talking about. Besides, what attorney would pass up an opportunity to crash a hearing and crush some hopes and dreams? That setting's like Disneyland for lawyers." Apparently, the IFBC core was getting pretty good in the game, because our shared hesitation to speak out in public now seemed like a distant memory.

The media was certainly ready. On Day 683, Patty Murray from Wisconsin Public Radio interviewed me during a report on the project. "The proposed plant will burn municipal trash at up to 1200°. Critics, including the Sierra Club, say it's an untested technology and would be the first of its kind in the country. Here is John Filcher, who co-chairs the citizens group Incinerator Free Brown County."

I was ready and recall saying, "This thing isn't a magic machine that can make dioxins go away, which is what you get when you melt or burn plastic."

Murray then stated, "Filcher says the Oneida tribe has not been forthcoming about exactly what trash would be incinerated, or how many emissions stacks there will be."

I further recall responding, "But they never disclosed that it's got all these emissions and these emissions towers and stacks and so forth. It's just never given out to the city. Yet, a mere few weeks later it IS disclosed to DNR, and they never seem to go back to the city and say, 'hey wait a minute, none of this was disclosed to you.'"

After hearing the report on public radio, my eldest child called from college. "Dad, I heard the radio report. It was great! Even my roommate flipped out when she realized, 'Oh my God, THAT's your dad on the radio!' And just guess what else just happened? I was in my advertising class and our professor was lecturing about persuasive forms of advertising, and he featured what he called one of the best examples of emotion-based messaging he had ever seen. Then he put up your billboard on the screen!"

"That's hilarious! How did he stumble across it?" I asked.

"He saw it when was visiting his relatives in Green Bay. Here I am, all the way over on the other side of the state, and I can't escape my father's influence — even here!" she teased.

"Ha! It's like ZZ Top once sang, 'I'm bad and nationwide, kiddo'."

After the call, I mused, she probably didn't understand the dated musical reference. *My children's musical knowledge is an appalling train wreck. Aaargh!*

The Plan Commission hearing took place after the radio interview, resulting in the expected unanimous vote in favor of keeping the permit in place. The fireworks had really begun prior to the hearing when Dean and I again spoke to a sizable crowd gathered at the downtown library. The folks in the gathering were already angry about the incinerator coming to their neighborhoods. One woman in her thirties thanked IFBC and CWAC for doing their best to protect their homes and families. It was an especially sensitive issue for her because her elderly parents lived near the site and lacked the financial means to move away. Other residents shared their concerns for their children, and of losing their investments in their homes when they become unsaleable.

After an hour, this very riled up crowd of over 150 residents marched to city hall and packed into the Plan Commission chamber where they glared at the board members while holding up hundreds of colorful signs protesting the facility. Greg and I were seated together in the crowd with Dean, who was scheduled to be the third speaker.

Shortly after stepping up to the podium and succinctly stating some of the initial objections to the incinerator, Dean then invited Incinerator Free Brown County to finish out CWAC's allotted time in a clever switcheroo and avoided any clumsy attempt to block IFBC from speaking because we hadn't been advised of the signup list.

My approach in addressing the Plan Commission was simple. It was time to rhetorically indict OSGC's plethora of project shortcomings while injecting a prosecutorial vibe. In logical order of descending issue importance, I discussed OSGC's lack of relevant experience, followed by its comedy of errors and misrepresentations over stack heights and emissions. I specified what toxins these residents could expect to inhale in and out of their homes, which were being deliberately hidden from their view. Next came the highly contaminated wastewater to be released into the bay waters. The truck traffic hauling garbage and ash…and the list went on.

Toward the middle of these remarks, I became acutely aware of the angry noises emanating from the crowd seated behind me, corresponding to the highlights of the presentation. But this time, I resisted turning around because I had already learned my lesson to avoid doing that. It was one thing to sit among an angry crowd of over 150, while it's an entirely different thing to glance back into the seething emotions in a mob of angry faces. While it was still a bit disconcerting to stand in front of a large, visibly and audibly angry crowd, the fun wasn't over yet! Someone rudely interrupted, shouting, "Madam Chair, tell him to speak with a more respectful tone. I don't appreciate his tone."

As the chair responded that she lacked such authority, I merely looked over with a raised eyebrow and a slight, humorless smile, and continued on exactly as before.

Back in the day a retired trial judge, my trial techniques professor, had often noted that this is how you deal with the other side when they try to disrupt your timing through the use of objections. Taking this advice to heart, I had learned firsthand over the years that this was a very effective way of dealing with such people.

When the interrupter was once more hushed by the chair, he grew angrier by the obvious lack of deference to his strong feelings. Maybe it was the small, humorless smile while soldiering on with the evening's discussion that irked the man. And just to torment him some more, I deliberately extended the remarks for a few minutes longer than originally planned.

At the conclusion I politely thanked the Plan Commission for their time and attention. And because it was getting late it seemed prudent to make like Elvis and exit the building instead of hanging around for the hearing to wrap up because there were a large number of people still waiting to speak.

That was when the man who couldn't stop himself from interrupting decided to get in my face near the doorway a few steps into the outside hall, in full view of the crowd. He was a fairly large man whose most memorable feature in an otherwise unremarkable visage was a dreadfully unkempt goatee. The man's manner gave off a 'don't you know how important I am' vibe.

Turning slightly and adopting a demented expression of delight, I just stepped in much closer than this confronter was obviously comfortable with, almost touching chin to disheveled goatee. It was a technique we taught to the lower belts in Tae Kwon Do to help diffuse a situation. Mr. Charming then announced who he was, snarling, "You people…," (by which he presumably meant IFBC) "…need to be better educated about this project."

Perhaps realizing from my expression how underwhelming his announcement was, Mr. Charming then retreated backwards a few steps, so I again moved closer, keeping this tormentor uneasy while still saying nothing. I merely cocked an eyebrow while holding the still demented expression. It appeared evident that Mr. Charming's confrontation wasn't playing out the way he imagined, so trying his luck a second time, he loudly stated, "You need to be better educated about this waste-to-energy system. We could teach you a thing or two about what it really is over lunch."

Whether or not this was a sincere offer, the IFBC gang just isn't into vacationing at a re-education gulag, so I replied, "Well, thanks. That's sounds fine but be prepared to be challenged while you re-educate us. Oh, and you're buying." I then accepted the man's business card that identified his role in tribal government, and with that, Mr. Charming finally disengaged.

Second later Greg caught up to me down the hall by the elevators. "What the heck was THAT all about? You guys were standing nose to nose!"

I shook my head. "Apparently he wanted a lunch date so we could talk about re-educating us in a gulag somewhere. What are your vacation plans looking like?"

Greg laughed. "Well, that just sounds like the trip of a lifetime. All expenses paid. Open bars. My wife will be so jealous she wasn't invited to come along."

"Those pesky mobs of protesters, they're just so darn inconvenient!"

Greg snorted. "Yeah, those protesters should be banned. They keep getting in the way of progress!"

The very next day Elaine called, sharing her amusement. "I have to tell you, we were highly entertained when we got a call from someone in the Green Bay government who was there at the meeting and she said lighting OSGC up like you did really rattled some cages. Because OSGC still isn't used to any criticism, enduring hours of it from a whole bunch of angry citizens was quite a shock to OSGC."

I chortled. "OSGC must be an exceptionally slow learner, because it's received a lot of criticism so far."

"The friend who called also said some of the Plan Commission stated that they were offended at the implication that they had failed to do their job the first time, thus having to hold another hearing. But, that's not on IFBC, that's on the council members who made them hold another hearing. By the way, you realize you can't go in front of the Council now, right?"

I responded, "I had assumed so, but walk me though it anyway."

"It's because you in particular are now some sort of — get a load of this — a 'villainous rabble rouser.' Isn't that terrific?"

I really laughed. "Seriously? I could learn to LOVE that label!"

"Oh, and my friends inside Oneida also said tribal members are growing increasingly upset at OSGC because of its bumbling antics that keep fueling the growing scandal," Elaine informed me. "The simultaneous co-community campaigns to expose OSGC is really starting to pay some serious dividends."

Villainous rabble rouser, I thought after the call. *That's good stuff! Simple, easy to remember. Maybe I could get some commemorative hats embroidered with that.*

As it turned out the night of the council meeting, I had another engagement elsewhere.

CHAPTER 23

DAY 687

Rescission Hearing

"Everyone has his day, and some days last longer than others."

—Winston Churchill

A day before the Conditional Use Permit reconsideration by the Green Bay Common Council on Day 687, Dean called and asked a question that he thought wouldn't be received well.

"Would you be offended if we thought it's better if you aren't present at the upcoming council meeting? Due to last week's performance at the Plan Commission, we suspect your presence might be a bit too provocative."

Surprising Dean, I merely laughed and responded, "We expected that! Plus, Elaine already waved me off. The plan was to light 'em up at the Plan Commission to rattle a few cages, then make myself scarce for tomorrow night's finale. So, Greg will be there instead."

Dean wanted IFBC's presence at the council meeting and was relieved to learn Greg was IFBC's designated hitter, so IFBC would still have eyes on the prize. "OK, that's great. Elaine and I had discussed sending you in to light 'em up at the Plan Commission, but I wasn't sure if she remembered to tell you on that call that doing so would make you radioactive in front of the council for a while."

"No worries. She did indeed. I knew that would happen anyway when she passed word along, but I couldn't pass up the chance to chew on the bone for a while. Turns out, I have another engagement with an opposition group citizen's meeting down at the Maribel Sportsman's Club over the proposed digester down there the same night anyway."

"That's the same night?" Dean responded. "Do you want someone from CWAC as a wingman for that? We have been hearing that it's a proposed wet digester that might leach enzymes into the groundwater. If it were a dry digester, we would be there to encourage it instead."

"Nah, I got this covered. The Maribel folks are pretty early in their process to try to stop the proposal. They also have some pretty good reasons to suspect it's another trash incinerator being disguised as a purported wet digester to try to get it approved because they said some preliminary plans they saw contained a line about solid waste processing buried among the verbiage about digesting organic waste."

After a second or two of silence, Dean noted, "That's concerning. We wondered why the developers were being so non-communicative. Good luck and let me know how it goes. I'll give you a call after the council meeting. There are some new Green Bay city council members due to the last election, and we think we might have the votes to overturn."

After Dean hung up, I had an *Uh, wait! What?!* reaction to Dean's remark about possibly having the votes. Obviously, there were behind the scenes developments to which IFBC had not been privy. I decided it was prudent to keep that news to myself for now.

The next night was a beautiful evening, and I enjoyed the short drive down I-43 to Maribel. The fall colors were in full glory, which in Wisconsin is truly something spectacular. Fall is my favorite time of the year to ride a mountain bike down the various trails that wind through the region.

The meeting at the Sportsman's Club kicked off at the same time as the Green Bay council meeting. Greg and I exchanged a long running series of text messages throughout the evening, as did Dean and me. When my turn to address the crowd arrived, I spoke about the need to organize, use a uniform name, and the importance of branding.

I emphasized avoiding the trap of getting sucked into discussing the digester using the developer's made up semantics. Most critical of all, I passed along the sage messaging advice of Elaine, Rich and Mike to stay reasonable, stay factual, and keep your sense of humor. Many in the crowd were disappointed to learn how critical was the need to remain persistent and to hound developers into making unforced errors, as was the vital need to uncover information. From my spot near a picnic table in the dining hall of this club, it was easy to see, among the many faces present, who would have the fight in them to follow through and who would not. I thought, *I just watched the anti-digester core self-select themselves right in front of my eyes!*

When I finally sat down, I checked my phone, which had repeatedly been vibrating with incoming messages. There were multiple updates from both Greg and Dean, saying that they were amused at the overhearing commentary — from persons who were seated behind them — about some guy who 'practically persecuted' OSGC at the Plan Commission hearing last week.

I thought with a laugh, *Yeah, he's a real mean one, that guy, a real heartless menace.*

Perhaps unsurprisingly, the Green Bay council meeting was still on-going even after the hours-long Maribel meeting concluded and I drove home on I-43.

As predicted in advance by Elaine during her phone call to me before last week's Plan Commission hearing, the Plan Commission had reported to the council the Commission's position that there had been no misrepresentations or misunderstandings in a written report contained in the city council minutes (only modified to remove unnecessary date references):

REPORT OF THE GREEN BAY PLAN COMMISSION

The Green Bay Plan Commission, having held a Public Hearing and considered all testimony and reports the following:

Notice of the Public Hearing to Review the Conditional Use Permit for the Oneida Seven Generations Solid Waste Disposal Facility was published (copy attached).

Numerous written comments were received and forwarded to the Plan Commissioners, the Oneida Seven Generations Corporation, and the Clean Water Action Council of Northeast Wisconsin. The Commission heard testimony with respect to the Conditional Use Permit (CUP) that had been approved for the Oneida Seven Generations Corporation solid waste disposal facility to be constructed at 1230 Hurlbut Street.

Prior to public testimony, the Plan Commission staff provided a detailed report on the history of the CUP application and the reasons for their original recommendation for approval with conditions, which was adopted by the Plan Commission. After considering information provided by representatives of the Oneida Seven Generations Corporation, representatives of the Clean Water Action Council of Northeast Wisconsin, alderpersons, and interested citizens, the Plan Commission unanimously approved the following motion:

> Based on the information submitted and presented, the Plan Commission determines that the information provided to the Plan Commission was not misrepresented and that it was adequate for the Commission to make an informed decision, and recommends that the CUP stand as is.
>
> The Commission further determines that the information the Plan Commission received was adequate, and based upon information then available, that the Plan Commission did understand that there were emissions and venting as a part of the system, and therefore made sure

that the Seven Generations Corporation would
need to meet the requirements of the EPA and
DOE, as well as meeting the requirements of the
municipal code through a normal process of give
or take.

Even though I wasn't yet aware of the written report from the Plan
Commission before the council meeting, it wasn't hard to guess the
gist of it because of Elaine's prior call predicting that the fix was in. It
also was obvious that this report would be another stumbling block to
IFBC's efforts to rescind the CUP or subsequent litigation arising from
a rescission. As a practical matter, it meant the IFBC gang hadn't managed to move the needle as far as Green Bay municipal government was
concerned, and this report was heard in full by all attending that night's
Green Bay council meeting.

Things were quiet at home when at I returned from Maribel. There
weren't even any new messages from Greg or Dean, and the late TV
news desk indicated the Green Bay council was still in session. But about
20 minutes later Greg came knocking at my front door.

He was the bearer of bombshell news which the local news was
about to announce. "Have you heard yet?" he asked when I opened the
front door.

"No, but I'm dying to find out!" I said, catching on from Greg's
huge grin that something big occurred.

"Alrighty then. The Green Bay council rescinded the CUP despite
the Plan Commission's report!"

I broke out into a huge grin and chuckled. "Dayamn! Time to crack
open a cold one!" The two of us went into the kitchen to rummage
through the fridge.

As I opened a beer for each of us, I thought, *from this point forward,
momentum has finally flipped in our favor. Now it's OSGC's turn to swim
upstream.*

CHAPTER 24

Beers for the Brouhaha

"As aptly observed by John Adams, during his defense of British
soldiers charged with the Boston Massacre,
"[f]acts are stubborn things ... and whatever may be our wishes,
our inclinations, or the dictums of our passions,
they cannot alter the state of facts and evidence."
— *United States v. Robinson*, 460 F.3d 550 (4th Cir. 2006)

Greg and I were understandably wound up over the night's huge developments. Even though it was now very late on Day 687, it was time to tip our beers (because it's Wisconsin... beers are mandatory here) and toast this development. "To victory!" said Greg.

"I love the smell of napalm in the morning," I responded. "It smells like victory!"

We were completely stunned that the permit had been rescinded despite the Plan Commission reporting it had been apprised of everything they thought necessary to approve it.

"I was pretty entertained over how upset the Plan Commission seemed from your performance at their hearing last week. Apparently, rumor is the mayor told the Plan Commission to expect only a few folks in attendance, and no fireworks. Instead, they found themselves in front of a large, hostile crowd with signs and angry glares!"

Greg laughed out loud when I wisecracked, "Hey, getting the Powers That Be all kinds of mad is a gift. You just can't coach something like that!"

Greg was animated as he described what happened when the vote was taken. "When they counted the votes and result was to overturn the permit, I looked back at the OSGC section. They didn't look so smug anymore. They were completely shocked! I was shocked too! Nobody saw this coming."

I decided it was time to tell Greg about the mysterious information Dean had shared by phone. "OK, now that the vote is done, I gotta tell you something Dean said to me on the phone a few days ago. He said there are some new City Council members due to the last election, and thought we have the votes to overturn."

"What!? Are you kidding?"

"No! I thought maybe I wasn't interpreting it right or something, but decided discretion called for radio silence for a couple of days, just in case. I haven't mentioned it to anyone."

Greg was really surprised. "How did they even know that?"

At that, I just leaned back into my seat, shook my head and said "I dunno, maybe sorcery or something. It's probably best we just don't know and I'm not going to ask."

Day 687's *Press-Gazette* article stated, "Several aldermen said they felt developer Oneida Seven Generations Corp. had misled the city about the proposed plant's pollution and public health hazards." City Council President Tom DeWane was quoted, "As time went on, things changed drastically," in describing both the previously omitted revelations and the knowledge of the residents. OSGC's attorney was already setting up for an appeal, saying the council lacked the authority to rescind the permit, and again trotting out the usual drivel that OSGC wanted to be a good neighbor. Never did the incineration proponents seem to sense that the public had clearly concluded that the act of bringing a toxic trash incinerator even remotely near someone's home is no one's idea of being a good neighbor. Even uttering such nonsense made homeowners ask themselves what a *bad* neighbor would do by comparison. All along, OSGC was never able to overcome the persuasive questions normal people always default to, which is the tried and true, 'Who you going to believe, me or your lying eyes?' The eyes win every time.

Sadly, since this was a legislative action by the Green Bay Common Council, the mayor had the power to veto the action and send it back to the council for reconsideration. Greg and I wanted badly to avoid a veto but were savvy enough to recognize that politicians were first going to gauge public reaction closely.

By the following day, TV reports about the rescission hearing were pretty devastating to the OSGC brand. Visible in the TV screen were many of the protest signs, with one memorably saying "No Biomass Incinerator for Green Bay. VOTE TO RESCIND. I can give you ten reasons" with pictures of ten stacks adorning the placard. Reporting that the City Council was greeted with another packed house, the camera lingered on a bright pink sign. This sign read, "A pattern of misrepresentation by OSGC. RESCIND THE C.U.P.". The report noted that plan opponents lined up near the entrance for the hearing. Dean, Greg and Joanne were all clearly visible in the pictures of the entry line.

A local neighbor was interviewed saying, "We talked to hundreds of people in this whole process, and the process worked. They sat down, they thought about it, they re-looked at it, and they said, 'yeah we agree with you, it was rushed'. And we appreciate and we thank the council for their due diligence."

City council member Andy Nicholson was seen saying, "My opinion is this. Why would we take the risk to place the citizens of Green Bay as guinea pigs for this brand new technology?" A final image of another hot pink sign simply stating "Fraud = Rescind" left a lasting impression on viewers.

Still other TV reports showed images of other signs saying, "Save Our Children From Gasification Pollution", which immediately preceded Greg being interviewed, noting the vote "is a clear message that when this CUP was originally approved it was ramrodded through very quickly."

The Day 688 episode of the Jerry Bader Show went in depth about the rescission. Jerry opened the discussion by stating, "What happened last night at city council, and I will confess I did not see this coming, and this creates a very complicated scenario for Green Bay Mayor Jim Schmitt."

Jerry later noted, "I agree with what the council did last night" while going on to correctly note neither the mayor nor the council adequately did their due diligence on the project and that he "strongly suspects that Oneida Seven Generations was deceptive" as he also voiced concerns whether the city can satisfy the litigation burden of proof pursuant to prevailing evidentiary standards.

And then, in what could otherwise have been a quiet period where both sides could take a breather, the *Press-Gazette* surprised IFBC by running a cartoon from editorial cartoonist Joe Heller, who worked for the *Press-Gazette* for 28 years. Mr. Hellers' cartoon lampooned "How a Gasification Plant Works" with several panels describing "Take Some Stuff…", "Apply Some Heat", and "Up it Goes in Smoke (Poof)".

Alette, Joanne, Greg and I loved the cartoon.

CHAPTER 25

DAY 694

The People Have Spoken

"This case lends credence to President Lincoln's remark that you can't fool all of the people all of the time."
— *People v. Haskins,*
171 Cal. App. 3d 344, 214 Cal. Rptr. 685 (Cal. App. 1985)

On Day 694, the *Press-Gazette* reported that the mayor had decided not to veto the council's rescission. The mayor's prepared statement said, "It is important that economic development projects are done through consensus and not through veto." Despite the self-evident nature of the truth of his statement, OSGC reiterated the company's extreme disappointment, and its intent to construct its trash incinerator, nonetheless. Following up on the mayoral and council actions, the Green Bay city attorney then sent a letter to OSGC on Day 703 setting forth the "basis for this decision." Only the dates have been edited out of the pertinent portion below:

"The Council's action to rescind the Conditional Use Permit (CUP) was based upon the following: information presented during the public hearing as well as a review of the history of OSGC's CUP application, including the materials submitted to the City of Green Bay by the Clean Water Action Council containing false statements and misrepresentations by OSGC." The city attorney then went on to state that OSGC "made untruthful statements before City governmental bodies while seeking the CUP. These false statements were made in response to questions or concerns related to the public safety and health aspect of the Project and the Project's impact upon the City's environment." He continued listing various offenses, saying that the "statements were plain spoken, contained no equivocation, left no impression of doubt or uncertainty, and his words were intended to influence the actions of the governmental bodies he was addressing."

The letter continued, stating the CEO "knew his statements were false" and that he "was not a new or uninformed member of OSGC; he was the CEO and had been involved throughout the Project's development; therefore, he was knowledgeable about the pilot work, the process and the equipment, the materials that would be used, the nature of the by-products and chemical releases."

After that, the core members of IFBC gathered together at my house to discuss the city attorney's letter. "What do you guys think about the letter?" asked Alette, sitting down in the easy chair with a glass of chilled chardonnay.

"Seemed kind of vague," mumbled Greg around a bite of peanut butter cookie. "I would have liked to see some more facts in there."

Joanne took a sip of her Merlot before responding. "Yeah, this was nice but I had the impression they could have gone a lot farther."

"They've kind of reached the stage of the festivities which I tend to call the Battle of the Letters, where this letter says this, and that letter says that."

I paused to take a sip of milk stout beer before continuing. "Ordinarily, it makes more strategic sense to give 'em a taste of the strength of your defense to get the claimant realistically thinking about how difficult it actually will be to pursue their claim because they typically tend to underestimate the defense while simultaneously overestimating their own chances. Wakes them up a little bit."

I paused for another sip, softly grunting approval of the frothy, cold dark beverage. "But sending some vague letter containing a couple of conclusory statements and zero facts to support your position, that also telegraphs some significant meanings. Mainly that the writer isn't confident enough of the facts or relevant processes to know how to use them or deliver a kill shot up front."

Greg took a swig of his honey ale and shook his head ruefully. "Man, I hope you're wrong but city hall's reputation for bureaucratic bungling says you're right."

By Day 717, the *Press-Gazette* reported that OSGC intended to sue Green Bay over the permit revocation, calling it "arbitrary and unreasonable" and suggesting that the City Council "didn't do its homework." The City Council President was concerned the comedy of errors between OSGC and the city would lead to 'bad blood', although it seemed to me that bad blood was inevitable just by proposing to construct a trash incinerator anywhere near city residents who clearly did not want it.

CHAPTER 26

DAY 717

Like a Good Neighbor, OSGC is There

"We caution that "'he meant well' has served as an epitaph for
many a futile endeavor, many a lost cause."

— *State ex rel. Leung v. Sanders,*

213 W. Va. 569, 584 S.E.2d 203 (WVA 2003)

By Day 717 OSGC had already started off the litigation festivities by filing a pair of lawsuits with the state court. Their lawsuits focused on Green Bay's alleged failure to appropriately move through the proper procedural steps to unwind the permit. As I subsequently noted to the core IFBC team, "OSGC's claim was basically a Due Process claim; the kind an aggrieved party files to say somebody forgot to check some procedural boxes in the order in which they should be checked before reaching a conclusion. Like we observed with the city attorney's letter, I'm afraid this won't be the only procedural hiccup on Green Bay's part."

Alette responded back. "Yeah. At least at this point, I think it's safe to say OSGC resembles an uninvited party guest who complains about the food but just won't leave."

Things did not improve when OSGC decided it would organize its version of a protest. On Day 743 a Green Bay council meeting was held behind closed doors, which the *Press-Gazette* article the following day described under the headline, "Oneida plant backers get loud". The paper said,

> Supporters of the trash-recycling project were particularly vocal in demanding that the City Council hear their concerns, then booing and shouting when their request was denied. One shouted that racism was driving opposition to Oneida Seven Generations, which is affiliated with the Oneida Tribe of Indians.

The paper noted that the only other interested parties at that meeting were the actual residents of the Mather Heights neighborhood, who were represented by their association president, who described the spectacle of non-residents who "booed and shouted." The president further stated, "I thought it was ridiculous. They showed no respect."

Within weeks, the attorneys for OSGC and Green Bay had reached an agreement to submit the matter to the court — on briefing only — for a possible early judgment. The IFBC core gathered together in Ashwaubenon to discuss the litigation and recent events.

"Wow, it's been a while since we all got together," noted Alette wryly.

Nodding his head and raising his eyebrows, Greg replied, "Yeah, you look kind of familiar. What's your name again?" Turning to face me, he asked, "I know there's been a lot that's happened since the permit was revoked, but what do you think about the litigation?"

I thought for a second, then replied, "Well, obviously it's a Due Process lawsuit like I said earlier. OSGC will have to prove Green Bay made a process mistake in rescinding the permit. Because we all experienced just how murky that whole process was and nobody understood what was happening nor why, and how Green Bay seemed to stumble through it with the Plan Commission and City Council reaching opposite conclusions, I have my doubts about the strength of Green Bay's CUP revocation. Not that I can publicly express those doubts beyond this group here, so let's continue to keep this opinion to ourselves."

"What do you think about their plan to seek a quick ruling by the court? Joanne asked. "I've never heard of that before and you've been saying all along that you would use the opportunity to grab all kinds of information if OSGC got us involved in a suit and make it all public."

I looked at her with a tilt of my head. "Yeah. But based on this suit's procedural posture, I'm shocked the City would be so unwise as to make that kind of rookie litigation mistake. If an entity is taking actions based on a party's misrepresentations and/or fraud, that entity better not take procedural jump shots and forget to establish sufficient supporting evidence for their actions during pretrial Discovery. And they need to establish that they followed a fair set of procedural steps as well. Skip that, and a party kneecaps itself by cutting off the opportunities to put meat on the bones of its defense and properly introduce it all into the litigation record."

Greg sighed. "I knew it. the City's reputation for bureaucratic bungling is going to bite them in the hinder again!"

"Here we go again," Joanne said, shaking her head sadly. "It took forever until I was able to sleep normally again after the incinerator relocated away from our homes. I can't handle that much stress."

"I can't stop thinking about what would have happened to my children if it had been built near our places," Alette joined in sadly. "They can't protect themselves, or just move away. Now I can't stop thinking about those poor people near the Hurlbut Street site. A friend of mine lives in that area. She cries every time the topic comes up. They're frantic and don't know what to do."

Green Bay's procedural jump shots in first rescinding the permit followed by the abbreviated defense of the rescission was a hot topic of conversation among the steering committee as well as with Elaine and Rich. We were unanimous in thinking that this abbreviated defense was a very bad decision by the City. At our next core meeting, Alette and Greg asked what I thought now that the suits had progressed a bit further.

"I've seen many fraud cases," I responded. "You always have to get the evidence in via Discovery so you can use it to later support a judgment in litigation. By now my view of it really isn't anything new you guys, but, geez! What a missed opportunity by Green Bay! To give up the ability to uncover even more damaging stuff, or to strengthen its procedural position by showing how OSGC's representations influenced the actions of Green Bay. The City also unwittingly forfeited the ability to defend based on the impossibility of the so-called technology and science. But no, Green Bay just throws all that away! Only reason they agreed to skip Discovery is probably because the City thought they could save time and money, but all it really tells me is Green Bay still doesn't know how to proceed with a fraud and misrepresentation defense."

Elaine, who was present at this meeting, piped up. "The City also probably thought they didn't want bad blood with their neighbor so they could be friends, but they aren't friends. Green Bay hasn't woken up to that yet."

Elaine's next comment caused even more grumbling among the group. "You've already uncovered some of the federal stimulus and state financing through the contracts from the Wisconsin Economic Development Corporation and the news articles identifying federal grants, but OSGC will try to build its incinerator somewhere with that money until whenever the drop-dead dates in the financing contracts expire. And the internal movement to expose OSGC's doings still needs more time before they're ready to move on it."

I was well aware we still needed to run out the clock on the government financing due to what we had uncovered from open records requests to the Wisconsin Economic Development Corporation, but that didn't make hearing about it again any more enjoyable. "OSGC still has the time and the clocks to succeed," I worried time and again.

I pulled out another document obtained from an open records request. "Listen up team, I thought you'd all find this memo to be completely at odds with Green Bay's litigation strategy to skip Discovery, because it's a memo from the city attorney that pretty clearly recognizes the city's need to obtain evidence from OSGC to help the city establish OSGC's intent to deceive the city way back for the Day 498 Council meeting." I then began reading aloud parts of the lengthy memo:

"Essentially, the City's legal options with respect to an already granted conditional use permit are limited. The first option is to do nothing because there is no legal basis upon which to take any legal action. The second option would be for the City to determine whether all actions being taken relative to the CUP are being met and whether City ordinances are being followed. If the actions are in violation of either the CUP or the Code, then the City may halt that action, require an amendment to the CUP, or begin the process to revoke the CUP through a quasi-judicial hearing."

I paused to take a breath before continuing with another excerpt from later in the memo.

> This is where things get muddy, both practically and legally, to make a decision right now. The question is whether OSGC engaged in any lies or misrepresentations. Each side has made allegations and countered the other's allegations; however, we do not have a full chronological, historical record of what was said, especially to other governmental agencies. To accurately determine what was said by OSGC throughout the permitting processes with other government agencies would require extensive fact-gathering that would take more time to adequately develop.

> This is present in the event that this legal process is not followed, there is not an adequate record, or if there is not a legal basis upon which to revoke the CUP.

Greg nodded his head, stunned. "You just got that memo from the city? Yikes, they have no idea how to prove a misrepresentation case, do they? Why did they rescind the permit if they knew in advance that they didn't know how to do it?"

"How do they manage to keep bungling EVERYTHING?" Alette muttered.

I just shrugged. "I know, it's just befuddling that they still have no clue how to substantiate, and just as importantly, articulate a fraud or material misrepresentation case beyond recognizing some rudimentary due process concerns. And, those are the process concerns which the city council then ignored anyway when it rescinded the permit, not to mention they didn't follow through and find the holes in their evidence as the memo warned. Now we can only hope the city's procedural hiccups in rescinding and defending aren't going to prove too devastating to the City's defense. I'm still shocked the City decided to skip establishing a record to support its defense."

Taking a drink of her lemon-flavored sparkling water, Elaine declared, "I suspect we'll never learn why Green Bay failed to check the boxes it needed to check for both the rescission and the litigation, so IFBC will just have to privately speculate about it among yourselves."

On Day 766, Green Bay's brief was submitted to the trial court. The facts recited in the brief stated, "The architectural rendering of the Facility showed a building with no rooftop stacks" and "OSGC's application materials also included materials purporting to show that the 'pyrolytic' process that would be used to 'bake' the solid waste was a proven technology."

The brief further included statements transcribed from the audio tapes of the initial OSGC presentation. Things like "there is no hazardous material," and "all the gas is taken off by a 'cherry scrubber' so it takes away any kind of harmful toxins that might be in the gas and the rest is burned as natural gas" and "the ash that comes out can be dumped in a landfill or mixed as a road base." Other statements were contained in the document, like, "there are no smoke stacks, no oxygen, and no ash" and "there is carbon and ash which actually could have been tested and go right in to organic farming," followed by "there are some dioxins."

After reading the brief, Alette called and asked, "Why didn't Green Bay question these statements at the time they were made? They contradict each other constantly."

Even though she couldn't see me I shook my head in disgust. "Yeah, it's unbelievable that the Plan Commission and City Council didn't do that. Didn't even seem to prompt the City to more aggressively look into the project. I've long wondered why someone didn't ask for more time to consider the matter back then."

"Wow. Just wow," Alette responded. "I guess this really WAS pushed through like some kind of no brainer."

Crucially, the city's decision to take a litigation short cut meant it gave up the golden opportunity to truly test how OSGC's word salads and other so-called evidence would hold up to even cursory judicial scrutiny. Despite all of that, IFBC's ever-present sense of humor caused us to immediately note that the city's briefing cited only to the Clean Water Action Council and the Midwest Environmental Advocates. Just like with the Plan Commission's report about its re-review of the permit, IFBC's efforts similarly didn't make the cut.

Well, we just can't get any respect from these guys, I thought with a note of amusement.

It was a different story in OSGC's briefs. During the Day 780 IFBC meeting at Greg's house, I mused that, "At least OSGC had the grace to mention Incinerator Free Brown County in its homework. Props for the call out!"

Elaine laughed at this attitude and said, "I couldn't decide whether OSGC would be so mad at you guys it would blame all their woes on you or continue to act dismissively towards the little people and just ignore you. Looks like it split the difference by giving IFBC an honorable mention!"

"OSGC's cognitive dissonance in simultaneously suggesting that we are both a small but vocal group of terribly uneducated misfits, while also suggesting we're this nefarious, shadowy group of puppet masters pulling strings behind the scenes is hilarious." I laughed. "I think everyone sees through both of those fake and contradictory descriptions, but it sure is entertaining to see which version OSGC will use at any given time."

"We should set up one of those odds maker boards with the various things OSGC says, and everyone can buy in dollar bets on which they think we'll get called," Greg proposed. "See who winds up with the most money,"

"I don't have that kind of cash!" Elaine responded to everyone's amusement.

In re-reading of the brief again that evening, I thought to myself, *OSGC's clumsy attempt to debunk IFBC through hearsay ginned up by someone with an interest in seeing the incineration project come to fruition wouldn't hold up to even the most minimal judicial scrutiny if we contested it. Since we aren't a player in the lawsuit, it's better to simply sit on the bench and watch how the legal proceedings play out. Meanwhile, we gotta keep applying public pressure as that was where the real fight always has been at.* At least the honorable mention in their briefs made me happy to know OSGC was still smarting from its wounds.

Interestingly, the whole group noticed that OSGC's media communications, from the point of rescission going forward, had been restricted to press releases with the occasional appearance by someone who probably stuck to a written script.

Greg had also noted to himself that, *OSGC has become rather averse to speaking to the media due to its constant blundering and the downward trajectory of media reporting. Gee, that's really just too bad.*

CHAPTER 27

DAY 772

All Lawyered Up

"The court's dilemma in trying to determine the order in which
the various motions and contentions should be considered,
is well illustrated by the old saying,
"Which comes first, the chicken or the egg?"
There being no conclusive answer to that question or to this
court's dilemma they will be addressed in what seems to be
the most logical order."
— *Graves v. Walton County Bd. of Education,*
91 F.R.D. 457 (MD Ga. 1981)

T he trial court hearing occurred on Day 772 at the Brown
County Courthouse in downtown Green Bay. The Brown
County Courthouse was added to the National Register of Historic Places in 1976 and is a beautiful copper domed building that was
completed in 1908. The former site of team practices and contentious

meetings during the early years of the local sports franchise, the four-story tall courthouse is now a stop on a walking tour.

After dispensing with various housekeeping matters, the court got down to business. OSGC's lawyers naturally made an opening statement designed to paint the project in the best possible light. It's their job. That's what they're there for.

"It's no accident, your honor, that this project found a home in Green Bay. Seven Gens approached the city staff here in the city. The city staff encouraged Seven Gens to find a place for this project in the city. It worked together to find a suitable location and ultimately decided on the site on Hurlbut Street just down the road from the Pulliam Power Plant and that property, Judge, was picked for good reason."

The OSGC attorney (a different lawyer than the one who sent the nastygram to us about the billboards back on Day 367) continued, making various statements including, "Seven Gens has not done anything wrong. It's in full compliance with the CUP, yet the Common Council decided to revoke the permit. This, Judge, it could not do." He went on to claim, without any evidence whatsoever, that the city employees who worked on approving this incinerator project would never have approved something which could cause harm to the residents. If the City had bothered to conduct Discovery, it would have been in a position to rebut these, and other, claims.

The attorney for the City delivered Green Bay's short opening remarks. "Did the city have authority to revoke? The answer to that question is the city does have authority. Under what circumstances is the issue before us right now? And here the question is, we're not exercising that decision, was there an arbitrary and capricious act by the city in doing do?

"That comes down to a review of the record. Is there information in the record that supports the position that they took? And a review of the record will show that is the case. There is enough in there to show that statements were made by the tribe to city officials, to the council members regarding the nature of this facility.

"Those statements turned out not to be completely accurate. Things were learned after the fact that when brought to the attention of the

City officials caused them to change their — to review and revoke the permit." The City's opening continued on for a while, with the attorney noting, "Reasonable minds may differ on the evidence. And that is the point here. Reasonable minds can differ on what's out there, and in this situation, there is a certiorari action, we must defer to the decision made by the city."

One of the first issues the judge raised was regarding the Plan Commission re-hearing and that the Plan Commission reported it found no misrepresentations of fact in the voluminous materials provided to the Plan Commission for its review. The court asked, "How do I reconcile the two separate findings from the body charged with determining whether or not it would recommend that permit be issued as against the city's decision, Common Council decision to revoke the permit?"

Interestingly, the City's attorney replied, indicating the City was not bound by the Planning Commission's approval to automatically approve the CUP and that the City retained the discretion to have denied the CUP.

In terms of legal jargon, I noted that this answer was a non-sequitur since it never addressed whether the City had the power to subsequently rescind a Conditional Use Permit AFTER it had issued. It only spoke to the power of the City to deny an initial application for a CUP prior to issuance. I thought, *denying an application is a very different proposition than unwinding an issued permit as the rights of a permit holder are much broader in scope than those of an applicant. If this guy's dancing on the head of a pin already, the City is in trouble. Suggesting the City's right to deny an application carries forward into an unfettered power to arbitrarily revoke a permit just isn't going to age well.*

Obviously, the court was unsatisfied with the City's carry forward argument, as it didn't explain what the Plan Commission re-hearing was supposed to accomplish back on Day 683. The judge asked, "Why did they use the review process? There's no basis." I thought this was an excellent question, as the IFBC core had often asked the same question.

The City's attorney responded with something meant to be plausible sounding "It was an opportunity to gather information, to allow the parties to present their information to the Commission." While fact gathering superficially sounded reasonable, the attorney went on to state, "Ultimately, it comes down to the Council acts as a body and its majority vote. So, we can't get into why each person made their decision, but it was a vote of the Council as a whole to make this decision."

I couldn't help but notice it didn't speak to the jarring disconnect between the Commission's re-review and the Council's disregard of that; as a practical matter, it was treated as procedurally irrelevant. As I listened to this, I thought *so the Plan Commission hearing really WAS just kabuki theater to waste everyone's time like some sort of diversion? I didn't see that coming.*

Neither IFBC nor the Court could seem to understand the City's position that skipping the evidence somehow explained why the City Council acted as it did, although that omission seemed unfortunately consistent with the City's abbreviated litigation strategy to avoid dealing with messy subjects like evidence.

To my way of thinking, it was difficult to reconcile how the City expected to establish how specific information influenced council members to rescind the permit by simply suggesting a majority vote nonetheless was taken with one mind and no further inquiry into the 'why' of it was necessary. Interestingly, the City's attorney noted for the Court that several members of the City Council were present the evening of the Plan Commission hearing where I had lit up OSGC. That made me think, *Well, well. I was previously unaware of that little nugget! Interesting, even though it really isn't relevant to the outcome or whether the Council acted of one mind or more importantly, WHY it took action because they skipped conducting Discovery.*

I felt the motion hearing by the trial court was filled with other interesting arguments as well. In response to the court's question about where in the audio of the original Plan Commission transcript was there "any discussion regarding the public health, safety, or general welfare of the City of Green Bay in issuing the permit" OSGC's attorney replied, "I think that's implicit, Your Honor, in the condition that the Plan Commission attached the permit in that it comply with all state and federal environmental regulations."

The judge's next remarks were devastating when the judge noted that the court would be surprised if there had been any such discussion because OSGC indicated there would be no hazardous material produced by this facility, so why would there have been such a discussion as the absence of hazardous material would not give rise to a concern regarding endangerment of public health? I nodded to myself, thinking, *I've been waiting for the city to say that. Why did they fail to do so? At least the judge caught it.*

Unfortunately for the City, its decision to skip Discovery also meant it lacked the ability to establish whether it agreed with OSGC's characterizations and suppositions about what was implied or what the Plan Commission could have reasonably believed was included or excluded. Starting well before today's hearing, I worried that this would become a figurative anvil tied around the City's neck in later judicial proceedings, although it didn't appear to impact the proceedings here in the trial court.

For the moment, however, arguments about smokestacks were unfavorable for OSGC as the judge asked, "And right after the CUP was issued, as we all know, after the CUP was issued and it was sent to DNR for permitting, DNR permitted the facility provided it had a 60 foot smokestack?"

OSGC's lawyer replied, "Correct." The stacks discussion began to go sideways for OSGC as OSGC's lawyer attempted to explain away OSGC's initial references to a lack of a stack. He stated, "What was said to the Common Council, and this is important Your Honor, because there is not misrepresentation here, is that there would be no stacks like the stacks associated with coal-fired power plants."

The trial court was not buying it. The judge noted that OSGC had said, "there are no smokestacks." The judge continued. "And in the CUP, as you and I both know, there's drawings that do not indicate any type of smokestack. In fact — and you know this. I'm not telling you anything you don't know. The record at 21-122-23 shows a flat roof warehouse building, which I think would lead any reasonable person to believe there are no smokestacks because it's a completely closed loop process. Nothing is going to come out of that building. There would be nothing

— there would be nothing to associate a smokestack with." My eyebrows shot up at the strength of that statement. *Poof!* I thought, using the IFBC joke born from the *Heller* cartoon. *That had to hurt.*

The judge was not finished. "The other visuals in the CUP showing sites, nowhere show any type of venting. They don't show any type of smokestacks. So again, let me take you back, because I think this is an important issue. I'm not finding any evidence in this record that would allow a reasonable person to conclude that there would (a) be a smokestack or that (b) there would be a smokestack of this type of dimension, which is required by DNR. The agency that you say is going to stop any concerns that one would have, has to be Emissions. Help me to understand."

The response compared the proposed incinerator's sixty-foot stacks to existing stacks from local paper mills and the old Pulliam power plant, which was hundreds of feet tall, suggesting that disregarding the massive difference in scale nonetheless implied OSGC's claims were truthful. The attorney then blamed the City's failure to prohibit stacks in the CUP, indicating such an omission implied that the Council actually permitted stacks, saying, "If it was important enough to the council" … "when it granted this permit that there be no stacks, that should have been a condition of the CUP."

With another small shake of my head I thought ruefully, *it certainly is muddled. How was the City supposed to ban stacks when it was unaware of the planned existence of any stacks? Pretty tough to establish whether the chicken or the egg came first when they came to court empty-handed.*

The parties in the two-hour hearing went back and forth, discussing the insufficient evidence in the record. The Judge made several references to the lack of evidence hampering his ability to thoroughly evaluate the record to his satisfaction. Then the courtroom discussion turned to the relevant case law cited by the opposing parties. The City continued to provide arguments stating that it was entitled to rely upon the information provided by the applicant. The City noted that if OSGC's information wasn't entirely accurate, the City was entitled to legally rescind the CUP in response to misinformation because it wasn't the land use which the City had been led to approve. The argument was honed even further when it was noted that the misrepresentation had to be material, and not over some inconsequential matter.

OSGC's lawyer did what all lawyers do, immediately drawing factual and legal distinctions to support OSGC's disagreement by stating the company's position that it had a vested property right in the CUP. He even suggested that OSGC did not commit fraud or misrepresentation merely because the City did not see fit to require a lack of stacks in the issued permit. As I listened, I again thought, *clearly the City's failure to conduct even rudimentary discovery to build its defense was a strategic error of such magnitude that it allowed the other side to speculate all sorts of inferences about the CUP process. That error again means the City just doesn't have what it needed to rebut such speculation.*

After considering all the arguments of counsel and reviewing a lengthy but still incomplete body of evidence, documents and relevant legal precedents, the judge issued a ruling from the bench. He stated that he was satisfied that OSGC's "representations simply were not correct" and that the City had relied upon them "as part of the basis to approve the CUP." He further stated, "I don't think the City was accurately and fully appraised. If anything, there is inconsistency, but to be frank, I think there was a misrepresentation." The findings also included noting the judge does not "know why, quite frankly, the City of Green Bay sent this matter back to the Planning Commission because they" [the Planning Commission] "simply had no authority to do anything."

The bench's remarks continued on, indicating the judge was satisfied with the City having met its burden, and that OSGC did not under a standard of review (called *certiorari* review) whereby deference is given to a municipality's actions under a rebuttable presumption of correctness. "And so, in light of the law, in light of the state of this record, the Court today denies Seven Generation's its petition for *cert.* review."

CHAPTER 28

DAY 772

Fallout Zone

"In law, as is life, the devil you know
is better than the devil you don't."

— *Am. Horse Prot. Ass'n, Inc. v. Veneman*, 200 F.R.D. 153 (DC 2001)

Despite the City's victory at the trial court, it's procedural missteps really bothered me. After the ruling, the IFBC core gathered with Rich and Elaine to discuss the hearing in an after-hours meeting in Ashwaubenon on Day 772 after the hearing earlier in the day.

During this meeting Greg revisited the issue, asking, "Given what we know about Green Bay being its own worst enemy and tripping itself up all the time, how can it be possible the City thinks they can rescind a permit at any time if a company made big investments based on the permit?"

"They can't just rescind without a good reason," I answered. "It takes a reason like fraud or material misrepresentation that wrongfully induces a municipality to issue the permit it wouldn't have otherwise issued. In the trial court's hearing, the City had all these lawyers show up, but they inexplicably decided to try to get it in front of a judge without first doing their pretrial homework. It definitely hurt the City's defense in the hearing, but they got lucky and overcame it anyway. It's like some rookie law students thinking actions speak for themselves without realizing that they have to explain why underlying reasons prompted said actions. Seriously man, it's the same thing I hammer into my kids for their school papers. You want the 'A' grade, you have to explain more than the Who, What, Where and When. You also have to explain the Why, and the Why is always the most difficult thing to articulate."

Greg, Elaine, Rich, Joanne and Alette laughed. Then Rich mentioned that, "It's possible that politics were behind the procedural irregularities, which will probably bite the City in the hinder. Again."

"I think we're getting pretty used to seeing that happen." Joanne replied.

Television news that evening carried the story out to the local area. NBC26 reported, "The judge agreed with the city council members who say they voted to rescind the permit in part because representatives of Oneida Seven Generations lied about environmental concerns, including the need for smokestacks, and actually told council members that there were no environmental concerns." After the reporter noted how both sides sought a quick decision, by the conclusion of the two-hour hearing, "The judge backed the city, saying they had every right to cancel the permit."

FOX11 reported, "Some city council members felt misled by the initial plan which, among other things, did not include smokestacks." Over on WBAY, it was indicated that "The judge ruled in favor of the city on grounds that the original proposal for the gasification plant that the city first approved a year and a half ago had inaccuracies and misrepresentations of the smokestacks."

The Day 773 *Press-Gazette* article stated the judge "agreed with Green Bay's lawyers that Oneida Seven Generations, in initially applying for the permit had misrepresented facts about the proposed plant, particularly concerning the amount and type of emissions and the need for smokestacks to vent those emissions." The article went on to note that the Council president defended the City Council's decision to rescind the CUP and denied that the rescission would discourage other developers because it would encourage those other developers of the city's commitment to a cleaner environment. Dean from CWAC stated the decision would strengthen the city's ability to prevent unwanted development. Wisconsin Public Radio also carried a report which interviewed OSGC, which interestingly claimed the pyrolysis variant of incineration was a relatively new technology, but that versions of it have been successful in Europe.

By now, my view of the 'but, but, but, success in Europe!' claim was that it was both somewhat sad yet fairly hilarious, because when questioned, not once had OSGC ever been able to prove such a claim. That same public radio report also carried a quote from some purported environmentalist neither IFBC nor CWAC had ever heard of claiming pyrolysis does not burn anything.

Immediately following this remark the reporter played my reply, which I remember was, "If you stuck your turkey in the oven too long, it would be incinerated. And that's really about the same methodology they're using as well. They're sticking things into a giant oven and melting it down. Eventually it'll be reduced to ash." WPR reporter Patty Murray concluded by noting Incinerator Free Brown County has a number of objections, including the size and height of discharge stacks, truck traffic, and exactly what type of waste will be burned if the permit gets reinstated.

I couldn't help but notice the Orwellian nature of the report's earlier quote from the purportedly lifelong environmentalist about "using inappropriate words" because it so closely resembled OSGC's dystopian notions about IFBC's thought-crimes by telling the truth.

CHAPTER 29

DAY 776

Hot Potato

"As the old saying goes, enough is enough."

— *Illinois Commerce Com. v. Interstate Commerce Commission,*
270 U.S. App. D.C. 214, 848 F.2d 1246 (Ct. App. DC 1988)

Unwilling to move on to more productive endeavors, OSGC
made the decision to try harder to escape the now hostile environment in Green Bay and find another happy home for its
incinerator. When I heard of the possibility of it moving elsewhere, I
thought, not for the first time, that *strategic thinking to apply resources
connecting predictable outcomes to identifiable goals is apparently not among
OSGC's strong suits.*

I further noted to myself its decision to shop the incinerator around
to a different location would have made more sense if OSGC's goal had
actually been to try to make the thing universally derided. Since universal condemnation was presumably not OSGC's goal, by now it was
abundantly clear the latest search for new home was just another bumbling misstep done in ignorance of public opinion. OSGC decided to
site its incinerator in the Town of Oneida just west of the Brown County

line and the Green Bay metropolitan area. This site is straight west of Hobart, which itself is west of Ashwaubenon.

On Day 776, the *Press-Gazette* reported that OSGC had unveiled plans for a facility, which OSGC now dubbed a 'plastic-recycling' facility. The irony was rich, as the *Press-Gazette* noted worries about the environmental effects "such an industrial operation would have on areas of the Oneida Indian Reservation" which were described as "pristine" despite having already had a large commercial building on the site.

No such concerns had been publicly voiced by OSGC about the earlier proposed sites in Ashwaubenon or Green Bay.

Significantly, the article stated the tribal zoning body — who must rezone the site and approve a development permit — was accepting public comment on the proposal for another few weeks. The *Press-Gazette* interviewed me for about half an hour over this new location, and I was surprised at the quote chosen for use in the article because it was just about the first thing I said.

"It's the same old stupid project," I blurted out when he broke the latest news to me because I hadn't yet heard of it. The article continued, saying "Despite its location outside of Brown County, the emissions generated by burning plastic waste would pose a health hazard to residents throughout the area, Filcher said. Some members of the Oneida tribe agreed."

"Yvonne Metivier, a tribal elder who lives in nearby Hobart, said she worries about harming the environment and also about committing more tribal money to another business venture." Metivier was quoted as saying, "This is another money pit. It's just unthinkable that this would be called progress." IFBC could not have agreed with Metivier more, and the core membership immediately began calling it the 'same old stupid project' to each other because we felt that it and it accurately described the boondoggle.

The next day Dean called to discuss the new site location. We shared a good laugh about my unintentional quote. I had to admit, "It was just something I blurted out at the beginning of the call. I didn't think he'd actually use THAT one!"

Dean laughed. "We thought it was a pretty good quote over at CWAC!"

Talk show host Jerry Bader also discussed the new location proposal on his Day 776 broadcast. While he lacked the details about the new proposal, Jerry noted the leadership seemed less concerned by the process itself, and more concerned about their putting any sort of facility on land considered 'pristine.' Jerry said, "The company is governed by its own board of directors and operates somewhat independently of tribal leadership. That's interesting. *Somewhat* independently. Because when OSG was rebuffed by the city, they went into hiding. And they had the tribe do all the talking." It seemed that Jerry was well attuned to OSGC's habit of disappearing and letting others bail it out of trouble.

It was at this time that IFBC's good friends at *OneidaEye* got in touch about the latest project site. They were determinedly collecting and distributing information concerning events impacting the Oneida membership. The breadth and depth of the documentary evidence they obtained, and their connecting of the dots between people, enterprises and events repeatedly left me breathless. Repeatedly. In fact, I consider it an awesome enterprise that continually uncovers many interesting documents and facts.

The communication of information between IFBC and *OneidaEye* was already at a high level, and Leah provided the contact information for me to cobble together and file lengthy comments with the zoning commission as follows [Some dates and designations have been omitted for this reproduction]:

IFBC respectfully submits the attached comments pursuant to the Public Hearing notice. IFBC is an all volunteer grassroots environmental advocacy group. IFBC has already established a storied history of supporting waste reduction, reuse, recycling, composting, extended producer responsibility and initiatives to limit dependence on landfills. IFBC has steadfastly maintained a "no incinerator" position since its founding and has joined with hundreds of groups across the globe in resisting initiatives which involve burning or otherwise melting down petroleum based plastics and has routinely been referenced as a leading authority on the subject.

IFBC asks the Oneida Land Commission to carefully consider all aspects of this latest proposal for the Oneida Seven Generations pyrolysis staged plastics incinerator. The issues to consider can be summarized as follows.

Proximity Hazards

- **Traffic.** The Oneida Turtle School is less than a mile from the proposed site, and the Turtle School playground is on the north side of the school so there's little other than Hwy 54 between the playground and the proposed incinerator. Prior editions of this project involved enormous levels of inbound truck traffic to haul sufficient petroleum based plastic fuel, as well as outbound truck traffic to haul away ashen residue. Outbound haulers must also be capable of sealing the residue to prevent it from spreading to surrounding areas of Oneida land which was described to the Press-Gazette as "pristine" in the article on this matter. To make matters worse, if this incinerator is to run 24/7, inbound traffic would either have to haul around the clock or triple the number of inbound haulers on Fridays to ensure sufficient petroleum based fuel for weekend operations. Monday outbound residue hauling will likewise triple corresponding to the Friday inbound hauling. All this truck traffic and possible leak exposures will take place in close proximity to the Oneida Turtle School.

- **Emissions stacks.** Prior disclosures to the DNR (information which the Brown County Circuit Court recently ruled was withheld from the City of Green Bay) reveals 10 emission stacks for this type of facility which was described for the Press-Gazette as using "the same technology as the proposed Green Bay plant." DNR records also reveal that 3 of these smokestacks will be 60 feet tall, 1 at 45 feet tall, 3 at 40 feet in height, and 3 at 7.5 feet. The height of these stacks will loom over pristine Oneida lands and cast very long shadows over a children's school and playground. See attached Exhibit 1.

- **Pollutants.** Prior disclosures to the DNR (information which the Brown County Circuit Court recently ruled was withheld from the City of Green Bay) reveals all the smokestacks needed by the facility aren't present merely for decorative purposes. They are there to discharge dioxins (which are currently being removed from the Fox River), which are the natural emissions of melted petroleum based plastics.

Operational hazards

- **Materials separation.** OSGC's prior Preliminary Draft Materials Separation Plan that it submitted to DNR suffered from many defects. OSGC's prior plan stated an "additional 10 trucks per weekday will be necessary to remove the unacceptable items, end product material, and recyclables." Although this facility is intended to operate seven days a week, due to the Monday — Friday tipping schedule it will need adequate room to store hundreds of tons for weekend incineration and melting. The following questions arise:
  - What is OSGC's plan to provide for adequate removal of each weekend's accumulation of unacceptable items, end product material, and recyclables?
  - What is OSGC's plan to remove char residue and ash after the pyrolysis fires incinerates/melts the petroleum plastics, because after two years OSGC was completely unable to identify a market or taker for this waste.
  - How will OSGC separate undesirable materials from those to be melted/burned/incinerated?
  - What is the formal staff training plan for safety and emergencies?
  - What safety equipment will be present?
  - What materials monitoring will OSGC conduct to ensure only petroleum-based plastics are melted/burned/incinerated?

- Will OBC question why OSGC plans suddenly shifted from trash to recycled plastics incineration when OSGC previously claimed it had more than enough tons per day to sustain this operation with independent trash haulers and did not require a Tri-County haulers/contract?

- Where are these loads coming from and what is the cost per mile to haul this plastic? This is especially questionable when Outagamie and Brown Counties already have a dedicated and well running recycling program of paper and plastics products.

- What are the costs per ton in getting this feedstock to the new location that will make this operation profitable (since most other OSGC projects have not been)?

- If the main feedstock is now going to be centered more on petroleum-based plastics, does OSGC need to submit its latest scheme to DNR for review?

- What, if any equipment has already been purchased to date when OSGC was intending to incinerate trash and what changes to the equipment are needed for a different feedstock? How much of the invested money could be lost due to this change?

Miscellaneous hazards

- **Sourcing.** A significant issue arises when the question is asked where all this petroleum-based plastic may be obtained. There are two important questions to ask as follows:

  — Can purity of petroleum plastics be guaranteed?

  — Are the petroleum plastics feedstock being imported from beyond out of state?

- **Truthfulness.** OSGC was held by the Brown County Circuit Court to have misrepresented the incinerator project to the City of Green Bay, thereby justifying the City's rescission of the permit for misrepresentation. There are two legal principles which apply to this situation:

— ***Falsus in Uno, Falsus in Omnibus.*** The United States Supreme Court has long upheld the foregoing Latin phrase describing when testimony is partially false, it is considered false in the entirety. "When it is once ascertained that a witness is capable of committing perjury, all he swears to is rejected as false. In reason and in law the rule is the same when a party is found to be capable of forgery: the papers not known to be fabricated must share the fate of those which are proved to be spurious; for everything is corrupt that comes from a corrupted source. *Falsus in uno, falsus in omnibus.*" See *United States v. Castillero*, 67 U.S. 17, 17 L. Ed. 360, 1862 U.S. LEXIS 247, 2 Black 17 (1862).

— **Half truths no different than any other untruth.** Another way of stating the above principle was also succinctly articulated by the U.S. Supreme Court in *Equitable Life Ins. Co. v. Halsey, Stuart & Co.*, 312 U.S. 410 (1941). The Court stated a "statement of a half truth is as much a misrepresentation as if the facts stated were untrue."

• **Do you trust your children to OSGC's care?** Given OSGC's loss in Brown County Circuit Court upholding the decision of the Green Bay Common Council for rescinding OSGC's permit because of OSGC misrepresentation, can OSGC representations be trusted regarding the health and well being of Oneida children and adults?

• **Reputational damage.** The Brown County Circuit Court held the City of Green Bay was justified in rescinding the permit for OSGC's misrepresentations in a widely reported decision. This ruling came down after more than two years of embarrassing publicity incurred by OSGC's botching of the entire incinerator debacle. When will this project and OSGC be stopped from further besmirching the carefully cultivated good neighbor reputation of the Oneida Tribe of Indians of Wisconsin?

- **Motivational disclosure.** The current proposal to site this project in the Town of Oneida is the fifth proposed site. In considering the prior rejections by each of the prior sites (Hobart, Oneida, Ashwaubenon, Green Bay), why would OSGC continue its mad quest to build an incinerator? There are several possibilities:

  — **Debt.** The State of Wisconsin loaned OSGC and OEI 4 million dollars (see attached Exhibits 2 and 3, which are the loan documents) to build an incinerator. If OSGC fails to build any facility, the loans must be repaid sooner.

  — **Risk exposure.** The recent D.C. Court of Appeals decision in Vann v. U.S. Department of the Interior, 701 F.3d 927 (D.C. Cir. 2012) creates potential personal liability exposure for members of the Oneida business committee, the land committee, and OSGC. Sovereign immunity now won't protect these persons from being sued individually by anyone who suffer injuries or damages from their official actions. Failing to properly apply government loans unquestionably creates both civil and criminal causes of action regardless what form the contracting entity assumes. Even if the incinerator is constructed, risk exposure for harm it creates still exists.

For these reasons, IFBC requests that the rezoning request be denied.

CHAPTER 30

Clawback

"In classic Keystone Cop fashion
(except that nothing here is funny), much of the work
of the fiduciaries in this case has consisted largely of
closing doors after the damage has been done."

- *In re Petit*, 291 B.R. 582 (DC ME 2003).

D ay 798 brought more than sending the IFBC comment letter
to the Oneida Land Commission. The second letter I mailed
was to the Wisconsin Economic Development Corporation
(WEDC). Ever since obtaining copies of the two WEDC loans for construction of the incinerator, we had been pondering when it would be
advantageous to open up a new front regarding the loans as a method of
ratcheting up pressure on OSGC.

"What do you guys think about trying to use the loans as a new
avenue to go after OSGC? Now that they're weakened by losing in the
trial court, this might be a good time to cause some more pain for that
outfit," I said during a small meeting of the core group members (plus
Elaine) at Greg's house.   176

"I like it. OSGC doesn't seem to get the message that nobody wants its incinerator," said Alette. Looking at Joanne, who was nodding with a big smile on her face, she said, "Oh yeah. Let 'em have it!"

Greg laughingly responded, "Let's pile it on. OSGC needs to go away".

"I thought you would like that idea. I'll cobble together something in my basement lair and copy everyone on it."

"Your lair?" asked Elaine with a grin.

"Yup. My much better half calls it that. Sounded like a less pretentious description than calling it the Incinerator Free Brown County World Headquarters, Beer and Coffee Bar."

"I kind of like calling it the World Headquarters, Beer and Coffee Bar!" giggled Alette.

Later that evening I sent the following letter to WEDC with blind copies emailed to our group and the *Press-Gazette*:

> IFBC writes to advise the Wisconsin Economic Development Corporation (WEDC) about our grave concern regarding possible misuse of the public funding made pursuant to the above two contracts (see attached Exhibits 1 and 2, containing the first pages of each) for a total of $4 million. While we are aware WEDC has been plagued with well-publicized issues of accountability and accounting for disbursements, recent events pertaining to these contracts (the "contracts") prompted IFBC to draft this letter to WEDC and request WEDC to rescind the public funding made pursuant to these contracts.
>
> As you can see from the attached newspaper articles in Exhibits 3 and 4, the contract funding to construct energy recovery facilities appears to be diverted to other purposes than permitted under the contracts. SEP FY10-20265 only pertains to creation of jobs in Green Bay, Wisconsin, and the City of Green Bay's rescission of the building permit for this project for misrepresentation was upheld by the Brown County Circuit Court.

LEG FY10-19812 pertains to establishing a "state-of-the-art energy recovery facility in Brown County...". The Press-Gazette article contained in Exhibit 4 details plans to shift this WEDC funded project to Outagamie County. Both misrepresentation and out of area geographic siting fail to comply with the strict terms of both agreements.

It is not difficult to imagine there are other failures to comply with each agreement not contained in this letter. IFBC believes this situation presents a unique opportunity for WEDC to remedy past issues by recovering disbursed funding and redirecting it to other, more legitimate ventures to create viable economic development in Wisconsin.

For these reasons, IFBC requests WEDC to rescind the contracts and claw back disbursed funding. Thank you for your time and efforts.

Thank you for your time and efforts.

Obviously, I did not expect the funds to be clawed back, especially since IFBC was advised that there may have been some sort of connection between WEDC's leadership and the law firm representing OSGC, but IFBC anticipated that, at a minimum, it would be another irritating burr under OSGC's saddle. IFBC members saw no need to let OSGC have time to catch its breath.

CHAPTER 31

Moving on over to Morrison?

"Defendant's argument brings to mind an old saying: 'Just because you're standing in a garage doesn't make you a car.'"

— *United States v. Raymer*, 941 F.2d 1031 (10th Cir. 1991)

While it was starting to become a zombie project, the corpse of OSGC's incinerator was keeping busy shambling around looking for another victim. Within a few days of mailing out those letters to the zoning office and WEDC, Alette received word from residents living in the nearby town of Morrison indicating that the town board had discussed the OSGC incinerator as a potential new development.

Morrison is a rural township located in a county adjacent to Brown County where many of the residents were still tuned into the local news emanating from Brown County. It took them little time to track down how to contact IFBC. One of those residents called Alette and asked if someone could lend a hand. Alette then called Joanne, and then she called me.

"Hey John," said Alette. "We received word of the next potential site for the incinerator. Do you know where Morrison is? About a half hour south of the metro using the back roads. I received a call from a few folks down there who are afraid the local town board is interested in the incinerator. They told me it's already been discussed once and it's coming up on their agenda for more discussion next Thursday. She said they heard about how successful we've been in derailing OSGC and was hoping someone from our group could meet with them before the town board meeting to get them up to speed."

Surprised and pleased, I quickly agreed.

"Oh! I almost forgot to tell you," Alette added, "Joanne is from that area originally, and wanted to tag along if you're going to the board meeting too."

"Perfect, I'll make the arrangements. Tell Joanne I'll pick her up and will get back to her with the time I'll be over." After disconnecting the call, I called the concerned Morrison resident to make the arrangements and was pleasantly surprised to learn that she offered to drop off copies of videos showing that the OSGC incinerator had been discussed at three prior Morrison meetings.

Watching the videos before attending next Thursday's Morrison meeting was truly enlightening for me and Joanne, especially because one video of a meeting held way back on Day 45 was the first time anybody in IFBC got to watch the initial sales pitch for OSGC's incinerator.

That Day 45 Morrison board meeting video was a relatively low-key affair held in a room with a kitchenette in the background. It revealed that the incinerator was portrayed as a "waste-energy management" system. As we watched the 15-minute presentation I muttered to Joanne, "Cripes! What an exercise in Orwellian euphemisms of incineration techno-babble and happy talk." It seemed to consist mainly of drawing distinctions without differences between combustion, plasma arc and pyrolysis.

Tellingly, the whoppers began with the statement, "We have a complete destruction of pollutants. So any type of toxins, PCBs even, so actually breaking them down to their original elements so it's a completely inert material at the end of the day."

I just shook my head. Joanne muttered, "Good heavens! Everybody knows 'inert' isn't a synonym for 'safe'. It merely means the material isn't chemically active and is certainly still capable of leaching those *inert* elements down into the groundwater."

"And how can they achieve 'complete destruction of pollutants' without splitting the atom?" I asked. "What a farce!"

Given the variable composition of solid waste, another whopper was, the "majority of the by-product at the end of the day is called carbon ash." It was simply amazing to watch of the lack of awareness of fundamental scientific principles. One of those principals was, "original elements" that aren't carbon cannot be transmogrified into the entirely different element of "carbon" merely by heating them up a little bit.

The presenter also attempted to trivialize the plant's emissions as "about two times more than what's coal plants are actually burning" while also casting such emissions in the positive light, stating that said emissions were much lower than plasma arc or combustion. I thought, *this was a unique way of missing the main point — akin to comparing radiation from uranium-based weapons to that of plutonium. It's like just noting the residual radiation levels just differ by degree, but failing to notice the target was destroyed by both anyway. Dead is still dead.*

Another bone I had to pick with this spectacle was the highly misleading definition of pyrolysis-based waste-to-energy. Arising from either a misplaced belief in rote repetition of technical sounding word salads or a fundamental lack of engineering acumen, it was described as "thermal decomposition of organic and synthetic waste material, or any kind of material really, at elevated temperatures in the absence of oxygen." Growing more irritated as the video progressed, I grumbled to myself (so Joanne didn't have to hear it all), *decomposition only refers to ORGANIC materials and has nothing to do with synthetic.*

Then came more nonsense about some scientist who created this system and who purportedly set the emission standard in California (where Greenaction has already clearly found there is no such approved system) and magnetized materials separation that pulls out steel, aluminum and copper. What gobbledygook! Aluminum and copper are not magnetic!

For me and Joanne, the very best part of the presentation was the Q&A, when someone asked, "How's everything going with that one in Packerland, the Oneida's?" The answer was entertaining. After describing it as a political problem the speaker stated, "We can refute pretty much anything they come up with."

Joanne smiled at that. "Yeah, it's not too tough to refute questions in a friendly Q&A where the attendees lack information, but it's a whole different proposition when IFBC comes to the table." I couldn't agree more. Then Joanne quipped, "Do you think they still believe they can refute anything we can come up with now?"

I laughed out loud. "Ha! Not a chance! Here's to doing our homework so we can drop in and stir the pot on Thursday!" We were together in agreement.

Unlike the Day 45 pitch, the discussion at the Morrison town board meeting on Day 806 didn't even last five minutes. It was relatively vague and there was no opportunity to ask questions. Since Joanne and I were deprived of the opportunity to 'stir the pot' I penned the board a follow up letter.

The IFBC letter was somewhat customized from the standard IFBC comment template to fit the situation, noting the prior dates the incinerator was discussed, and adding "IFBC has also obtained video of the above noted meetings where the OSGC incinerator was discussed by Morrison officials. IFBC also requests the Morrison leadership permit an IFBC representative to meet with them at the next meeting."

In the letter, IFBC questioned why Morrison would even entertain any discussion of a disgraced project that lost its last permit due to misrepresentation. IFBC continued, "A natural corollary to disregarding the dangers posed in working with a developer whose project is so tainted by such a public scandal is whether the board members would potentially waive any governmental immunity and be exposing themselves to personal liability exposure arising from any disregard to the dangers of working with a tarnished developer who has previously misrepresented its project."

Within days the local resident in Morrison called me. "My contact on the town board called! IFBC's letter prompted the town board to shelve the matter until some later point in time! She said to tell you and Joanne, 'Thank you so much!'"

"That IS good news! I'm really happy to hear that," I replied. "You might want to stay vigilant and monitor the situation down there closely to see if the board decides to pick it up again at a later point, just to be cautious."

"Oh, we will, don't worry about that. Any changes and we'll give you a call right away."

On Day 809 a Press-Gazette article said the Morrison town chairman thought the OSGC incinerator sounded like a good concept, but he did not know if it belonged in Morrison. Another board member said he would consider the project, but, "We would have to study it some more." It was time to move on to the next thing as events were swiftly moving along.

CHAPTER 32

DAY 808

All You Need is Love

"[T]here is no indication that [it] … was simply an inadvertent misstatement … for which the applicant should be given a mulligan."
— Springs Window Fashions LP v. Novo Indus.,
L.P., 323 F.3d 989, 996 (Fed. Cir. 2003)

Thanks to information provided by Elaine and a call from the *OneidaEye*, we were advised that the zoning commission would approve the rezoning for the incinerator prior to submitting IFBC's comments because there was some sort of nepotism connection between OSGC and the zoning commission. Nonetheless, although the commission should have abstained from considering the matter, it proceeded — while the conflicted member sat this one out. In my opinion, the core IFBC membership was risking ocular injuries from the tremendous eye rolling this news wrought. I couldn't help but think, *truly, the jokes write themselves on this one.*

The *Press-Gazette* article on Day 808 proclaimed, "New Oneida plant site zoned on tribal land" in a large headline. Noting that many hurdles remained "for the controversial project," the paper said, "Tribal members have submitted a petition signed by more than 80 people opposing the development on the former Tower Foods grocery store site just west of the Brown County line" In a bit of journalistic future telling, the article noted the petition sought a public referendum to decide the future of the proposed gasification facility.

Leah had already brought IFBC up to speed on her plan to seek such a petition. While the petition was fully supported by IFBC, the process was not a topic IFBC should publicly comment upon. Accordingly, IFBC maintained radio silence about the petition. Meanwhile, IFBC advised our Oneida members that Leah's petition was *not* a matter for the group to publicly comment upon, although individual members were certainly encouraged to follow their hearts on the topic.

The *Press-Gazette* even went so far as to quote elders who brought the hurt to OSGC by voicing disappointment in the zoning commission, stating, "A few people who stand to gain have completely abandoned the welfare of their own people." The same news hilariously indicated OSGC could not be reached for comment.

On Day 871 the *Kalihwisaks* carried the banner headline, "GTC to hear petition asking for ban on energy projects." Leah was quoted about protecting the people and all life sustaining us because it depends on protection from dioxins. She also said, "tribes face increased exposure to dioxin and other pollutants due to our land-based culture, and that dioxin is a known carcinogen causing severe health damage. OSGC admits their previous proposals would emit dioxin and that their latest proposal is a stepping-stone to the large facilities they sought before." The report also quoted OSGC admitting the new facility will emit dioxins.

After reading these great quotes the IFBC members cheered, as if watching an out of the park home run! Leah had absolutely crushed it. Alette was heard to mutter with a smile, "Remind me never to tick Leah off. She's really feisty!"

CHAPTER 33

Appealing

"The outcome of this appeal validates the sage advice once given by Yogi Berra to the effect that 'it ain't over 'til it's over', and the also famous saying that 'it's not over 'til the fat lady sings.'"

— *State v. Oliver*, 30 Kan. App. 2d 665 (KS Ct. App. 2002)

While the battle for the Town of Oneida was being waged, other events were also in motion. OSGC filed notice of an appeal on Day 833, with the Wisconsin Court of Appeals, which is the intermediate level of courts in the Wisconsin judicial system. OSGC's brief, filed two months later was 68 pages long.

Leah called from the *OneidaEye* offices to talk to me. "Have you had a chance to review OSGC's brief yet," she asked.

"Uh, no, was that filed today?"

"I didn't think you'd seen it yet. We got a copy of it already which I will email to you. Can you look it over and send me your thoughts on a private email? I'm working on some talking points over here."

"Can do. You'll have them later tonight," I promised.

Within minutes I was reading OSGC's brief. In the brief's Issues Presented for Review section, OSGC took care to emphasize every discussion of emissions during the CUP application phase, noting "A small but vocal group of opponents claimed the facility would harm local air quality and urged the agencies to disapprove the facility."

OSGC's statement continued, describing the opposition as having "failed to persuade the state and federal agencies, the opponents of the project then went back to the City, claiming that OSGC had misrepresented the nature of the Facility during the CUP application process by saying there would be no air emissions. In fact, OSGC had told the City many times in writing and orally that there would be emissions, and that those emissions would be subject to state and federal environmental standards."

I thought, *I probably would have adopted a similar approach had I been representing OSGC when describing the city's murky procedural detour back to the Plan Commission before reappearing in front of the City Council for final reconsideration. Geez! We even thought at the time it played out it seemed procedurally questionable. Now here it is. Poof!* I chuckled as I again recalled IFBC's adoption of 'Poof' after the *Heller* cartoon.

OSGC's attorneys indicated in the brief that the Planning Commission had thoroughly reviewed an abundance of documents and testimony in order to arrive at a considered opinion that there had been no misrepresentation. The attorneys then made an unfavorable comparison between the detailed Planning Commission review and the abbreviated City Council rescission, describing it as "without conducting any inquiry of its own." I mulled this over, thinking, *unfortunately, this was a key element missing from the City's litigation record. Now the city can't put meat on the bones of its defense. Can't even rebut claims of procedural improprieties. Not like everybody couldn't see that coming once the City basically skipped the pretrial festivities.*

I realized that another failure on the City's part was not to have made a record of OSGC's claim that the City's meeting minutes were "replete with errors," as well as the more obvious mistake of the City failing to explain the reasons for the rescission with any specificity. This had left OSGC relatively unencumbered in creatively inferring what the City Council members allegedly thought.

OSGC did give IFBC one small shout out in its brief, stating, "In fact, one of the more vocal opposition groups called itself 'Incinerator Free Brown County.'" I smiled to myself. *Nice to know OSGC is still smarting from one small wound.*

OSGC presented two issues on appeal: 1) May the CUP be rescinded based on implied conditions not originally included in the permit, and 2) May the CUP be rescinded for misrepresentation of facts to the City.

In contrast to OSGC's position claiming sufficient disclosure of emissions and stacks, the City's brief declared that there was substantial evidence of misrepresentation and that, "The primary issue before the Court is whether a municipality has the authority to void a CUP when inaccurate and misleading statements were made by the applicant during the CUP approval process."

Despite its well documented litigation failures, the City's attorneys nonetheless wrote that, "Because the record contains ample evidence that inaccurate and misleading statements were made by OSGC during the CUP application process, the City believes it acted within its lawful authority in voiding the CUP." I couldn't help but notice the heavy reliance of the City on materials filed by the Midwest Environmental Advocates compared to little of the City's own work. With a sinking feeling, I thought *the City is over relying on someone else's homework, which telegraphs a massive problem for the defense. Pay attention to what they're not telling us. What they're not telling us is the City belatedly realized they didn't adequately develop its own facts for the defense.*

Now it was up to the appellate court to review whether or not the evidence was adequate to support the rescission of the permit.

After reviewing the briefs, the IFBC group gathered together over wine and beer at one of the Ashwaubenon bars and grills on Oneida Street near the stadium. "Kudos to the city for citing — at length — the comments submitted by the Midwest Environmental Advocates, but it sure seems as if the City's heavy reliance on third party comments is a tacit acknowledgment of the city's scant litigation record."

Sipping his amber ale, Greg asked, "Am I correct in assuming that it's because skipping the chance to build its record now means the City is trying to substitute third party comments in place of facts establishing a thorough deliberation and permit reconsideration?"

Startled, Joanne, Alette and I all looked at Greg. "Holy cow! Look who went to law school this week!" I was very impressed. "Best you not be talking to OSGC's lawyers. That's the most succinct description of the situation I've heard yet."

Greg laughed. "Yeah, pretty sure I won't have much to say to them."

I continued. "The remainder of the City's brief focuses on statements by OSGC which the City says were untrue, or red herrings of irrelevant topics introduced to divert the attention of listeners or readers from the original issue. The red herrings consist of the same clumsy prose and techno-babble we've all experienced since Day 1."

Not surprisingly, OSGC's reply brief, which was filed somewhat later, latched on to the City's over-reliance on third party comments. The brief stated that the City's defense was "built entirely on the Unfounded Assertions of the Political Opposition Groups".

Now it was time for the Court of Appeals to reach its conclusion about the situation. It would be months before the parties would hear the result.

CHAPTER 34

DAY 846

Keeping the Pressure On

"If you get three strikes,
even the best lawyer in the world can't get you off."
— *King v. Burris*, 588 F. Supp. 1152 (DC Colo. 1984)

Since the exchange of briefs at the Court of Appeals did not give the core IFBC members any confidence that Green Bay would prevail, we decided to keep applying pressure and maintain our momentum during this period of relative quiet. To my surprise, the impetus soon arrived in the form of the *Press-Gazette*.

The reporter called me, asking, "The *Press-Gazette* wants to run an article about IFBC itself. Would you and the other group leaders be agreeable to interviews so I can collect the article background?"

"I'm fine with that," I told him. "But I can't really speak for everyone else yet. Let me take their temperatures and get back to you?"

The reporter sounded excited. "That would be great. Let me know as soon as you can. We would like to make a long essay article about it."

A few days later, the reporter and I met for coffee at a La Java in Howard, Wisconsin, to talk about the situation for an hour or two. After our discussion the reporter said he would soon be interviewing the other IFBC core members for their stories.

The lengthy article appeared on the *Press-Gazette's* front page on Day 846. In a totally consistent IFBC move the steering committee elected to go without a picture in the article due to our functioning as a team, and also because we preferred to keep OSGC guessing for strategic reasons.

The Day 857 edition of the *Press-Gazette* also carried significant news (that Leah had already given me a heads-up about). Under the headline, "Oneida plant faces some more opposition" the article described a potential doomsday scenario for OSGC. "But now that the Oneida Tribe of Indians-owned company is trying to locate the plant on tribal land, some of its own people are talking about doing away with the company. Opponents say they are considering taking steps to dissolve Oneida Seven Generations to prevent the company from exposing the tribe to any more financial or political turmoil."

Because Leah had unleashed this bombshell news — like trying to dissolve OSGC — I quickly called IFBC core members together at a coffee shop in Ashwaubenon. "To help capitalize on this momentum, IFBC should write a second letter to the WEDC requesting the return of contract funds," Alette suggested.

"OK, seems like a good time to take another shot at it. There was no joy earlier, so let's try again," I agreed after a sip of some wonderfully potent coffee. *This stuff will curl the hair on your face*, I thought with satisfaction as another sip was on the way.

IFBC's letter noted that, "the contract funding to construct energy recovery facilities appears to be improperly diverted to other purposes than permitted under the contracts without state approval." The *Press-Gazette* article attached to the letter detailed plans to wrongfully shift WEDC funding project to Outagamie County. The letter also stated, "Obviously, misdirecting state funds to a different project in Outagamie County breaches the terms of both contracts. It is unclear why WEDC failed to respond or initiate an investigation to recover taxpayer funds."

The Jerry Bader Show, *Press-Gazette*, and a local TV station were copied on the letter.

The *OneidaEye* also sent a request letter that spoke to a somewhat different aspect. As usual, Leah was devastating in her articulation. After noting that the state funds were being misdirected, she stated the General Tribal Council is scheduled to vote on a resolution to "prohibit OSGC from building an industrial commercial incinerator anywhere on the Oneida Reservation."

Leah also questioned the validity of the loans, pointing out that the contracts with the WEDC were signed by former OSGC officials whose terms had already expired, and that there was a lack of financial transparency going on with OSGC. "It is the appearance of nepotism, 'cart before the horse' decision making, slipshod mismanagement, an utter lack of transparency and accountability, as well as outright fraud that has some Oneida Tribe members discussing dissolving OSGC altogether."

That month also brought the conclusion of the waste wet digester saga down in Maribel. Although IFBC had little involvement since crashing the DNR open house way back on Day 499, our friends in Maribel had been keeping IFBC informed as the project progressed. The Ledge Guardians citizen group had done an excellent job opposing this proposed project over the past year. And now, just prior to board hearing the Guardians had advised Joanne and I that they feared that the vote was likely predetermined because they said one board member may have ties to the developer. It was time to see if we could lend a hand and be the element of uncertainty for the hearing.

Joanne and I drove down on a crisp, cool spring evening to the village board hearing. Citizen comments lasted about an hour and a half, during which there were no favorable remarks for the project. Comments were so one sided that there was nothing which could rationally be construed as being even marginally favorable to the developers. The numerous statements touched upon the suitability of the chosen location, waste dispersion from the proposed facility and its attendant environmental impacts, costs, property value losses, lack of transparency, the ever-changing outward-facing corporate identities, inconsistent representations, litigation potential, compliance with existing long-range planning, probable stench and runoff. I was very impressed at how well the folks there had done their homework.

Rather than being mere observers, Joanne and I both spoke to the board on a variety of topics. Joanne touched on the lack of honesty and transparency, and environmental impacts. Not wanting to beat a dead horse by reiterating comments already well articulated by the others, I took a chance, noting the possibility of personal liability exposure if a possible relationship between a board member and a developer were to be discovered. That might involve lawsuits by citizens whose homes dropped in value due to proximity to the digester, cleanup costs, remediation and so forth. I figured all we needed was to wake up just one board member as a unanimous board vote was required to approve the zoning application. Since a 3/4 vote in favor is required to pass and it's a 3-member board, the math works out to mean a unanimous vote was necessary to pass.

The Ledge Guardians and attending citizens were shocked and pleased when the outgoing board member voted against instead of in favor. He presented thoughtful reasons for his vote, including the potential litigation costs, fairness of spending substantial village resources to benefit only one business, dislike of the odd procedural deviations used for the issuing of the permit, distrust of an entity with a checkered past a lack of transparency as well as a constantly changing identity, and suitability of location.

The next morning, Joanne received an excited phone call, which she summarized in an email:

> John, just got a call at 9:40 this morning from Mike thanking us for coming. He said that the fact another group showed up to voice concerns made all the difference, especially with the dissenting board member. He said people listened because he heard comments after the meeting about legalities and damage to the environment being irreversible, especially damage to the water table--- with no recourse. (A man at the meeting told Mike that the worst thing he ever worked on professionally was damage to the aquifer in the U.P.) Also, the lawyer from Hobart was very impressed according to Mike. Mike said that next month they will be trying to

ram this thing through again and that they also fear that OSGC's incinerator might be targeting them next. He thanked us once more and said that we will be in touch.

Going forward, Joanne and I were advised that the incoming Maribel board member was against the project. He will have assumed office by the time of the next board meeting and his presence means that the project's future prospects flamed out. The Ledge Guardians would be keeping a close watch and would let IFBC know if anything begins to stir.

Ultimately, the proposed facility wasn't built.

CHAPTER 35

DAY 888

Hallelujah Chorus

"Call itself what it will, a spade is a spade."

— *Gentile v. Orthodontic Ctrs. of N.D., Inc.,*

2007 U.S. Dist. LEXIS 72322 (DC Colo. 2007)

Things truly heated up at the Day 888 General Tribal Council (GTC). It was recorded.

After the GTC got underway, one elder spoke at length about matters affecting the members' per capita distributions. Part of her comments referenced OSGC. "I also wanna say that this business committee is left with bad decisions made by previous business committees, and so are we. And what are some of those bad decisions?" she asked. "For almost 20 years we absolutely threw $500 million down in the toilet and got nothing for it. No apologies from leadership. It's good now that we have stopped the bad investments, to some degree. What does the Tribe continue to do not so well? Seven Generations and Thornberry Creek."

The speaker paused for a moment and then continued with a quick recitation of the audit reports detailing OSGC's financial misadventures, next noting they don't have the current "audit yet, but we do know that they claimed to the City of Green Bay that they spent $4 million that will be a loss if they don't retrieve it. Um, the BC voted, I just learned last week, to put aside $750,000 for their legal fees, and now they want $33 million for this new project. Seven Generations will tell the General Tribal Council that they're making money, but the paperwork, the evidence, does not support their untruths. Seven Generations is losing money for the Tribe."

Later she stated, "So I am asking you to support for three years while this Business Committee resolves the money that we're losing, the millions we're throwing away, they're trying hard, it needs to be done. We're spending $20 to $40 million a year that we don't need to be doing. We should be getting a $3 million a year profit from Seven Gens. They have $30 million of our real estate, they're supposed to generate income, not borrow from us. Not lose money. If we could stop that loss, we would be all very, very comfortable."

Later in the agenda a motion was made on the resolution to stop OSGC from building any gasification, waste-to-energy, or plastics recycling facility within the Oneida Tribal Reservation boundary. Leah stepped up to the microphone to speak about the motion. "I think the Oneida Tribe of Indians of Wisconsin should re-embrace the brand that was widely created in November of 2000, which makes it clear that we oppose noxious emissions, incinerators and dioxins anywhere."

Leah read aloud a prior official statement issued by a GTC several decades earlier, which put their collective opposition to dioxins and organic pollutants on record because of the dangers they represent to a land-based culture like Oneida's. After noting prominent members who affirmed the previous GTC statement, Leah continued. "The Business Committee was wise to take seriously the harms dioxin causes. IQ deficits, behavioral disorder, disrupted sexual development, immune system damage, birth defects, diabetes, and cancer. And a mother's womb exposes her offspring to dioxins that accumulated in her body in the years before conception. After they're born, babies continue to receive dioxins from their mother's breast milk."

Leah then asked, why would the Business Committee enthusiastically vote to support "OSGC taking the Oneida Tribe into millions of dollars of debt to invest in the incineration industry and build an incinerator on the Oneida Reservation as the resolution states?"

Leah then added, "Somehow, OSGC convinced the Business Committee that trying to turn a profit on dioxins was more important than protecting the people who'll be stuck with debts and disease. Here's what we know about OSGC. From bogus claims of 'not incineration' to 'no harmful emissions', to 'no stacks', to 'renewable energy', and 'plastics recycling', OSGC has told the public and elected officials several untruths.

"OSGC admits they plan to use pyrolysis and gasification to convert garbage into combustible materials, and then to burn, incinerate them and bury the ashes. Garbage sources they have talked about include tires, municipal solid waste, dairy waste, human sludge, and medical and hazardous waste. OSGC admits they will emit the following hazardous substances: dioxins, furans, formaldehyde, acetaldehyde, arsenic, lead, cadmium, chromium, fluoride, antimony, mercury, nickel, iron, copper, selenium, chlorides, hydrogen sulfide.

"OSGC's partner, Alliance Energy's DNR application identified their proposal as an MSW combuster. According to EPA.gov, the NSPS regulations define municipal waste combuster to mean any device that combusts gassified municipal solid waste, including gasification combustion units. A municipal waste incinerator combusts solid waste and thus is functionally synonymous with a municipal waste combuster. According to an email by Richard Angelbeck from EPA's Region 5 Permit Section, Gasification equals Combustion equals Incineration."

The audience began to grumble over what they were hearing because it most certainly was not aligned with OSGC's earlier presentations on the subject.

Returning to the podium, Leah finished her presentation. "Here's the justification for Gasification = Combustion. We look to the NSPS definition of Municipal Waste Combustion Unit, which includes equipment that combusts, gassified municipal solid waste, including pyrolysis combustion units. So, incineration equals combustion, and combustion includes gasification, therefore incineration includes gasification. Incineration turns landfill into sky-fill and sends one truck of toxic ash to the landfill for every 4 trucks of garbage burned. The gas, smoke and liquid solid waste that leave the facility will have the same mass as the solid materials entering the facility. Masses of gas and particulates will go up the stack, toxic ashes and solid waste will need to go to landfill, and liquid waste will also need to be managed.

'Now OSGC claims they want to recycle plastics, but incineration is not recycling. The EPA says recycling is activities by which materials that are no longer useful to the generator are collected, sorted, processed, and converted into raw materials and used in the production of new products. But this definition excludes using these materials as a fuel substitute or for energy production, which is exactly what OSGC proposes.

"Here's the truth about plastics-to-oil. Some companies have been caught lying about their finances to attract new investors. Companies are admitting feedstock costs are going up because they need higher grade plastics to make oil they can sell to refineries. Companies are admitting they often have to go offline to repair parts or fully replace parts more frequently than expected.

"Companies are admitting that the machines they originally proposed must be switched to newer models, and those have higher emissions than first claimed. The entire plastics-to-oil industry is totally dependent on society expanding the use once and toss mentality despite the true cost to humanity.

"Instead, we should toss out that short-sighted mindset and create incentives to dispose of the manufacture of non-recyclable goods in the first place and refuse to give corporations a way to falsely make their garbage seem like some kind of renewable energy resource." Leah finished shortly thereafter.

Following that were some parliamentary discussions moderated by the GTC chair, the resolution was presented for a vote. After the long meeting, Alette, Greg, Joanne and I exchanged high-fives when the GTC voted to adopt Leah's resolution and stop the proposed siting of the incinerator in the Town of Oneida.

"Poof! That's another painful checkmate for OSGC!" said Alette excitedly.

"Yes, and it really showed the common sense of the community members," Joanne agreed.

Later, Greg snorted a small laugh as we sat in my basement lair with a pair of beers. "Sure sounds like no one believes OSGC's baloney anymore."

I nodded. "Yup. Now we know for sure all the communities believe the same thing — that OSGC's promises to keep contamination out of the environment is like roping off a peeing section in a public pool!"

Congratulations for Leah's work poured in. Bradley Angel from Greenaction emailed:

CONGRATULATIONS AND THANK YOU FOR YOUR WORK ON BEHALF OF THE ONEIDA PEOPLE AND ONEIDA NATION, AND EVERYONE WHO CARES ABOUT OUR ENVIRONMENT, PEOPLE'S HEALTH, THE TRUTH, AND JUSTICE. Please extend my thanks and best wishes to the other tribal members who joined with you in fighting the terrible project."

A tribal elder's message to Leah, IFBC, Greenaction, CWAC, WEAL and others said:

The internet was alive yesterday nationally and internationally for your courage to save the Oneida people from harm and the great fight against the corrupt ones among the tribe.

American Indian pro Environmental groups and Sierra Club et al are spreading the word. There is much more work for you....

GAIA's email said:

Your powerful presentation and truth telling is inspiring to all of us!

The list of congratulations went on and on.

The story in the *Press-Gazette* on Day 889 stated that the GTC blocked the proposal to build the incinerator on sovereign tribal lands. Also included was a statement noting that the Wisconsin Governor had called a WEDC meeting after a "scathing audit" of the agency that stated WEDC "repeatedly failed to follow state laws, didn't track loans and awarded money to ineligible projects, among other things."

After reading the part of that article noting WEDC's problems in addition to the GTC outcome, I decided to keep up the momentum and sent a third letter to WEDC on Day 891 requesting claw back of the loan proceeds. I provided copies to a number of state legislators and media outlets, including a copy to the *Press-Gazette*.

The Sierra Club also sent a letter to WEDC. In a coordinated effort, it was sent the same day as the IFBC letter, appending the entirety of our letter and stating, "We wish to monitor this situation and ask to be added to any communications regarding this issue as pertains to the IFBC request. Please inform us of any communications or changes in the situation."

The third event occurring on Day 891 was a pleasant surprise. It was a large opinion piece representing the *Press-Gazette's* point of view about the incinerator. The headline read, "People have spoken; time to move on." This powerful editorial noted the staff sought process comparisons from OSGC about similar facilities to its proposal, and OSGC vaguely referred the editorial board to working plants far away, elsewhere in the U.S. and Europe. "We asked for specific examples and were never provided with them." The editorial also noted they were unable to locate any similar plants anywhere.

The editorial board concluded that there were a lot of questions that would need to be answered before any kind of waste to energy or other similar trash processing project could be re-proposed. The article concluded with, "The people of three communities have spoken. It's time for a different approach or to drop this project altogether."

I was surprised when the WEDC finally responded a few days after my Day 891 claw back request, stating the unsurprising position that WEDC will await the outcome of litigation and the appeal process. But

I thought, *at least it was FINALLY an acknowledgment*, although one which merely prompted additional letters.

Dean from CWAC and Charlene from WEAL sent letters to the WEDC on Day 893, expressing their desire to reinforce the requests coming from IFBC requesting the WEDC reclaim the unspent funds distributed and seek to recover funds already spent due to OSGC's misuse of funds. As WEAL had a number of unanswered questions, they were included in Charlene's letter with the proviso the WEDC was to consider them an open records request.

The WEDC's off-putting non-responses to the other's letters now prompted me to write a fourth IFBC letter, asking, "As WEDC has chosen to monitor an irrelevant lawsuit rather than recover clearly misappropriated taxpayer funds (evidenced by the news article clippings provided to you in IFBC's prior correspondence), can you advise IFBC under what circumstances WEDC will move to recover misappropriated funding?" WEDC failed to respond to that fourth letter.

The Day 899 edition of the *Kalihwisaks* carried an article about the adoption of the petition banning OSGC's proposed venture on tribal lands. OSGC's technical acumen was on full display with the article noting OSGC's "presentation featured technological glitches" so it was unable to present its show. Leah's comments in the article spoke to the growing rift between the GTC and OSGC.

"I'm proud of GTC for defending itself against OBC and OSGC which is the first step in showing the world that GTC isn't buying what OSGC is selling, and the next steps are to divest the Tribe of the incineration business and dissolve some corporations, while setting and enforcing higher standards for corporate behavior."

Leah meant every word.

CHAPTER 36

DAY 954

The Gathering Storm

"Accordingly, the clock began to tick..."

— *Paterson-Leitch Co. v. Massachusetts Municipal Wholesale Electric Co.*,
840 F.2d 985 (1st Cir. 1988)

For the next few short weeks things were relatively quiet. I put IFBC meetings on hiatus due to the nice weather and the lull in events. All messages were handled via email, texting or by phone. As the weather was so favorable, Greg and I spent a lot of time outside independently enjoying long rides on the bike trails. The other core team members were likewise busy enjoying the great outdoors.

I hope this incinerator project is dead at last, I thought. *It'd be nice to be able to stop worrying about it for once.*

However, this tranquil moratorium did not last. At the next after-hours IFBC meeting in the conference room of a local manufacturer in Ashwaubenon, Leah had arrived to guest-star for the evening because she carried incredible news. Over cookies and coffee, she told the group that the *Press-Gazette* was "interested in the Oneida movement to dissolve OSGC" and would soon run an article about it. "I'm helping orchestrate a full court press to consign OSGC to the dustbin of history, and the effort has a lot of moving parts to it."

Greg, Alette, Joanne and I were stunned. "You mean the time has come to go for the jugular?" I asked while still trying to process this bombshell news.

"You bet," Leah replied. "It took a long time to get a hold of the actual documents and verifiable financial figures, but myself and a few others think we've now got exactly what we need. OSGC went off the rails a long time ago, but all this time it had its financial hooks into the just the right people to keep the heat off.

"Now, between its mismanagement, environmental missteps, and documents proving how much money it has actually been losing, OSGC has finally managed to make everyone really upset. So, we think now is the perfect time — while it's weakened."

"Wow, you have done some incredible work, Leah!" Elaine exclaimed as she passed along the plate of cookies as it was migrating down the table. "Did you let the *Press-Gazette* in on the plans?"

Leah nodded. "I received a call from the paper about OSGC when I messaged about possibly dissolving the company. The *Press-Gazette* editorial staff was wondering whether we have a realistic chance."

"Well, I sure hope you do. You've done an awesome job!" I added. "But we sure don't have a crystal ball giving us insight into the chances, for obvious reasons."

Elaine nodded. "My Oneida Nation friends are pretty certain that the people are fed up with OSGC and have had enough of its antics. They have had it with all the money the company has thrown away, all the bad business deals, the bad press, and the problems that go on and on."

"Well it will sure be great to finally get the true numbers out there," Greg added. "The project financing was a constantly moving target all along, since OSGC kept throwing out inconsistent numbers to the public."

Taking a bite of her cookie and then wiping the crumbs off her mouth, Leah responded. "I'm hearing the same thing over and over again from everywhere in Oneida. There's just so much anger over the lost money, and the people are tired of being embarrassed by OSGC. Naturally enough, people don't like being lied to. While we don't have an official poll, our sense is that the numbers are there to finally do away with that company.

"We also think that the data on losses and lack of responsibility has been uncovered enough to really move the needle for people who have been undecided."

Elaine shook her head, saying, "Wow! Just wow! Actually dissolving OSGC would just be huge. Earthquake huge. What a message it would send!"

The *Press-Gazette* article came out on Day 954 under the headline "End of Oneida company sought" with a subheading reading "Petitioners are fed up with Seven Generations Corp." Noting that only 50 signatures were needed to call an *ad hoc* GTC, the petitioners collected hundreds of signatures to send a message to tribal leaders. "This was just a sign of solidarity," the article quoted Leah as saying. "The people are speaking."

OSGC continued as if tone-deaf, issuing a statement that read, "questioned whether the petition effort was based on correct information about the company's activities." It seems again that OSGC can never see past the trees into the forest, where its actions continually caused an uproar.

The *Press-Gazette's* article also noted another individual, who was backing the petition drive to dissolve OSGC, who said an audit shows OSGC paid more than $600,000 a year in salaries to just four employees. "The people see this now; they see what's happening. They want to stop this."

Another noteworthy effort was that of obtaining hundreds of signatures in a parallel effort to oust the tribal chairman for his support of OSGC. The *Press-Gazette* reported on it, stating that the chairman, "and his backers suspect the petition is motivated by support for Oneida Seven Generations Corp., a tribal owned economic development company that has stirred controversy with a waste-to-energy plant proposal." The ousting failed, but the message it sent was loud and clear.

FOX11 reported on Day 953 that several Oneida Tribal members "walked their latest hopes of dissolving Oneida Seven Generations Corporation into tribe headquarters, Tuesday." One of them was reported as saying, "getting rid of OSGC would save family time, possible investigation by the federal government, and most importantly, money spent fighting a lawsuit against the City of Green Bay."

And then, on Day 1010 I was utterly astounded to see that NBC26 broke unexpected news, reporting that the OSGC CEO had resigned and moved out of state. Leah Dodge stated to reporter Brian Miller that she was "surprised, but not shocked." She continued, "For OSGC to continue to promote or to try to sell incinerators to other reservations is unconscionable." *Are we seeing the beginning of the end?* I asked myself as I watched the news unfolding.

One thing IFBC had repeatedly observed over the prior thousand plus days was the phenomenon of unaccountable companies (and government bureaucrats) continuing their behavior because they have come to believe they need not abide by the mundane rules applicable only to the *little people*. While providing fodder for IFBC members to jokingly imitate OSGC's approach as 'Don't you know who we are?' and 'You're not smart enough to understand our genius' it was clear that such behavior would continue until someone put a hard stop to it.

Once again, that stop came when OSGC was caught flouting the GTC's new ban on burning. On Day 1045, both Leah and a tribal elder joined IFBC's core members for some after hours coffee and snacks at a meeting. We all enjoyed an enthusiastic discussion to see what could be spun up after a relatively quiet summer. I could immediately see that both Leah and special guest were really angry that OSGC had blatantly disregarded GTC's burn ban by operating a small, test sized trash incinerator in Oneida.

"This flagrant disregard of GTC's ban has really infuriated many in Oneida," said the elder. "It smells like a 'Rules for Thee, but Not for Me' attitude, and that doesn't sit well with the people."

Leah agreed. "Wow, people really hit the roof when they heard OSGC got caught incinerating, especially near the daycare center. How stupid was that?"

Alette was shocked, although not entirely. "What, OSGC didn't think it would get caught? Don't the rules apply to OSGC?"

I laughed. "C'mon! Rules are only for us little people! They don't apply to big, important companies. Just ask OSGC. It'll be happy to tell you how important it is."

Greg chuckled in response. "OSGC has been happy enough to bend or completely ignore the rules from day one. And then tell everyone we don't know what we're talking about. I'm going to enjoy watching OSGC get hoisted by its own petard!"

It didn't take long for the *Press-Gazette* to report on the flap. The Day 1090 report, opening with, "Oneida company questioned about 'open burning'" was brutal. It said tribal leaders were taking action against OSGC for "allowing a business that critics describe as an illicit trash incinerator."

The discovery was made by a fire inspector, who reported it improperly included 'open flame devices.' Absurdly, after getting caught ignoring the rules OSGC again promised to respect and obey GTC law, but by then few believed the veracity of OSGC's promises.

CHAPTER 37

DAY 1110

Judgment Day:
Doctrine of Just Desserts

"You hear that Mr. Anderson? ... That is the sound of
inevitability... It is the sound of your death."

— Agent Smith, *The Matrix*

D ay 1110 was Judgment Day. It was the inexorable day of reck-
oning for OSGC. We listened to a recording of it while sam-
pling some adult beverages and enjoying the festivities.

The specially called GTC that day was highly contentious. After
the motions and voting in the lengthy parliamentary portion of this
recorded session, a member was granted fifteen-five minutes of unin-
terrupted time for his presentation about OSGC and the debt bombs it
incurred.

Thus began a remarkable presentation. "Thank you. Before I get into
my speech, I know it's the Christmas season so I want to wish you all
goodwill no matter how this turns out. I trust the judgment of the Gen-

eral Tribal. When I say General Tribal, that means you, and you, and you."

The speaker paused for a breath, then continued. "And because this is a General Tribal, it's a special General Tribal. Normal ones occur in December and July. This is not a business committee, so I'm going to respectfully request that all the members of the business committee with the exception of the chairman, and the secretary to record it, leave the stage and find a place in the audience." As he paused, applause could be heard in the background. The business committee chairman declined to acquiesce to the request.

The speaker continued. "Today, Seven Gen has run up a debt of over $20 million. Where there are federal dollars involved, the federal court will come after the federal recognized tribe. And we could end up in Chapter 11 bankruptcy in federal court. If you get the FBI in here, somebody's going to jail and we could lose some of our income. If we allow this to continue, it will affect our per capita. But today, we don't need the business committee to tell us what to do. We together, the GTC, can do what we want to do. Something that the business committee hasn't done in 17 years. Dissolve Seven Gens. Show the first slide please. Seven Gens has collected over $2.5 million in one year alone in rent money for the Tribe. $1,862,675 in rent alone for the Tribe. Our money! They use this money as collateral to borrow more money for themselves. They kept the Tribal money and use our rent money as collateral. Show the next slide. This is against Article 4, Section 1C of the Constitution. You cannot encumber Tribal assets. The Constitution says that the General Tribal Council, that's you, of the Tribe shall veto any encumbrance of Tribal assets."

"Article 9 — show the next one — of their own charter, it states under Distribution of Profits, directs them to turn that profit back to the Tribe. They could keep 25% for managing the contract, and the net. We'll get 75% of the net back. Seven Gens has waived its sovereign immunity in all financial transactions. Look at the bottom of the slide. In other words, they agreed to be sued in state court, and agree it'll apply to the judgments. Show the next slide. Seven Gens is grantor on bank notes of failed business ventures to the millions of dollars. They said that these notes were secured by real estate. 'Grantor' is one who makes a guarantee, and a guarantee is a formal pledge to pay back the obligation."

The speaker again asked for the next slide. "This is against Article 4, Section 1, paragraph C of our Constitution, the Powers of the General Tribal Council. It states, the General Tribal Council, you of the Oneida Tribe of Wisconsin, shall veto any encumbrance of the tribal lands or interest in tribal lands. Show the next slide. Their own charter, Article 17, Limitations of Power, under Paragraphs C and D, states that the corporation may not encumber any real property of the Oneida Nation or secure a loan or incur indebtedness, or require an obligation or a guarantee on the part of the Nation. Seven Gens is not paying back the principle on some of the notes. Show the next slide. You'll notice that a certain paragraph, the last paragraph, that they're interest only payments."

The speaker then discussed the audit reports in everyone's printed meeting handouts and noted the current liabilities. "If we don't pay that required, it'll go up to $10 million by the end of the contract." He continued revealing even more details. "We're going in the hole every day. On top of that, they're trying to extend the contracts. They have no intention to repay these loans! Read the auditors note below. And the auditor's note reads, the corporation and its lenders are negotiating extending the terms of the loan.

"The corporation expects to renew the current agreement on a long-term basis with terms sooner than the arrangements. Accordingly, the debt remains classified as long term as management does not anticipate repayment of these notes in amounts in excess of the estimated scheduled payments. This is in violation of the contracts and their charter. Only the business is going to profit from this. They are supposed to repay us, the tribe. That's our profit." The speaker then discussed salaries and meeting expenses of the corporation.

After further financial discussion, the speaker concluded with the following, "If we dissolve Seven Gens today, we can assign the rental units to the property manager in the Division of Land Management. And we could collect the $2.5 million. Show that last slide, please. We could pay off all the debts and it would take us four years and nine months. Then we could increase our per capita. We only have 16,808 Indians on the tribal roll, and we're getting $2.5 million profit. You guys figure it out. Last month on the 22nd, you just saw what Seven Gens, they were caught again, experimenting with an open burn project in their head office. It was written in the *Press-Gazette*.

"They're in violation of the tribal laws, they're in violation of the charter, and they're in violation of the Constitution. Now I'd like to propose, show the next one, a resolution to dissolve them. I hope you'll second that motion.

"I motion that we accept that resolution to dissolve Seven Gens. You get that one the board? We have a motion made and second, Mr. Chairman. I call for the vote. Thank you."

There was a loud round of applause at the conclusion of the informative presentation.

Following that presentation and a parliamentary procedural discussion, a report was presented detailing a third-party auditor's predicted financial impact of dissolving OSGC. The 'significant financial risks' were described such that "the tribe and OSGC do not have unilateral rights to transfer its interests in the various business ventures that Seven Generations holds. The operating agreements of each business venture have specific provisions governing the transfer and withdrawals of interests on a both voluntary and involuntary basis. On a voluntary basis, Seven Generations should get fair market value for their interests. But if the joint venture partners view this as an involuntary transfer, the tribe and the Seven Generations might get book value."

After hearing the counter presentation, I grunted with satisfaction before saying, "Well, *that* was less than compelling. OSGC is suddenly worried every last penny can't be squeezed from selling off a few small ventures while the company hopes no one sees the debt elephant in the room."

Greg nodded. "Red herrings to distract."

"Red herrings indeed," I agreed. "Even now OSGC keeps trying to distract."

OSGC's presenter continued. "The other issue that is of great importance is the debt agreements that Seven Generations has. There is approximately $25.3 million of debt that is being held right now at this level, and in order to transfer these debts on to the books of the tribe, consent needs to be given by the lenders. If the lender does not give consent, it is possible under the loan agreement, that they could call the loans in for early repayment and cause significant financial strain to the tribe."

The presenter recommended a thorough due diligence regarding moving the debts to the tribal balance sheets, plus a thorough legal analysis, and cautioned the audience to expect significant transactional costs to accomplish a dissolution. The speaker concluded by pointing out that most concerns with OSGC can be addressed through lesser measures to limit its freedom to act instead of dissolution.

Alette couldn't contain her surprise. "25 freaking MILLION in debt? That's way higher than they had been letting on before. Oh wow!"

Greg sat up straighter, too. "With OSGC having hidden that much debt, I'm thinking they sealed their fate. Listen to the rumbling of the audience. They're sounding pretty upset. This isn't going well for OSGC."

The GTC, after more parliamentary discussion, voted to dissolve OSGC!

The IFBC foursome and Elaine all high-fived each other, whooping our approval at hearing this the taking of another huge step in the beginning of the end of OSGC.

WFRV reported on Day 1110 about the dissolution vote and interviewed the chairman stating that they will try to provide the most orderly process for the dissolution. The Day 1113 edition of the *Press-Gazette* reported on the dissolution and quoted Leah as saying, "We couldn't trust [the corporation] to do the right thing and we couldn't trust the business committee to hold them accountable, so we had to."

IFBC core members were still jubilant at our meeting later that week in the Ashwaubenon business park in a company's conference room. Elaine also attended, and our discussion quickly grew serious. "You all were the bravest group of citizens I have ever had the pleasure to meet. You never wavered, never got down, always maintained a great sense of humor, and never let OSGC get to you. But now, it's important not to be perceived as gloating over OSGC's fate," Elaine cautioned.

Echoing Elaine's comments, I added, "Like usual, we can make all the fun of OSGC we want just among ourselves, but always show our game face to the public. Besides, just like any other internal tribal politics, OSGC's dissolution isn't a subject IFBC ever discusses as that is in someone else's wheelhouse if it comes up. We don't have a comment on such things, and we as a group have never directly spoken to those topics."

"Is the company just gone now, or does it need time to wrap up its affairs?" Alette asked.

"If it follows the dissolution trajectory of other entities, it will take a fair amount of time to wrap up its affairs however long that takes," I replied.

Focusing on the dissolution process, Elaine shared what her sources were saying. "The powers that be are already maneuvering to prevent the dissolution. They will try to portray dissolution as too costly and try to use that as a justification to continue."

We all discussed the dissolution at length and arrived at the determination that we would have to keep applying pressure until there was no chance of OSGC rising from the dead. Once started down the path to oblivion, until OSGC was completely dissolved, IFBC and OSGC would be in a race against time. But at this point it looked like a race where OSGC might still have the clock, but it was IFBC who now had the time.

At about this same time there was more welcome news. First, we saw a well written letter from an opponent of the incinerator thanking all the fellow tribal members for their commitment and partnership in dissolving OSGC. "Years from now those of you who stood up and forced the BC to dissolve 7 Gens will be remembered as helpers; and those who did not will be judged by the passing of time as non-supporters of honest government."

And second was a public congratulations of IFBC from the Center for Health, Environment & Justice for putting "an end to a proposed gasification plant in both Ashwaubenon and Green Bay."

CHAPTER 38

DAY 1172

Undead

"We've passed the point of beating a dead horse--now were
tenderizing it."

— *Texas Instruments, Inc. v. Hyundai Electronics Industries, et al.,*
49 F. Supp. 2d 893 (ED Tex. 1999)

Although one court of appeal opinion memorably called it flag-ellating a deceased equine, to me this phase of the campaign felt more like zombie hunting. Just to remind the WEDC that IFBC's love and attention was still focused on ending OSGC's influence in the incineration world, I sent a fifth letter requesting claw back of the funds now that OSGC's end was approaching. As expected, the WEDC again failed to respond to us beyond acknowledging receipt of the letter. However, the WEDC did react by sending out a default notice on one of the loans.

"Dissolution of Seven Generations constitutes a business failure and Event of Default under Section 6 of the Loan Agreement referenced as SEP FY10-20265 (Agreement). Additionally, Seven Generations failure to meet the Deliverables in Exhibit A Section 3 of the Agreement results in interest escalation to four (4) percent retroactive to the date of disbursement under Exhibit A Section 4. If Seven Generations fails to cure the default to the reasonable satisfaction of WEDC," the letter read. "WEDC will, without further written notice, declare you in default and demand payment from you of the entire balance of the contract $2,063,730.92."

Below that, in bold text, was the statement "We ask you to pay $2,063,739.92 to WEDC immediately." It was unclear why there was a $9 difference between the amounts unless it was attributable to its being a typo since the letter was also mis-dated, but I was happy to see the state agency finally start to move on the loans.

I also received a copy of WEDC's Day 1172 follow-up letter to OSGC memorializing an extension agreement on the loan. It made me think of the GTC presentation last month. *A loan extension. Of course, OSGC couldn't pay any principle, only interest. Just like the speaker had pointed out in the dissolution meeting when he addressed OSGC's debt troubles.*

In exchange for WEDC delaying legal action to recover the funds while OSGC pursues legal appeals and new financing to pursue the project or pay off the WEDC loan, OSGC will make interest-only payments for a few months. After that, OSGC will begin to make monthly payments of $34,998, and repay the loan balance in a few months — or demonstrate that the contract deliverable goals will be met. As I read those terms, I thought, *if OSGC can demonstrate it is still going to build an incinerator, then the loan balance doesn't come due right away. Unacceptable!.*

Although IFBC members were delighted our persistent letter writing stung OSGC yet again and caused a bit more bleeding, our core committee was unclear about our next actions. But momentum unexpectedly picked up a few days later when the Sierra Club published a write up on the incinerator saga. "No plasma or pyrolysis gasification plan has ever been successfully deployed for managing municipal solid waste in the United States. Wisconsin should not be a guinea pig for the rest of the nation taking an expensive economic and environmental gamble on this technology." This from a Sierra Club volunteer with decades of experience in waste management.

The write up detailed the extravagant government waste just to fund OSGC's proposed incinerator, and concluded, "Considering the unproven nature of pyrolysis and plasma gasification, the potential for toxic air emissions and hazardous ash, and the risk of undermining recycling and renewable energy, the John Muir Chapter urges communities to invest in better alternatives to these "magic bullets" for handling municipal solid waste. More energy and more jobs can be created with projects that encourage recycling, foster real renewables, avoid landfilling and incineration, and hold producers."

CHAPTER 39

The Bills Come Due?

"No rogue should enjoy his ill-gotten plunder for the simple reason that his victim is by chance a fool."

— *Chamberlin v. Fuller*, 9 A. 832, 59 Vt. 247 (VT 1886)

Leah called IFBC together because of some news she had received from her work as editor of the *OneidaEye*. She routinely kept everyone up to speed on the dizzying array of OSGC business dealings, and she now advised us that OSGC was about to be sued by a vendor. While this wasn't a surprise to me that unpaid vendors would sue to obtain payment from a troubled company facing dissolution, the enormous amount of damages claimed in the suit was rather staggering. Greg asked, "Do you think the tribe would be on the hook for that kind of cash? The numbers around this proposed incinerator just never seem to consistently add up."

"Hard to tell as I don't know exactly what's in the complaint and it's impacted by an area of law which isn't in my wheelhouse," I responded. "I suspect not, for a variety of factors, including the discrepancies between the dollars being requested and the public claims of how much OSGC suggested it would reap by incinerating trash."

"It's been a longstanding concern for the tribe, that as sole owner of OSGC, there could be exposure for OSGC's acts if a lawyer out there would try to use that to pierce the corporate veil," Elaine mentioned. "That and the financial missteps are just some of many reasons why OSGC has been getting a brighter light shined on its activities."

As predicted by Leah, on Day 1193 OSGC and the Oneida Tribe were named as defendants in a lawsuit over the incinerator lease/facilities management contracts signed by OSGC. The *Press-Gazette* carried a top of the fold, front page headline which stated, "Oneida tribe targeted in $400 million suit over energy deal". As Leah had indicated, the suit was filed out of state by a business vendor for lease payments, revenues and other benefits. Neither tribal leadership nor OSGC offered any comment to the media over the lawsuit.

The article continued, "John Filcher, a leader of Incinerator Free Brown County, a group opposed to the waste-to-energy development, said he was surprised by some revelations in the suit. He noted that the disputed contracts allegedly were signed long after Oneida officials had encountered widespread opposition to the project. 'You have to wonder what in the world they were thinking,'" Noting the large amount of damages sought, I had also told the paper that naming the tribe as a defendant was potentially significant and recalled saying, "The deep pocket here would be the tribe itself."

I found it interesting that the article didn't mention my statement to the paper that it's hard to comment on a litigation complaint that I had not yet read, but I was certainly gratified to see some of the remaining discussion made it into the article.

CHAPTER 40

DAY 1220

New Life

"Were this case not so tragic,
it could quite properly be classified as 'A Comedy of Errors'."
— *United States v. Applewhaite*, 195 F.3d 679 (3rd Cir. 1999)

IFBC's run of good news against OSGC was about to hit a rough patch. On a blustery spring Day 1212 the Court of Appeals reversed the trial court's judgment in favor of the City. Feeling it did not need to address all of OSGC's arguments, the Court of Appeals stated that a municipality possesses the authority to revoke a CUP based on misrepresentations made during the permit process, but the "operative questions are whether the City exercised that authority in an arbitrary manner, and without substantial supporting evidence." When IFBC gathered that evening to discuss this ruling, I noted, "The court's analysis means the City's procedural shortcomings are coming back to bite the City in the butt."

"Check this out," I pointed out to our gang. The "operative questions are whether the City exercised that authority in an arbitrary manner, and without substantial supporting evidence."

The court continued its analysis regarding the City's too-clever-by-half method of slyly publishing a the original permit application notice that barely suggested anything about OSGC's project to the reader, which was coming back to bite the City in the butt. "Fickle and inconsistent fairly describe the City's action here. The City's initial Plan Commission and Common Council meetings were noticed public meetings. It does not appear there was any significant opposition to Seven Generations' proposal. Public opposition grew during the state and federal environmental review process.

"Having failed to persuade those agencies, project opponents turned their attention back to the Common Council, which they successfully persuaded to revoke the CUP on misrepresentation grounds. The City did so despite the Plan Commission's specific finding that there were no misrepresentations and without ever identifying the allegedly false statements."

As we had discussed what we perceived to be a major problem for the City over a year ago, the City's procedural shortcomings in rescinding the CUP continued to cause it problems. "Even more dismaying than the City's failure to mention the findings of its own Plan Commission, though, is its failure to articulate any rationale for its revocation decision" and that none of the City's findings "identify the supposedly false statements with any specificity." As would be expected by the City's procedural deficiencies in both rescinding the CUP and skipping Discovery, the City came to court empty handed, so the Court found that the "absence of any identifiable false statements in the City's decision is troubling." Accordingly, "We cannot trace the City's reasoning because it prematurely stops."

On Day 1213 the City Attorney said in a written statement that the city is "reviewing its options." The Council President's statement indicated he did not believe the City had done anything wrong.

I responded to the *Press-Gazette* by noting that IFBC found the decision disappointing, and that it was unclear how this decision impacts the $400 suit by the vendor.

Dean from CWAC also cautioned that the decision "opens the door to companies coming in and saying what they think the city needs to hear and doing something totally different."

On Day 1242 the City filed an appeal with the Wisconsin Supreme Court. When I heard about the appeal, I thought, *unfortunately OSGC's suit was still alive, because a dissolving company is entitled to wind up its operations, including ongoing litigation.*

Meanwhile, IFBC and WEAL were getting involved in opposing another proposed trash incinerator for the Village of Mukwonago, elsewhere in Wisconsin. Using the numbers OSGC had filed with the DNR and the DNR's calculations of wastewater, I noted that, for the Village, it might similarly expect its proposed project to discharge 1,935,960 gallons of highly contaminated wastewater into the Mukwonago River each year.

The proposed Village of Mukwonago incinerator was never granted an operating permit.

CHAPTER 41

DAY 1421

Very Appealing

"In law, as is life, the devil you know
is better than the devil you don't."

— *Am. Horse Prot. Ass'n, Inc. v. Veneman*, 200 F.R.D. 153 (DC 2001)

Realizing Green Bay had some 'splaining to do, and having very limited facts to work with, the City's initial brief to the Wisconsin Supreme Court on Day 1421 focused on articulating why it believed the Court of Appeals used the wrong legal review standard and substituted its judgment of the evidence in place of the City's.

The information contained in the Midwest Environmental Associates letter submitted by CWAC again figured prominently in the City's briefing. As has been repeatedly mentioned earlier, the City's decision to skip Discovery meant it had to keep including things like letters in its briefs because the City inexplicably tied its own hands.

About the actual permit rescission hearing on Day 687, the brief had this to say: "At that same meeting, a vote was taken on a motion to declare the CUP void based upon the following conclusions:

"That representatives of OSGC 'made untruthful statements before City governmental bodies while seeking the CUP. These false statements were made in response to questions or concerns related to the public safety and health aspect of the project and the project's impact upon the City's environment.' Those statements were 'plain spoken, contained no equivocation, left no impression of doubt or uncertainty, and the 'words were intended to influence the actions of the governmental bodies.' Finally, the representatives knew such 'statements were false' and they 'provided false information'."

Ultimately, there were few substantive differences between this version of the City's brief and prior editions filed with the lower courts. As I looked through the by now familiar briefing styles, I noted for the hundredth time, "Procedural hiccups continue to be a festering problem for Green Bay."

OSGC's briefing by now had acquired a decidedly more polished and aggressive tone to likewise repackage the same information for the next level of review. By now, OSGC heavily emphasized the mutually irreconcilable conclusions of the Plan Commission and the Common Council for the permit rescission. Try as it might, the City's efforts to explain away mutually irreconcilable actions by characterizing the Planning Commission's conclusions as having no weight simply never sounded persuasive. The City wouldn't be getting hoisted by its own petard now if it hadn't purportedly fixed the outcome of the Plan Commission hearing back on Day 674.

OSGC's lawyers peppered their brief with claims of statements having been "ripped out of context", that OSGC "is outraged at the City's position", and that the City's argument was "novel". As I read the briefs and looked beyond such argumentative new language, OSGC's brief seemed to otherwise just be a rehashing of the lower court briefing — with the noteworthy addition of a section titled, "The Opposition Groups Change Tactics". In this section, OSGC said, "Instead, the opposition groups began to pressure the Common Council to reconsider the CUP." The brief also stated, "OSGC objected, pointing out that it had presented extensive information about potential emissions to the Plan Commission and the Council, and that DNR and DOE had reviewed the potential emissions in detail as the CUP had specified."

"OSGC objected." I couldn't help but go back to the video of the hearing to compare what had been said. In the video of the Day 498, Common Council meeting, OSGC's then attorney clarified his response after duly noting an objection. "I'm telling you that the Conditional Use Permit has been issued. I will recommend to my client to get back to the city here if there are some specific questions that want to be answered. I would recommend that they answer some questions that you may have that are relevant to the Conditional Use Permit, and I think that's what I would recommend and take back to my client. I'm not prepared here to speak for my client on behalf of whether it should be referred under the circumstances that I've heard today, back to the Planning Commission. And I urge you to remember two things that I've said here. It will be built in accordance with the zoning requirements, including stack heights."

After reviewing that video again, I was left with the impression that the objection was clarified to be merely that attorney's personal objection and not OSGC's. I don't know why the full context didn't seem to be communicated in the briefs. *Maybe it came at some later hearing or meeting or something?* I wondered.

The City's Day 1467 reply brief began by noting OSGC began its "brief with a quote from Casablanca to advance the notion that the City of Green Bay ("City") was 'wholly insincere' when it revoked the Conditional Use Permit ("CUP") at issue. OSGC's brief is indeed littered with phrases like 'pure makeweight' and 'sandbagged' to describe its view of the City's decision." To which the City responded with a quote from Hamlet, noting OSGC "doth protest too much" in describing OSGC's "indecorous posturing."

Again looking past the unnecessary theatrics and pejoratives, the main theme in the reply brief argued that the Court of Appeals simply applied the wrong standard of review and that, had it applied a more deferential standard, it would have upheld the City's rescission as there was sufficient evidence to support the City's action. The City also high-lighted another change in OSGC's posturing in the briefing. "OSGC now concedes that its proposed Facility would not be identical to facil-ities elsewhere. OSGC's Br. At 66. OSGC could have easily shared this same information during the application process but did not. Instead, OSGC touted the technology as proven."

After I finished reviewing the multiple exchanges of filed briefs by the parties, I leaned back in my desk chair in my basement lair and took a sip of tonight's beverage of choice, a peanut butter nitro porter. Sitting quietly for a few moments, I finally thought, *the City is going to lose. Again.* Appropriately, a raspy blues song about changing luck was softly playing in the background.

CHAPTER 42

Follow the Dollar

"The district court, however, as the finder of fact, heard substantial evidence that these efforts were, at best, a day late and a dollar short."

— *Cobell v. Norton*, 345 U.S. App. D.C. 141, 240 F.3d 1081 (Ct. App. DC 2001)

One of the prescient statements by Alderman Guy Zima way back at the Day 498 City Council meeting had been to "follow the dollar." Coupled with his cautionary verbiage at that time to look into who was receiving campaign donations, that dollar trail might well lead to interesting places. And lo and behold, that trail led directly to City Hall for Green Bay!

On a cold, bright sunny Day 1498, unexpected news broke about improper campaign donations to the mayor. Hearing this news, IFBC core members were soon busy on their phones. "What does it mean?" Alette asked when I answered her call.

"I dunno. We need some more context to help make sense of why this is important because we don't know what the alleged impropriety actually is yet."

Some context was soon provided by Wisconsin Public Radio's Patty Murray, who reported, "the audit will review three years of incumbent mayor Jim Schmitt's records."

The next morning, the *Press-Gazette* reported that the audit was requested by three members of the City council, including one supporting an opponent of the mayor in the upcoming election race.

The mayor's statement referred to the audit as a "theatrical, and a political attack."

The Day 1499 *Press-Gazette* ran a long front page article headlined "POLITICALLY MOTIVATED?" with the sub header, "Alleged violations go beyond campaign finance reports, attackers say".

Mr. Schmitt's old nemesis, Alderman Guy Zima, held a press conference with another alderman to call for an audit pursuant to what the paper described as "The news conference followed a Press-Gazette Media story that Schmitt's campaign finance filings show about $10,000 of possibly illegal donations." The *Press-Gazette* said Mr. Wery made it clear they were not caught "off-guard" by the reports, suggesting they had been examining the mayor's campaign finances the past few weeks.

Reading and listening to all these stories and watching the Aldermen's press conference, I couldn't help but wonder, *Yes, but up to $10,000 in illegal contributions from WHOM?*

While it was unclear why it would take weeks to examine the mayor's 24-page Campaign Finance Statement listing the donations, I decided to get busy connecting the dots. The first dot seemed to be Mr. Zima's statement back in the Day 498 council meeting about following the money to see who benefited, and to look at campaign donations. "I think we have to watch where campaign contributions come and go from. I think we have to pay attention to who stands to gain, and who stands to lose. I mean, at this point in time the public, I think rightfully so, is more than suspicious about this," Mr. Zima had said at the time.

Talking among ourselves, I surmised for Greg and Alette, "Back on Day 498, I'm guessing Mr. Zima may have already been alluding to the now breaking kerfuffle over campaign donations. I'm now thinking he already suspected something at that time and has been waiting for years to spring a trap coinciding with the next upcoming election!"

Greg just shook his head. "Oh man! How would he have known? Or is it a coincidence?"

I shrugged. "No idea. Could be either of those. Could be something else entirely. No way to tell because we have no line of sight into what's going on for that kind of stuff."

If nothing else, we thought the political gamesmanship of dueling statements in the *Press-Gazette* between the mayor and his foes made for an interesting spectacle of local politics.

The mayor initially tried to stay out in front of the matter by characterizing to the effort as a smear attack, and protested with the following: "Make absolutely no mistake, if there were errors made they were made with no malicious intent … and they will be promptly dealt with." He further threw down the rhetorical gauntlet by welcoming the audit to put the matter to rest. The mayor also dismissively referred to his accusers as "unhappy" with a "need to be angry at somebody".

My personal view was that perhaps the mayor failed to heed the Hamlet quote, "doth protest too much" in the City's own brief to the Supreme Court just a month earlier.

This linked directly to the second, more obvious dot which appeared a few days later. On Day 1499 the *Press-Gazette* wrote, "reports also indicate a few instances of donations coming from corporations, which is forbidden under campaign finance laws."

My personal attitude towards campaign finance limits is that they are both likely unconstitutional (as infringing upon the freedom of speech) and are just a farcical way for politicians to play 'gotcha' with each other. On the other hand, I am much more interested in who made these donations rather than in some artificial dollar limits.

The *Press-Gazette* also reported that, "One of those donations, for $500, reportedly came from Oneida Seven Generations, a corporation," and noted Zima and another alderman both "suggested a donation not only was illegal but also may have influenced Schmitt into supporting the corporation's failed efforts to build a waste incineration plant in the city."

Finally, I thought, *connecting the dots is actually forming a picture!*

At the next IFBC meeting that evening, Elaine commented, "The second dot connects OSGC and the mayor to the incinerator in a way that really lit up the IFBC Christmas tree! I can't imagine how damaging this is for everyone's reputations!"

I smiled. "I know I keep joking during our meetings that math is hard, and I like to keep things simple, so two was the limit of my dot connecting here. We just don't know if OSGC's campaign donation is the missing puzzle piece that helps partially explain a whole lot of stuff, like why the city was so reluctant to re-look into the circumstances of the permit's quick approval, the hiccups during litigation, and so on. Quite an interesting little scandal, really."

My own review of the mayor's 24-page long Campaign Registration Statement was also intriguing. Greg and I identified at least one other donation from someone we suspected had a connection to the contractors who were supposed to build the incinerator. "We had better stay silent on those, since the OSGC campaign donation speaks for itself," I suggested.

"Yeah," Greg agreed. "We're not involved in the campaign finance scandal. We don't have a role to play here."

The Day 1499 broadcast of the Jerry Bader Show on WTAQ was interesting. Jerry, who was not a fan of the mayor, played it straight. After an interview with one of the aldermen and some discussion, Jerry posed a thoughtful question. "But is there more there, there?" Exactly the same question we found ourselves asking.

The protesting too much, personally attacking the aldermen and OSGC's 'donation' had clearly made Jerry suspicious. "The dumbest thing you can do is posture as though you have something to hide if you really don't have something to hide."

This far, I was still strongly leaning towards treating these campaign finance foibles as a moderately interesting sideshow ultimately leading to little meaningful change. Over coffee at a coffee shop in Ashwaubenon, our little core group gathered to assess the situation on Saturday morning.

"I'm just thinking this is no different than the other campaign finance dust-ups that seem to make the news. It's a 'gotcha' formula that always seems to feature a little smoke, some mirrors, ritualistic denunciations and pearl clutching," I summarized. "Then the kerfuffle concludes with the accused muttering a few contrite sounding but empty statements about clerical mistakes having been made before they return the contraband donation. Once the political class finishes dunking on each other in this bizarre ritual, everyone moves on."

"I was afraid you were going to say that," Alette responded. "I always hope someone will pay a price for these shenanigans, but it seems like they never do."

This sentiment seemed to be echoed by the Brown County District Attorney, who told WLUK on Day 1498, "And this is what the mayor turned over to the city clerk, which to me suggests that it's more likely an accounting error, an inadvertent error. If they knowingly violated the law, they wouldn't necessarily turn that information over to the city clerk."

The Day 1505 edition of the *Press-Gazette* confirmed reports that the mayor's campaign finance reports were sent to the district attorney. Little did IFBC know the campaign finance debacle had more in store for the future.

The 'future' swiftly arrived with the announcement by the aldermen calling for an investigation, asking the district attorney to bring in an outside prosecutor to examine the data and ensure that there would be no undue influence by local politics. Radio host Jerry Bader again brought it up on his next show.

When speaking again to the same alderman as the last time on this topic, Jerry announced that the state's Government Accountability Board advised the city clerk about the requirement to give her results to the DA (district attorney). Jerry asked, "Do you believe it is possible that this goes beyond sloppy record keeping and that the record keeping as it was done possibly hides improprieties"

Jerry echoed the *Press-Gazette's* reporting and IFBC's feelings about the dust-up. It would just go away if the mayor would file some amended reports and refund the contraband donations, including the one from OSGC.

It did not escape my attention that politician's immunity from prosecution seems apposite to a shoplifter offering to return the pilfered goods. The little people go to jail for their crimes even after they offer to unwind the act, while the political class is allowed to skate free. I therefore agreed with Jerry, noting to myself while listening to the broadcast, *nothing more than the standard kabuki theater is likely to occur before the mayor gets away with it.*

As this was a rapidly developing current event, the widely reported news the next morning reporting that the Brown County District Attorney farmed out the campaign finance investigation to the Milwaukee County District Attorney caught my attention. *Evidently, the county attorney sees at least some there, there,* I thought. And then the Day 1509 *Press-Gazette* ran a front-page article reporting that the mayor returned $2,000 to his donors. Prominently, the article stated, "Schmitt's campaign has filed updated reports with the city clerk's office indicating donations were returned to Oneida Seven Generations Corp. and other supporters."

Once referred to the Milwaukee County District Attorney, I figured that would be the last we would hear of it for a while. However, I was wrong.

Within a few days, I unexpectedly ended up responding to a message from the Milwaukee County District Attorney requesting a copy of the IFBC timeline documenting the dates of events and identifying the source document for each event. *Wow. Didn't see that coming. I'm surprised the prosecutor down there ever heard of me. Crazy world,* I thought as I emailed the timeline.

CHAPTER 43

DAY 1501

Sloppy Mistakes
Continue to Haunt

"Baseball is almost the only orderly thing in an unorderly world.
If you get three strikes,
even the best lawyer in the world can't get you off."

— *King v. Burris*, 588 F. Supp. 1152 (DC Colo. 1984)

Meanwhile, as the campaign finance debacle continued to unfold there were other events occurring. Briefings accomplished, on Day 1501 the Wisconsin Supreme Court heard oral arguments in the suit between OSGC and the City. It was the third case of the day heard by the court in its main hearing room in the east wing of the Wisconsin State Capitol building in Madison, Wisconsin, on a day featuring heavy snow, and was observed by students from O'Keeffe Middle School. Chief Justice Shirley Abrahamson welcomed the students and introduced each member of the state's highest court to them.

Green Bay's attorney began first. He was undoubtedly aware that he was in for a rough ride in the saddle because of the presence of the school kids and he was less than two minutes into his opening before one of justices interrupted. After some clarification, the justice reworded his question by saying, "So, what specifically, what is it to pinpoint the reasons that were put on the record by the City to say Planning Commission, we don't agree. You were misled on these several points. What is it, specifically?"

The attorney explained the Council's vote to reject the Planning Commission's recommendation, and that the City's position is contained in an Alderman's comments in moving to repeal the CUP. At that point another justice asked for clarification regarding if the Common Council was looking at whether the Council was misled, or whether the Plan Commission was misled. The attorney indicated they were looking at whether the Common Council was misled as the Council is the ultimate authority for granting the CUP.

There followed a succession of questions by the justices seeking clarification on which government body decided what, and when. The Court's questioning focused on representations originally made before the Plan Committee, and whether the Council had directed the Plan Committee to determine just whether the Plan Committee had been misled, and not whether the Council had been misled. Key among the procedural errors for the City included its failure to introduce an intelligible audio recording or transcript of the original representations to the Plan Committee for the justices to review, because of the meager evidentiary record.

Once again, this meant the City continued to fumble the procedural disconnects behind the purposes of the separate Council and Plan Committee reviews and linking the Council's rescission to what was originally presented to the Plan Committee. It continued to be a fatal error. The City could not identify for the court how it went from A to C due to the missing evidentiary links to the gap between B and C.

As I listened to this questioning, I just shook my head ruefully and asked myself the same, frustrating question. *WHY did the City skip Discovery at the trial court level and try for the early win?*

CHAPTER 44

DAY 1642

Decision Day

"[a] party with the burden of persuasion who arrives

emptyhanded on decision day must expect to lose."

— *Monroe v. Children's Home Ass'n of Illinois,*

128 F.3d 591, 593 (7th Cir. 1997)

Little happened between the Supreme Court arguments and issuance of its judgment on Day 1642, affirming the Court of Appeals. In a lengthy opinion authored by Justice Bradley, the Court held that, "Like the court of appeals, we conclude that the City's decision to rescind the conditional use permit was not based on substantial evidence."

The Court even went so far as to footnote its displeasure with the unsatisfactory record by stating, "Counsel are reminded that it is incumbent upon them to provide the court with a sufficient record of the proceedings that we are to review. In this case, that should have included transcripts of the proceedings at issue." Had the City done that, not only could it have mounted a more adequate defense but the City would also have then been in the position to attack the impossibilities in the underlying 'science' as an alternative ground of defense.

Interestingly, as the litigation appeals continued to be refined for each court, the City ended up suggesting to the courts that IFBC did not influence the City's decision to uphold the CUP at the plan commission hearings and the subsequent decision to rescind the CUP at the rescission hearing because the MEA letter was the only basis for the actions as stated in the City's defense. Comments during the Supreme Court oral arguments reflected this reality.

Jerry Bader covered the ruling that same day, discussing the suit and again noting that the permit was approved without any real scrutiny because the scrutiny did not begin until after the project was unmasked by the environmental groups to reveal what appeared "like an incinerator." Jerry also described the project as a "bogus green miracle." He concluded that this debacle and sordid tale was a lesson when a green miracle gets pitched to any community.

After the dust settled from the Supreme Court loss, both litigants backed off and remained quiet for several months to attend other matters. Nine months later, OSGC eventually settled the $400 million vendor lawsuit that had been filed in another jurisdiction for an undisclosed amount.

Meanwhile, other proposed incinerators were continuing to occupy IFBC's attention. On Day 1612, I coordinated with WEAL and wrote a separate opposition to a proposed trash incinerator at a major zoo out west. Based in part upon IFBC's standardized resistance training materials, I recommended that the zoo ask many specific questions of the developers, and then to compare the answers. "While IFBC understands the issue of trash disposal is difficult, we believe predatory schemes to incinerate trash that are occasionally dressed up in green energy clothing do nothing to solve the issues while bringing many more unintended consequences directly into the zoo.

"Please investigate these projects with an eye towards protecting the zoo based on IFBC's experiences. Thank you for time. If you desire additional information (there is plenty of documented information in our possession which you might find interesting) or wish to discuss the proposed incinerator for the zoo, IFBC would be happy to provide documents to you or help in any other way it can."

After this letter, no IFBC meetings took place for months as the number of newly proposed incineration projects finally seemed to be dying down. It was the beginning of a relative period of quiet.

CHAPTER 45

DAY 2081

Watching and Waiting

"Unlike the beleaguered trial judge, we have the advantage of reviewing this play in slow motion, somewhat like the instant replay booth of professional sports."

— *Briseno v. City of Santa Ana,*
6 Cal. App. 4th 1378, 8 Cal. Rptr. 2d 486 (Cal. Ct. App. 1992)

This quiet interlude was a remarkable holding-your-breath-to-see-what-happened-next phase. And sure enough, on Day 2081 an attorney advised the General Tribal Council on the wording of a motion for OSGC to continue litigation against the City of Green Bay because dissolution of OSGC in its current state may impact OSGC's standing to litigate anew. IFBC forwarded the video of that to the Green Bay city attorney, and asked, "If the attached GTC action report draft purportedly (see page 2) permits OSGC to continue its litigation with the City of Green Bay, shouldn't the City consider the impact of Wis. Stat. § 808.08(3)? It provides if further action/proceedings other than those in (1) or (2) is ordered (the summary judgment was reversed by the court of appeals, so it would seem neither (1) (trial judge ordered

236

to take specific action) and (2) (new trial is ordered) are relevant), the action shall be dismissed except that an extension of the one-year period may be granted by the trial court if the order for extension is entered during the one-year period."

I also noted the filing date of the Remittitur listed on CCAP is "13 months ago. Arguably, the City might consider a long dissolved corporation with possible issues impacting its legal standing to pursue litigation (see First Commercial Bank, 969 S.W.2d 146) that waited past the one year permitted by Wis. Stat. § 808.08(3) cannot initiate new actions following revocation of its charter".

After sending those questions, I thought, *that should at least clue them in to a possible procedural defense if a suit pops up.*

I received no response. After the long break, however, the Mayor's campaign finance kerfuffle resurfaced one again on Day 2109 when the *Press-Gazette* reported about several alderman calling for the mayor's resignation. Noting that the investigation took 20 months, the *Press-Gazette* reported that the mayor was "charged Wednesday with making false statements on his finance reports, attempting to accept funds from someone other than the reported contributor, and attempting to accept funds in excess of the allowable individual contribution limit."

WLUK reported that the mayor will plead guilty to multiple campaign finance violations. The criminal Complaint (filed in Brown County) stated on page 3 under the heading "Corporate Contributions", the "Oneida Seven Generations Corporation contribution of $500" were "publicly reported in the name of the business. These were returned to the contributors. While it was ultimately determined that over the years a number of corporate checks were accepted and not returned, the investigation concentration on violations of a different nature." The mayor's press-release stated, "I want all of you to know that I have made mistakes in the handling of campaign finances."

The mayor's sentencing occurred on Day 2198. Local media widely observed that he pled to "three misdemeanor violations" and "accepted responsibility for dozens of campaign finance violations" in raking in over $10,000 in illegal campaign contributions. In sentencing the mayor to a $4,000 fine and 40 hours of community service, the judge disagreed with the attempt to characterize the acts as simple mistakes. The transcript contained this devastating rejoinder: "If it was simply a matter of you making honest mistakes, I don't think you'd be sitting here today." This was said by the Outagamie County judge during the sentencing hearing. *WLUK* also reported, "As part of a plea deal agreed to before the charges were filed, Schmitt has also dissolved his campaign fund. The $23,000 he had in campaign money, like other campaign finance violations, has been put into a state fund to help school libraries."

That evening the core members of IFBC all gathered with our coffee of choice at an Ashwaubenon coffee shop and waited for Rich to share his insider news. "Good to see you guys again," Rich said, taking the unlit cigar out of his mouth. "It's been a while! I have some news you'll find very interesting, and I wanted to tell you all face-to-face. As you know, the mayor is being forced to forfeit his $23,000 campaign fund. What you may not know is, as a practical matter, that is functionally a political death sentence. Even though he had once been a rising political star, the state prosecutors effectively decided to end the man's political career."

"Oh my!" Alette exclaimed. "I didn't think he would get anything more than a small hand slapping."

"Oh man, now I almost feel bad about slipping those cartoons I drew under his office door at city hall one night," Greg remarked, causing a burst of laughter at Greg's sly antics.

I thought about this whole adventure as I drove home later that evening while listening to some blues guitar on my truck's radio. *As awful as this whole mess was for all of us to endure, we sure made some fantastic new friends we wouldn't have otherwise met. I wonder how much longer we'll have to keep combating these schemes?*

On Day 2216 OSGC decided to file yet another lawsuit against Green Bay, this time in federal court. It's 23-page Complaint stated OSGC was "seeking to recover damages sustained as a result of the City's violation of OSGC's substantive and procedural due process rights" arising from the muddled procedural history of the attempted CUP revocation. The damages were explained in the Complaint as, "The City's irrational decision to revoke the CUP based on a manufactured rationale shocks the conscience and constitutes a violation of OSGC's constitutional right to due process. As a proximate result, OSGC has sustained over $5 million in out-of-pocket expenses, lost profits of approximately $16 million, and substantial legal expenses, including attorney's fees to try to convince the City to reconsider its decision, and to pursue the state court and these federal court proceedings."

As I read this derivative complaint, I thought back to when I had suggested a possible procedural defense. *I wonder if they'll use it or if they've completely forgotten about it by now?* Before I called it a night, I emailed a copy of the complaint to Elaine, Rich, Leah and the IFBC core members. "Here they go again," I noted.

CHAPTER 46

DAY 2272

Second Bite at the Apple

"His argument qualifies for one of our 'chutzpah' awards."

— *Dainippon Screen Manufacturing Co. v. CFMT, Inc.*,
142 F.3d 1266 (Fed. Cir. Ct. App. 1998)

By Day 2272 Green Bay had already filed a motion to dismiss the latest OSGC lawsuit, stating in its brief, "Rather than enforce the state court judgment as Wisconsin Statutes §§ 815.01, 815.02, and 785.03 entitle OSGC to do, OSGC" the City states plaintiff now seeks "federal review of the same decision along with damages." The irony in the role reversal of the City filing a brief noting OSGC's procedural irregularities did not escape my notice where the brief stated that the suit should be dismissed for lack of corporate capacity to sue.

The City's brief said, "[T]he Oneida General Tribal Council—the governing body of Oneida Nation—voted to dissolve OSGC. The subordinate entity Oneida Business Committee has not dissolved OSGC. Instead, the Business Committee has stripped OSGC of its powers and limited its purpose to strictly 'commercial leasing.' Then, shortly before OSGC filed this Complaint and in the face of tribal pressure to dissolve OSGC, the General Tribal Council considered a motion specifically designed to allow OSGC to pursue this lawsuit. After debate and consideration, however, the General Tribal Council voted to table that motion and never took any additional action. As such, the filing and prosecution of the present suit has never been authorized or approved."

The City's brief further noted, "[C]orporate capacity to sue is determined by the law under which a corporation was organized. Under Oneida Nation law, OSGC should not exist. To the extent OSGC exists at all, it is not authorized to bring the present lawsuit as it does not advance OSGC's authorized commercial leasing activities. OSGC's lack of capacity was confirmed when the General Tribal Council tabled the motion to prosecute this suit."

On Day 2381 the federal court agreed, but for differing reasons based on procedural grounds. It dismissed the suit. "Leaving aside the question how a project OSGC claims would have generated $16 million in profit could have lost its economic viability in five years, OSGC successfully utilized the procedural safeguards that were available for restricting the City's authority to impose zoning limitations on the use of its land. OSGC's procedural due process claim therefore fails." Regarding the second claim, this time for substantive due process, the court further ruled "the fact that OSGC ultimately prevailed and could have completed the project had it chosen to do so also makes the City Council's decision less shocking or egregious than a substantive due process violation requires. There is no suggestion that the City Council members were aware that delay would essentially kill the project because it would lose whatever economic viability it might have had. In the final analysis, the City's action caused a delay in the project; it was apparently a change in other factors over which the City had no control that caused OSGC to abandon it."

Dean called that night. "Hey, what do you think about the dismissal of the new lawsuit between Green Bay and OSGC?"

"Probably the correct decision," I replied. "OSGC failed to enforce its prior judgment from the first suit. Instead, OSGC started bouncing around trying to find a new home for it, which blew up in OSGC's face, but the company didn't move ahead with building it in Green Bay after the win like they should have. At the end of the day, the court ruled the City's action merely delayed the project. A change in other factors over which the City had no control caused OSGC to abandon it."

"That's what we were thinking on our end too," Dean agreed. "Sounds like everyone has the same opinion. In the end, it was OSGC that ran out the clock on itself."

I thought the additional irony was OSGC's failure to build a record to support its new claims, which caused problems for the litigant. That was a role reversal from the original lawsuit in state court where it was the City that experienced the same problem.

OSGC appealed the dismissal soon after. Inexplicably, the City chose to buy its peace rather than rely upon the dismissal up at the Seventh Circuit Court of Appeals, and the parties settled for $2.5 million.

CHAPTER 47

For Whom the Bell Tolls

"In this confrontation, ask not for whom the bell tolls:
it tolls for thee."

— *Thompson v. Calderon*, 120 F.3d 1042 (9th Cir. 1997) (dissent)

T he finalized dissolution of OSGC occurred on Day 3117, which is 8 and a half years after Greg first knocked on my door regarding Joanne's little red flyer. In my basement office lair, listening on the stereo to a popular Texas style blues artist work his guitar, I pored over some new documents and reflected back on the past years. *OSGC never built its incinerator anywhere in Wisconsin.* I tipped an icy cold Kolsch from Hinterland Brewing in Ashwaubenon to celebrate OSGC's finalized dissolution. *Unfortunately,* I thought, *trash incineration schemes continue to be proposed to unsuspecting communities under the guise of being miraculous green energy machines.*

And sure enough, it wasn't long before IFBC once again joined with our close allies, CWAC and WEAL, and filed opposition comments with DNR against yet another incinerator proposal seeking a research and testing permit exemption from the state for continued testing of a proposed solid waste trash incinerator.

The joint IFBC and CWAC letter noted the striking similarities in impossible claims originally made by OSGC and the current claims made by the current permit exemption applicant. IFBC also noted for the DNR this applicant was attempting to place itself in the position of vouching for its own credibility through the ludicrous situation of submitting testing results from what it portrayed as an independent third party despite the applicant's own board including a member from that same third party.

IFBC and CWAC also drew upon the instructive federal court documents from the recent sentencing of a person resulting from another fake green energy scheme in Brown County as they should provide a cautionary note to grandiose and complex business schemes involving trash incinerators — unverifiable claims of commercial viability, and miraculous suggestions of a closed system lacking wastewater discharge. The sentencing documents certainly provided some insight into the uncannily similar claims of this applicant.

We highlighted for DNR the sad tale of fraud that included the federal prosecution's sentencing memorandum which stated, "His pitches" … "were rife with material falsehoods, including claims of 'zero waste water discharge'; displaying fuel pellets that were actually made by a different company; and claims of patents and business relationships that did not exist."

We then compared those fake claims to the application attachment which even stated, "No water is used in the … gasification process and no wastewater is produced." I found those claims almost breathtaking. The sentencing hearing transcript stated, "none of the reports demonstrate the plan was commercially feasible, meaning that it could be profitably operated to generate pulp, pellets, fuel, tissue rolls, and consumer products for post-consumer — from post-consumer waste with no wastewater at the volumes and speed" that the perpetrator "promised his investors and friends."

The sentencing hearing transcript succinctly stated, "None of the reports demonstrate the plan was commercially feasible, meaning that it could be profitably operated."

CHAPTER 48

End of the Beginning

"Now this is not the end. It is not even the beginning of the end.
But it is, perhaps, the end of the beginning."

— Winston Churchill

The lack of accountability for incineration schemes remains of concern to IFBC. The final piece in the local incineration puzzle became clearer to me when, a few months later, I watched local television reports on the implosion of an incinerator located in South Sioux City, Nebraska. Located half an hour from my alma mater at the University of South Dakota, sections of Sioux City are located in Iowa, South Dakota, and Nebraska.

As I watched the WLUK report, I noted that Nebraska's regulator revoked the company's permit for numerous violations, and the station duly reported it in Brown County because the parent company appeared to be the same company IFBC had opposed in Maribel, Wisconsin, way back on Day 499. Very concerned, I thought, *this latest incineration scheme is alarming because it styled itself a "biofuels" plant. This "biofuel" scheme was dressed up as a green energy facility processing organic food waste feedstock to "create renewable natural gas", also referred to on its web page as "green gas". Its web page was replete with various "facts" and information*

246

on restaurant waste; however, the key was the first bullet on a graph under "Source Input" that said, "municipal solid waste".

After researching the situation I discovered this outfit's web page was replete with various "facts" and information on restaurant waste.

As a result of my sleuthing I discovered that, after just a few years of operation and polluting the air by repeatedly venting hydrogen sulfide gas, dumping contaminated wastewater into the regional wastewater treatment plant, and dumping thousands of tons of trash outside its facility, the company had lost all its city, state and federal permits. It was also deeply in debt, owing massive tipping and hauling fees for solid waste, bills due to unpaid suppliers, and water treatment fees. There was even a class action lawsuit from residents whose homes were now contaminated. The afflicted community had indicated the company now also owed millions in unpaid treatment fees although the company disputes the amount. The local newspaper there noted litigation judgments against the company were "beginning to mount" when describing a list of the known judgments.

I just shook my head as I continued researching. *As far as I'm concerned, communities are far better off staying away from these miraculous green schemes pitching fake solutions solving the problems of solid waste or that try to hide a plan to use solid waste as feedstock, so IFBC will have to continue our efforts going forward. Someone needs to be able to tell communities these schemes are harmful, wasteful, and their faulty financial assumptions inevitably seem to cause outlandishly severe financial problems for every host community. They also have no credibility regarding possible health effects.*

Throughout this entire adventure against OSGC's incinerator, I couldn't help but notice the glaring gap between engineers claiming an incinerator is safe for humans, and the utter lack of actual medical professionals supporting such dubious claims.

Perhaps project engineers are chasing dreams of becoming the next unqualified mechanical engineer with a television gig to start pontificating about a science unrelated to their actual credentials and experience, I thought.

Just as I again realized that IFBC will have to remain vigilant in protecting our locals from these abominations my email chimed. It was a message from Charlene from WEAL on that very issue.

"Hi John," she wrote. "Wisconsin has attracted several proposals for gasification projects over the past several years. Fortunately, not one full-scale facility has been built. However, the state may continue to attract startup companies pursuing gasification projects since two laws offer valuable incentives. The 2009 Wisconsin Act 406 gives renewable energy status to fuels produced by pyrolysis of waste materials and synthetic gas created by plasma gasification. The 2017 Act 284 exempts pyrolysis and gasification projects from being defined as solid waste facilities and will not require that type of permitting."

Charlene went on to say that "IFBC deserves a great deal of credit for developing an effective opposition through networking with CWAC, WEAL and numerous other groups in Wisconsin and across the USA. There were many twists and turns but the opposition persisted. Much can be learned from the OSGC saga on what to expect and how to effectively mount an opposition."

Of constant concern for IFBC, WEAL and CWAC, state law unfortunately continues to attract incineration developers.

So ends the saga of the OSGC trash incinerator — for now...

About the Author

John Filcher lives in Ashwaubenon, Wisconsin. Due to the large cast of heroes he encountered during this adventure, not all of them were included in this accounting. Their omission was merely for the purposes of keeping this writing more manageable, and no slights were intended.

If ever you should find yourself in the unfortunate situation of facing one of these *magic* machines moving into your neighborhood, he hopes you will find this book helpful during your struggle to halt this detrimental and unhealthful development.

www.ingramcontent.com/pod-product-compliance
Lightning Source LLC
Chambersburg PA
CBHW031845200326

41597CB00012B/280